Treasures from Native California

Location of Russian, Spanish, and native settlements in early California (after Milliken 2010).

Treasures from Native California

The Legacy of Russian Exploration

Travis Hudson and Craig D. Bates

Edited by Thomas Blackburn and John R. Johnson

Foreword by Stephen Watrous

Afterword by Glenn Farris

LONDON AND NEW YORK

First published 2015 by Left Coast Press, Inc.

Published 2016 by Routledge
2 Park Square, Milton Park, Abingdon, Oxon OX14 4RN
711 Third Avenue, New York, NY 10017, USA

Routledge is an imprint of the Taylor & Francis Group, an informa business

Library of Congress Cataloging-in-Publication Data:
Hudson, Travis.
Treasures from native California : the legacy of Russian exploration / Travis Hudson and Craig D. Bates ; edited by Thomas Blackburn and John R. Johnson ; foreword by Stephen Watrous ; afterword by Glenn Farris.
pages cm
Includes bibliographical references.
ISBN 978-1-61132-982-7 (hardback : alk. paper)—ISBN 978-1-61132-984-1 (institutional eBook)—ISBN 978-1-61132-753-3 (consumer eBook)
1. Indians of North America—Material culture—California—Catalogs. 2. California—Discovery and exploration—Russian. I. Bates, Craig D. II. Blackburn, Thomas C., editor. III. Johnson, John R. (John Richard), 1949- editor. IV. Title.
E78.C15H83 2014
979.4'01—dc23
2014026772

ISBN 978-1-61132-982-7 hardback

Contents

List of Illustrations *6*
Foreword by Stephen Watrous *9*
Editor's Preface *15*
Acknowledgments *19*

Chapter 1. Introduction: The Kunstkamera's California Collection *23*
Chapter 2. Documenting a Collection: The Collectors and Their Objects *29*
Chapter 3. A Superb Collector Visits California: Il'ia G. Voznesenskii *47*
Chapter 4. Describing a People: The Russians as Ethnographers *51*
Chapter 5. Objects of the Quest: Hunting and Gathering Equipment *61*
- Hunting Equipment *62*
- Gathering Equipment *90*

Chapter 6. Objects of Home and Hearth: Food Preparation and Shelter *95*
- Food Preparation and Serving *98*
- Household Items *103*

Chapter 7. Interacting With the Supernatural: Ritual Dress *109*
- Headwear *112*
- Bodywear *132*
- Ornaments *147*

Chapter 8. Objects for Festive Occasions: Music, Gifts, and Games 159
- Musical Instruments *159*
- Ceremonial Basketry and Presentational Items *162*

Chapter 9. Some Comments on Significance *185*

Afterword: The Bicentenary and Beyond by Glenn Farris *187*

Appendix *191*
Notes *197*
Bibliography *203*
Index *223*
About the Authors, Editors, and Contributors *231*

List of Illustrations

Unless otherwise credited, all sketches were made by and all photographs were taken by Travis Hudson in 1983 and 1985.

Frontispiece: Location of Russian, Spanish, and native settlements in early California.
1.1 Fort Ross as depicted by two early visitors, Duhaut-Cilly and Voznesenskii. *24*
2.1 California exhibit at the MAE, St. Petersburg. *33*
2.2 California objects on display at the MAE in 1873. *35*
2.3 California items collected by Georg Langsdorff in 1806. *38*
2.4 Munich shell necklace (SMV 213) matching Langsdorff's illustration. *39*
2.5 California artifacts depicted by Choris (1822). *41*
2.6 Some prominent Russian visitors to early California: Kotzebue, Golovnin, Wrangell, and Voznesenskii. *43*
4.1 Native Californians depicted by Choris (1822). *55*
4.2 Additional Native Californians depicted by Choris (1822). *55*
4.3 Tikhanov depiction of Coast Miwok man at Bodega Bay, 1818. *56*
4.4 Tikhanov depiction of Coast Miwok woman at Bodega Bay, 1818. *57*
5.1 Two views of a model balsa canoe (570-114). *63*
5.2 Balsa passing the Presidio of San Francisco in 1806 (Langsdorff 1814). *63*
5.3 Balsa on San Francisco Bay (Choris 1822). *64*
5.4 Front (a) and side views (b) of a decoy headdress (570-122). *68*
5.5 José Cardero depiction of a Monterey Indian hunter in 1791. *72*
5.6 Two "Cholovoni" (Chulamni) hunters near San Francisco Bay (Choris 1822). *73*
5.7 Sketches showing different types of bow nocks. *73*
5.8 Two views of bows (570-127, -130, and -129). *74*
5.9 Nocks of bows (570-129, -130, and -127). *75*
5.10 Bow (570-128). *75*
5.11 Bow (570-132). *75*
5.12 Bows in Helsinki collected by Etholen and Cygnaeus (FNM VK-336, VK-337, and 4911:23). *77*
5.13 Characteristics of arrow types. *79*
5.14 Assorted arrows in Bundle IV, showing (a) point and (b) nock ends. *80*
5.15 Assorted arrows in Bundle VII, showing (a) point and (b) nock ends. *81*
5.17 Assorted arrows in Bundle VIII, showing (a) point and (b) nock ends. *81*
5.17 Barbed and self arrows from Bundle VIII. *81*
5.18 Sketch of riband markings, Type A arrows. *82*
5.19 Sketch of riband markings on arrows of types B–F. *83*
5.20 Arrow quiver (570-133). *88*
5.21 Net bag (570-69). *89*
5.22 Seed beater (570-109). *90*
5.23 Conical burden basket, probably Pomo (MAE n/n). *91*
5.24 Headband of carrying net (570-72) displayed on mannequin. *92*
5.25 Carrying net (570-73). *93*

6.1 Tikhanov painting of Coast Miwok household near Bodega Bay, 1818. *96*
6.2 (a) Winnowing tray (570-89); (b) starting knot; (c) rim detail. *98*
6.3 Winnowing tray (570-88). *99*
6.4 Sifting tray (570-87). *99*
6.5 Basket hopper mortar (MAE n/n) and pestle (570-117). *99*
6.6 Basket hopper (570-84). *100*
6.7 Chumash serving tray (4296-6). *101*
6.8 Serving tray (570-86). *101*
6.9 Chumash serving bowl (570-85). *102*
6.10 Fire-making kit (570-115 a-b). *103*
6.11 Depiction by José Cardero of Monterey Indian woman wearing what appears to be a woven feather or fur blanket. *105*
6.12 Feather blanket (2520-8). *106*
6.13 Feather blanket (2520-9). *106*
6.14 Chumash storage jar (570-113). *107*
6.15 (a) Bottom and (b) bead decoration of Chumash storage jar (570-113). *108*
7.1 Flicker quill headbands 570-16, -17, and -18. *112*
7.2 Chris "Chief Lemee" Brown, southern Sierra Miwok, in dance regalia about 1936. *113*
7.3 Chochenyo Ohlone dancers at Mission San Jose in 1806 (Langsdorff 1814). *115*
7.4 Dancers at Mission San Francisco in 1816 (Choris 1822). *117*
7.5 California Indian men in dance regalia (Choris 1822). *117*
7.6 Death of Coast Miwok chief at Bodega Bay, 1818. *118*
7.7 Two views of young Coast Miwok man named Valthazar, 1818. *119*
7.8 Central Sierra Miwok dancers in Sonora, California, in the 1870s. *120*
7.9 Sketch showing topknot construction. *121*
7.10 Two views (a, b) of feather headpiece (570-4). *121*
7.11 Feather headpiece (570-7). *122*
7.12 Feather headpiece (570-8). *123*
7.13 Topknot headdress (WKM E-0169). *125*
7.14 Hairnet (570-67). *126*
7.15 Hairnet (570-68). *127*
7.16 Hairpins: (a) MAE 570-35, -36, and -30; (b) FNM VK-343. *130*
7.17 Two views (a, b) of woman's skirt (1-1061). *133*
7.18 Photo showing details of ornamentation on skirt 1-1061. *134*
7.19 Two views (a, b) of feather cape (570-3). *135*
7.20 Two views (a, b) of *mollok* cloak (570-2). *138*
7.21 Clamshell disk bead belt (570-14). 139
7.22 Feather belt (570-13). *140*
7.23 Helsinki feather belt (FNM VK-1036). *141*
7.24 Sketch of feather belts collected by the Russians. *143*
7.25 Sketch of extant feather belt patterns. *144*
7.26 Ear rods made from incised bird-bone tubes (570-39 to -48, -50 to -52, and -119). *148*
7.27 Ear ornaments (570-53 and -54). *150*

7.28 Sketch of ear pendant collected by Wrangell (WKM E-0170). *151*
7.29 Shell necklaces (570-20 to -23). *153*
7.30 Feather rope (570-10). *157*
8.1 Gourd rattle attributed to Langsdorff (SMV 183). *160*
8.2 Bird-bone whistles (570-63 and 570-62). *161*
8.3 Ceremonial basket (570-78). *166*
8.4 Ceremonial basket (570-79). *166*
8.5 Ceremonial basket (570-90). *166*
8.6 Feasting basket (570-91). *168*
8.7 Feasting basket (570-96). *169*
8.8 Feasting basket (FNM VK-342). *169*
8.9 Gift basket (570-92). *170*
8.10 Gift basket (570-93). *171*
8.11 Gift basket (WKM E-0173). *171*
8.12 Gift basket (570-95). *172*
8.13 Gift basket (FNM VK-203). *173*
8.14 Gift basket (570-101). *173*
8.15 Gift basket (SMV 142). *174*
8.16 Two views (a, b) of gift basket (SMV 143). *174*
8.17 Gift basket (570-102). *175*
8.18 Gift basket (570-105). *175*
8.19 Gift basket (570-104). *175*
8.20 Gift basket (SMV 9-48). *176*
8.21 Gift basket (570-94). *176*
8.22 Gift basket (570-106). *176*
8.23 Gift basket (570-97). *178*
8.24 Gift basket (570-98). *179*
8.25 Gift basket (570-99). *179*
8.26 Detailed views (a, b) of gift basket (570-99). *179*
8.27 Gift basket (570-100). *180*
8.28 Gift basket (570-103). *180*
8.29 Gift basket (4291-13). *180*
8.30 Gift basket (WKM E-0172). *181*
8.31 Men gambling with stick dice at Mission San Francisco in 1816 (Choris, 1822). *183*
8.32 Gaming pieces (570-37 and -38). *184*

Tables

2.1 California Items in European Museums Collected by Russians *30*
7.1 Dimensions of Feather Belts *141*
7.2 Ear Rods in the St. Petersburg Collection *149*

Foreword

Stephen Watrous

With the publication of this richly illustrated volume, a major aspect of the short-lived Russian presence in early California suddenly becomes clearer and more illuminating. A new perspective on Russian settlement, exploration, and relations with the Indian population in northern California during the early nineteenth century is opened. For over a century we have been left with few visible signs of the Russian impact and legacy. Since 1841, when the Russians withdrew, only a few Anglicized place names, several dozen Russian loan-words in local Indian vocabularies, and the abandoned structures at Fort Ross have served to remind us of the Russian presence long ago. The early Russian contribution to California's subsequent development, in terms of ethnic population, customs, institutions, or economic impact, was virtually nonexistent.

And yet for 35 years, in and about northern California, a handful of astute Russian observers established a literary, pictorial, and ethnographic legacy that has long gone unrecognized. The memoirs and sketches they produced and the material objects they collected all reflect, to a surprising degree, their keen interest in the native populations of northern California—or New Albion, as they often called it. These observers were indeed far more intent on describing and evaluating the indigenous inhabitants than they were their own settlers and colonists. Only in recent years have we gradually become aware of this fascinating, but long neglected, aspect of the Russian experience in early California. The very intent of the present book is to reveal and assess, systematically and definitively, the most colorful, visible, and valuable component of this tangible Russian legacy—the remaining ethnographic objects now scattered throughout various museums of European Russia and Central Europe.

The extant artifacts that derive from Russian activities in early California (1806 to 1841) are by origin almost exclusively Indian. Whereas the few materials or objects of Russian provenance known to have survived remain in California or Alaska, the Indian items acquired and conveyed back to European Russia have been preserved in large numbers.

Treasures from Native California: The Legacy of Russian Exploration, Travis Hudson and Craig D. Bates, Edited by Thomas Blackburn and John R. Johnson, 9–14.

Thus, the largest group anywhere of California Indian artifacts from before the Gold Rush has been housed in St. Petersburg, almost half a world away, for over 150 years.

These unique treasures were originally obtained (or sketched) by a few non-resident Russian visitors, who in their ethnographic interests were avid and casual, amateur and professional. The collectors themselves comprised a varying mix of military officers, scientists, physicians, artists, administrators, and navigators. They were men of Russian, German, and Swedish background, yet all were in the employ of the Russian-American Company. They were far enough ahead of their time so that in their own day and long afterward the artifacts they acquired were largely ignored. Not until the early twentieth century did the first Russian scholar publish a brief summary and appreciation of some of these materials (Gil'zen 1916). In the United States itself, only within the last generation has a realization of the existence and extent of these invaluable collections begun to emerge. Awareness of these objects has been enhanced by recently published reproductions of sketches of Alaska (see Smith and Barnett 1990, a catalogue of a traveling exhibition of original artifacts and prints).

Easily the two most active and talented among the select group of Russians who described Indian life and collected local artifacts were Baron Ferdinand Petrovich von Wrangell (1796–1870) and Il'ya Gavrilovich Voznesenskii (1816–1871). Were it not for the ethnographic efforts of these two persistent individuals, the present volume could scarcely have been compiled. As visitors to California, Wrangell (1833) and Voznesenskii (1840–1841) reflect a study in contrasts. Paired together, their differences complement one another in ways characteristic of the many-sided Russian presence in early Northwest America—in their age and social backgrounds, their interests, their professional capacities, and their writings. The objects they collected, the vast majority represented in this book, are invaluable to our understanding of traditional Indian life and culture in early California.

Ferdinand von Wrangell (in Russian: Vrangel'), a nobleman of Baltic German origins, was educated among the elite of the Russian Empire. A graduate of the Naval Academy and a science student at the University of Dorpat, in Russian Estonia, Wrangell first visited the New World (and California) with Captain Vasily Golovnin in 1818. After directing explorations in northeastern Siberia and heading a scientific voyage to Kamchatka in the North Pacific, Wrangell in 1828 was appointed the manager-in-chief of the Russian-American Company colonies. Arriving in Sitka (New Archangel), Alaska, with his family in 1830, he served for five years as the Company's top executive officer in North America. We can assume that by the end of his term he had collected the seven California Indian objects now located in Frankfurt (see Blackburn and Hudson 1990:103).

As manager-in-chief, Wrangell visited Northern California twice, in 1833 and 1835 (the latter visit on his return home to Russia via Mexico). His encounters with Indians north of San Francisco Bay were occasioned primarily by a reconnaissance expedition up the Russian River valley to seek a future, preferable site for the company's California outpost (in place of the deficit-ridden Fort Ross). Wrangell's detailed account of his inland journey provides us with an idyllic picture of an untouched wilderness and its indigenous population, just before Mexican and Anglo-American penetration began.

Wrangell writes, for example, of his party's approach to the Santa Rosa plain (north of San Francisco) and his first exchange with the local inhabitants:

> Before evening we reached the largest of the plains. At first it is unforested, completely level, luxuriantly overgrown with fragrant plants, and so immense that its distance is no less than twenty-five miles across....
>
> Nightfall took us unawares in one of those splendid oak groves which shade the plain here and there.... The campfires blazed up amidst the dark foliage of oaks a century old. Deep silence settled upon this land so richly endowed by nature. Scarcely had the night watchman—the coyote—intoned his plaintive howl, than our new friends, the Indians, arrived at the campfires. After we gave them tobacco, biscuits, glass beads, and other trinkets, they sat down with their fellow countrymen, our interpreters and vaqueros, in a circle and began their favorite activity...playing at odds-and-evens. (Wrangell 1839:71–72; 1974:3)

The next day the expedition visited its first Indian village. Despite an appearance of fright on the part of the women and old men,

> they behaved in a friendly way and showed us everything that belonged to their meager economy. In a few blankets lay provisions of paste made of ground acorn mush and of a kind of grits made of wild rye and other seed grains. Moreover, there were fish, which they catch in the stream by sprinkling on the water's surface a powder made from a bulb they call "soap-root"; with this the fish become stunned and float along the surface. Hunting is the men's activity. By contrast, the women must carry all the heavy loads and undertake the difficult jobs in general. This unusual division of labor probably stems from the peculiar fact that the women here are generally of a much stronger physical constitution than are the men, who, although large and well-proportioned, still seem to be weaker than the women. (1839: 73–74; 1974:3)

Wrangell sums up the engaging impact that the California Indians left upon him. An inborn propensity among these Americans for independence, he asserts,

> is reflected in all their games, their songs, their speech, their handicrafts, and whatever serves as their ornaments. Headdress, belts, ear-rings, etc., for the most part made of feathers, reveal not only their inventive spirit, but also a certain sense of the beautiful. Their speech, their melodic voices and singing all make a pleasant impression upon the ear. (1839:76; 1974:5)

Wrangell was no naive, romantic observer of undifferentiated "noble savages." He compared California Indians favorably to the Tlingits, Aleuts, and Chukchi in the north, whom he had already observed first-hand, with their unpleasant, "out-of-tune, guttural sounds" (1839:76; 1974:5).

With Wrangell we gain a glimpse of Indian life from the 1830s through the first detailed, semi-anthropological sketch of California natives extant. Although he omits mention anywhere in his account of acquiring Indian artifacts, his sympathetic, keen interest in recording Indian life of the time sets off his observations as almost unique in the Russian literature of early California. A comparable, but more topically organized account was written by Peter S. Kostromitinov, resident manager at Fort Ross from 1830 to 1838 (1839:80–96). Other, briefer ethnographic descriptions were recorded earlier by Langsdorff, Chamisso, Kotzebue, Matiushkin, and Golovnin. Wrangell in later life rose higher in the world of government administration (as minister of the Navy and member of the State Council) than did any other Russian who visited California. His legacy in North America is notable in that more locations in present-day Alaska bear his name than that of any other Russian.

Even more focused in his ethnographic interests and objectives was the young Russian scientist Il'ya Gavrilovich Voznesenskii, who visited California for 13 months in 1840–1841 while in his mid-20s. Son of an invalid officer, Voznesenskii was a self-taught, self-made man—a rarity in his time, within the socially stratified *ancien régime* of Imperial Russia. In one capacity or another he worked for the Imperial Academy of Sciences in St. Petersburg from age five onward, and at 13 he participated in his first scientific expedition—to Transcaucasia—under Academy auspices. After working his way upward in the Academy's Zoological Museum, Voznesenskii in 1839 was sent by the academy's museum directors to Russian America to gather zoological, botanical, mineralogical, and ethnographic materials for their collections. All in all, the young scientist's travels in North America—from Alaska's Kenai Peninsula to Baja California—lasted five years.

Voznesenskii's descriptions of his Caliornia stay are not as ordered or extensive as Wrangell's, nor were they published upon his return home to Russia. His notes, however, edited and published in part since World War II by various Russian authors, reveal an ardent collector and intrepid traveler, anxious to observe and acquire as much as possible within the relatively short period of time at his disposal. After his debarkation at Bodega Bay, he made his way to Fort Ross and northward along the Mendocino Coast; from there he went to the missions and ranches of San Francisco Bay; and lastly he traveled up the Sacramento River to Captain John Sutter's vast holdings.

Thus, Voznesenskii tells us that his first ten days, at Bodega Bay (in July, 1840), were devoted "solely to ornithological excursions, botanical trips, etc." Upon his arrival at Fort Ross, he relates:

> Of the many trips I made before I left..., the trip north from Ross to Cape Mendocino deserves mention. I spent a few days there in the mountains amidst dense forests of gigantic redwoods (*Pinus Lambertiana* [*sic*])[1] and majestic cedars (*Pinus Californica* [*sic*]). Such forests as these shelter the untamed Indian tribes of New Albion, who roam like animals and, protected by impenetrable vegetation, keep from being enslaved by the Spanish. (Liapunova 1967:14; Lipshits 1950:417)

In order to further his collecting activities, he set off on horseback for San Francisco Bay. Between October 1840 and February 1841, he writes,

> my time was spent successfully, for each day the collections were enriched by new acquisitions. Over these four months I visited many localities along the shores of the immense bay: on its southern side, Santa Clara and the Pueblo [San Jose]; to the east, San Leandro, San Antonio, San Pablo and Pinole; on the northern shore, Napa, Petaluma, Sonoma (the residence of the military general of Upper California [Mariano Vallejo]; and to the west, Mission San Francisco, Cape Drake, Sausalito, Angel Island, Alcatraz, and other islands. (Liapunova 1967:14)

By late February, Voznesenskii's "long-awaited opportunity" to proceed up the Sacramento River arrived. He thereupon visited Captain Sutter's headquarters at "New Helvetia."

> I spent 31 days on the then virginal banks of the Pele (as the local Indians call it). Upon the recommendation of Mr. Rotchev and others Sutter welcomed me quite cordially, and I stayed the entire time with him under the squalid roof of his cabin. Accompanying Mr. Sutter around his land, which the Mexican government had just ceded to him, we reached

> the Three [Sutter] Buttes, crossed the (now) gold-bearing Plumas and American Rivers a few times, and spent nights along their banks.... With Capt. Sutter's help I acquired some rather rare items in the area of ethnography. (Alekeseev 1987:21; Liapunova 1967)

Unfortunately, Voznesenskii gives few details regarding the "items" he acquired from the Sacramento Valley—the 26 arrows (Liapunova 1967), and the two shamans' capes of crow and condor feathers (Alekseev 1987).

In May 1841 he explored and charted the Russian River basin, and in June, together with Yegor Chernykh, resident agronomist at Fort Ross, he climbed "one of the highest mountains [St. Helena], whose summit no one till then had succeeded in reaching" (Alekseev 1987:24). With this feat Voznesenskii appears to have concluded his explorations of interior California.

Upon returning to Fort Ross, Voznesenskii set to work assembling his "rich harvest of acquisitions from all the branches of natural science." For assisting in his collecting and field work, Voznesenskii gave special credit to Fort Ross manager Alexander Rotchev, the like of whom he "could hardly have found elsewhere." Consequently, with Rotchev's help he prepared 15 cases of materials to send back to the museums of the Imperial Academy of Sciences. The collections were shipped from San Francisco in October 1841 on the steamer *Nicholas I* (Alekseev 1977:16).

The first systematic cataloguing of all of Voznesenskii's acquisitions occurred only in the early twentieth century, when biographer K. K. Gil'zen compiled a single comprehensive list of 1,071 items. Despite difficulties, Gil'zen attempted to arrange the artifacts by tribe or site of acquisition. Thus, the California portion of Voznesenskii's collection comprised only 152 objects: 68 hunting artifacts, 31 articles of clothing and ornamentation, 45 utensils and tools, and 8 religious items (Liapunova 1967:26). However, Travis Hudson subsequently attributed the majority of the 307 California items in the St. Petersburg Museum of Anthropology and Ethnography to Voznesenskii (Blackburn and Hudson 1990:149–152).

Overall, Voznesenskii provides the most extensive and geographically exact itinerary of any Russian traveler in early California, establishing a framework of time and place within which his collecting activities took place. However, his notes (written, or at least revised, well after his travels) correlate poorly with the specific objects acquired on his many field trips. Altogether, Voznesenskii describes no more than a half-dozen ethnographic items in any detail; for example, a hairpin, belt, headband, and earrings attributed to the Suisun people of the Sacramento Delta (Liapunova 1967:16). All in all, his heretofore published notes serve more as diary or travel entries than as a helpful source for accurately identifying the several hundred ethnographic objects he collected in California.

By September 1841, Voznesenskii brought an end to his many activities in California and set sail for Alaska, only four months before the Russian-American Company was to complete the ownership transfer of its Fort Ross holdings to Sutter. In effect, Voznesenskii's departure represents the end of Russian scientific interest in California, just as Russia's economic, demographic, and political investments in the area were also drawing to a close.

The second largest group of California artifacts that are known to have been collected under Russian-American Company auspices once belonged to Arvid Adolph Etholen (in Russian, Adolf Karlovich Etolin). A Swedish Finn from Helsinki, Etholen (1799–1876) was the company's manager-in-chief in America from 1840 to 1845. As a former sea-captain in the company's service, Etholen arrived in Alaska in 1818 and made five voyages to California between 1824 and 1833 (Pierce 1990a:136–137). Although he twice visited Fort Ross, Etholen's activities were primarily maritime and commercial in nature, and it is unlikely that in this context he acquired California Indian objects first-hand.

Not only did Etholen become Wrangell's chief assistant during the latter's tenure as manager-in-chief, he later became closely associated with Voznesenskii when the two sailed together from St. Peterburg to Russian America in 1839. After Voznesenskii completed his California activities, Etholen (now the company's chief executive) proposed that he next sail to Baja California with a Russian crew to continue his scientific research. Later, in 1842, Voznesenskii accompanied Etholen on an inspection tour of Alaskan outposts. Thus, one may surmise that Vozneskenskii, out of friendship and gratitude, presented a few of his remaining California acquisitions to Etholen before his final departure from Russian America in 1845. Indeed, of the California artifacts that Etholen once possessed, a majority (six of ten) have been identified as coming from interior California (Blackburn and Hudson 1990:59).

We are especially fortunate that the authors of this study have for the first time drawn upon such a wealth of available resources, world-wide in scope, to compile the most comprehensive account and photographic replication of Russian-derived Indian objects from early California ever attempted. Not only have they provided us with an attractive, orderly description, both textual and visual, of the known extant items, they have also compared them meticulously with analogous California artifacts now located in museums and collections throughout the United States and Western Europe. Their photographs and conclusions persuade us of the unique beauty and craftsmanship of these objects, which date back to a time when almost no other collecting of California Indian materials took place and photography was not yet born.

Moreover, the authors contend that Russian contacts were with California natives about whom we now generally know the least. Their careful study of the Russian-derived items provides them with enough evidence to observe an evolution in artifact design, use, and material (in the light of objects of later origin) over the course of the later nineteenth century. Despite intensive research efforts, however, the authors conclude that a majority of the objects, and the scanty descriptive data relating to them, fail to allow for a very exact or even approximate determination of their ethnic origin or locale.

The present work stands before us as a landmark in several respects. It testifies to the fruitful results of Russian-American cooperation (even in the pre-glasnost years of the early 1980s) in exchanging historical and ethnographic data of mutual interest and value. Moreover, it enhances substantially our appreciation and understanding of both Indian cultures and Russian accomplishments in early California. With the revelation, to us in the West, of these virtually long-lost objects, our astonishment and delight at the intricacies and skills of native arts and crafts becomes all the greater. Moreover, our lack of awareness of the talents and sophistication of Russian visitors in frontier California is once and for all dispelled. Through a century-long process of collecting, listing, systematizing, and photographing hundreds of artifacts, the long-vanished world of California Indians is, in the following pages, all but brought to life again.

October, 1993

Editor's Preface

Thomas Blackburn

The path followed by most books—from manuscript to publisher, from printer to reader—is usually relatively swift and straightforward. For others, however, the journey can be slow, tortuous, and as full of obstacles as any classic heroic quest. The present volume is certainly a case in point.

In March 1983, Travis Hudson, then Curator of Anthropology at the Santa Barbara Museum of Natural History, was given the rare opportunity of visiting the Kunstkamera and the Peter the Great Museum of Anthropology and Ethnography in St. Petersburg, where he spent three weeks examining and documenting what is arguably the finest collection of early California ethnographic objects ever assembled. Upon returning to the United States, and filled with enthusiasm as a result of his visit to the Kunstkamera and other European museums, he began working on a manuscript intended to provide detailed descriptions of the many amazing items collected by the various Russian travelers to California, as well as an explanation of the historical context within which those collecting activities took place. He also enlisted the support and collaboration of Craig Bates, Curator of Ethnography at the Yosemite Museum and a noted authority on the material culture of the native peoples of central California. A rough draft of the book was completed in 1984 and submitted to the University of California Press for consideration. Unfortunately, the Press declined to publish the manuscript at that time, although numerous suggestions for revision were offered. Hudson began incorporating the suggested revisions in the manuscript, while simultaneously working on at least three other major projects, one involving a series of volumes on Chumash material culture (with myself as coauthor), and another a general survey of the California objects held in European museums.

In May, 1985, Travis Hudson and I went to Europe, where—either separately or together—we visited some 18 different museums, and compiled additional information on their holdings of California materials to supplement the data that Hudson had accumulated in 1983 and 1984, and that he intended

Treasures from Native California: The Legacy of Russian Exploration, Travis Hudson and Craig D. Bates, Edited by Thomas Blackburn and John R. Johnson, 15–17.

to present in a separate, future publication. Tragically, Travis's sudden death in July 1985 brought these plans to a devastating halt, and resulted in a lengthy hiatus in the publication of the different sets of valuable information that he had accumulated in the course of his research. For a variety of reasons, I felt that it was incumbent on me to complete these projects as best I could. With the encouragement and assistance of Jan Timbrook of the Santa Barbara Museum of Natural History, I gained unlimited access to Travis's voluminous notes and photographs, and began the lengthy task of wrestling the mass of data into publishable form. My first priority after Travis's death was to complete volumes four and five of *The Material Culture of the Chumash Interaction Sphere*, which were subsequently published in 1986 and 1987. I next worked on completing and expanding the European museum survey, which was published in 1990 as *Time's Flotsam: Overseas Collections of California Indian Material Culture*. Finally, in 1992, I was able to turn my attention to the task of editing the present book on the spectacular Russian collections and to begin shepherding it into print.

I began by digitizing the text, putting it into an electronic format, and carefully editing the entire manuscript. In addition, Stephen Watrous was invited to revise and update his original forward to the book, which he did in October, 1993; that version is the one that is presented here. The manuscript was then sent to Craig Bates for what I rather naively believed to be a few minor additions and corrections that could be accomplished quickly and with relatively little effort. Unfortunately, Bates was deeply involved at that point in a number of other critical projects, and felt that he simply did not have the time in his busy schedule to revise the text properly and with the care that he believed it deserved. Thus matters stood for several years.

In May 1998, Craig Bates, Brian Bibby, David Roche, and a group of nine dancers from Grindstone Rancheria went to Russia in conjunction with a cultural exchange program to participate in an international music festival, and to concurrently conduct research at the Kunstkamera. Bates thus had the opportunity to spend two intensive days personally examining the collection at length, to photograph many of the objects, and to clarify a number of troubling issues regarding details of construction or the nature of the materials used in certain items—issues that had arisen because of ambiguities or seeming gaps in Hudson's original notes. As a consequence, his interest in the Russian collections was renewed, and circumstances seemed to once again favor successful completion of the long-delayed project. Fate, however, appeared to have other ideas.

In February 2002, Craig Bates suffered a sudden, massive stroke that left him physically handicapped, unable to read or write, and able to communicate verbally only with great difficulty. It seemed to me at the time that this final twist of fate had delivered a nearly fatal blow to any chance that the book could be completed as originally envisioned, and I resigned myself to the idea that the great Russian collections might continue to languish in obscurity for many more years. However, Craig's condition began to slowly improve with time, and by the summer of 2008 he was able—with the unflagging assistance of his wife, Sheila Deeg—to once again begin making necessary revisions to the manuscript. Those revisions were satisfactorily completed, and the way was finally clear to bringing the long delayed project to a successful conclusion.

The task of turning a complex manuscript into a finished publication has been rendered considerably easier because of the many contributions of two valued colleagues, John Johnson and Glenn Farris, to whom I owe a profound debt of gratitude. John, ably assisted by Fred Schaeffer, took on the arduous task of reviewing, organizing, and digitizing the many photographs and drawings that Travis compiled in the course of his research, sought out additional images when there were gaps in the visual record, and obtained necessary permissions from often far-flung institutions. He has been instrumental in obtaining funding to defray the costs associated with the use of many of the images reproduced here, and has played a critical role in arranging for publication. In short, his editorial help has been invaluable.

While both the wording and structure of the text are essentially the same as originally penned in 1985, I have chosen to make some necessary, minimal alterations, guided to a great extent by suggestions made by Glenn Farris. The text and citations, for example, have been updated to reflect both advances in scholarship and Bates's reexamination of the St. Petersburg collection in 1998, as well as the wealth of new historical accounts that have become available as a consequence of such publications as James Gibson's invaluable *California Through Russian Eyes, 1806–1848* (2013). Glenn has also contributed a useful summary of some of the more significant developments that have occurred during the last few years involving Russian activities in early California, and outlined the current status of research in what is becoming an increasingly active field of scholarly interest. He has also suggested a number of additional citations and emendations that have added materially to the value of the text. Several tables and a number of figures that provided detailed measurements of certain artifact classes or contained data that seemed redundant or superfluous in light of recent publications have been deleted. At its heart, however, this is, I feel, the book that Hudson and Bates originally envisioned, and that it is an enduring testament to their scholarship. I believe that it has been well worth the wait, and hope that you, the reader, will feel the same.

July, 2014

Acknowledgments

This study is not, of course, the product of our efforts solely, but rather of those of many institutions and individuals—and we would like to take this opportunity to extend our sincere appreciation and heartfelt thanks to them all.

First, the authors would like to thank those who helped us locate obscure or rare publications, many of which were in Russian or German, and those who translated them into English: for library resources, Stephen Watrous, Nicholas Rokitiansky, Glenn Farris, E. H. Crownhart-Vaughan, the staffs of the Bancroft Library at the University of California, Berkeley, and at the Santa Barbara Museum of Natural History, especially Clifton Smith and Shirley Morrison; for translations, Carl Moody, Stephen Watrous, M. W. Kostruba, George Brown, Paul Hodireff, Jeanie England, Mariehelena Kakonen, Ruth Puckett, and Sister Victoria of Our Lady of Kazan Skete. A special thanks also to Carl Moody for the transliteration of Russian citations in our bibliography.

Next, there are a number of institutions and individuals which allowed us to study their California collections for comparative purposes. Foremost among these are the European museums containing Russian-collected materials. For St. Petersburg's Museum of Anthropology and Ethnography, we wish to thank Doctors Rudolf Its (Director), Rostislav Kinzhalov (Head of the American Department), Aleksander Terukov (Deputy Manager of Collections), and curators Elena Okladnikova, Roza Liapunova, Elena Vasilieva, and Galina Ivanova; for Moscow State University's Museum of Anthropology, Dr. Nina Smirnova (Curator); for Frankfurt's Weltkulturen Museum, Dr. Mark Münzel (Director) and Herbert Wagner (Conservator); for Munich's Museum of Mankind, Dr. Helmut Schindler (Curator); for Oldenburg's Natural History Museum, Dr. K. O. Meyer (Director); and for Helsinki's National Museum of Finland, Dr. Pirjo Varjola (Curator). Other museums which provided support and cooperation, along with the abbreviations we use to cite the objects in their collections, are the following:

AMNH	American Museum of Natural History, New York
BKM	Brooklyn Museum, Brooklyn
BM	British Museum, London
DAM	Denver Art Museum, Denver
FM	Field Museum of Natural History, Chicago
FNM	National Museum of Finland, Helsinki
HMA	Hearst Museum of Anthropology, University of California, Berkeley
LBNM	Lava Beds National Monument, California

LVNP Lassen Volcanic National Park, California

MAI Museum of the American Indian, New York

MAE Museum of Anthropology and Ethnography, St. Petersburg

MAP Musée de l'Armée, Paris

MER Musée d'Histoire Naturelle et d'Ethnographie, La Rochelle

MC Mission San Carlos, Carmel

MH Musée de l'Homme, Paris

MPM Milwaukee Public Museum, Milwaukee

MSU Moscow State University Anthropology Museum, Moscow

MVB Museum für Völkerkunde, Berlin

NMD National Museum of Denmark, Copenhagen

OPM Oakland Public Museum, Oakland

PM Peabody Museum, Harvard University, Cambridge

PRM Pitt Rivers Museum, Oxford University, Oxford

RMAC Redding Museum and Art Center, Redding

SBM Santa Barbara Museum of Natural History, Santa Barbara

SC State of California, Parks and Recreation, Sacramento

SDM San Diego Museum of Man, San Diego

SMD Staatliches Museum für Völkerkunde, Dresden

SMV Staatliches Museum für Völkerkunde, Munich

SNO Staatliches Museum für Naturkunde, Oldenburg

SVZ Sammlung für Völkerkunde, University of Zürich, Zurich

ULM Ulster Museum, Belfast

UMP University Museum, University of Pennsylvania, Philadelphia

USM United States National Museum (Smithsonian), Washington, D.C.

WKM Weltkulturen Museum, Frankfurt

YPM Yosemite National Park Museum, Yosemite

Manuscript production required the services of many people. For photography, we wish to thank the Brooks Institute of Photography, Santa Barbara, and Michael Dixon, Staff Photographer for the National Park Service, Yosemite National Park. Artwork was undertaken by Kathleen Conti; editorial reading was provided by Carla Martinez. Becky Cleek helped with preparing photographs for use in the book.

Identifications of wood, feathers, basketry materials, and so on were provided by several fellow staff members at the Santa Barbara Museum of Natural History: Paul Collins, John Schmidt, Waldo Abbott, Jan Hamber, and Jan Timbrook. We would also like to thank William Cain and Dorothy Washburn for providing sample basketry materials for comparative purposes; a similar kit for feathers was provided by Charles Woodhouse, Jan Hamber, and Paul Collins. Aid with the identification of projectile point distributions was provided by David Fredrickson. Larry Dawson aided in the identification of some of the basketry items, as did Bruce Berstein; Brian Bibby assisted us considerably with information regarding dance regalia, and provided several photographs of artifacts. The complexities of native village names, when recorded in nineteenth-century Russian and later transcribed into English, provided us with no small problem, and it is a pleasure to acknowledge the assistance of Randall Milliken in untangling these and providing us with a clearer understanding of which particular village was associated with a specific people. Thanks also to Adrienne Kaeppler for her help on the feather blankets in Leningrad, and to Thomas Blackburn for his drawings of the two feather belts in La Rochelle, France.

Although not consulted directly in terms of this project, a number of native people also contributed to our work by sharing knowledge of their culture, especially material culture objects. Foremost among them was the late Henry Azbill (circa 1896–1973), whose knowledge of his own Chico Maidu people and their neighbors contributed greatly to our knowledge of their material culture and ceremonial life. Others include Elsie Allen (Pomo) and Brown Tadd (Sierra Miwok); many more enriched this study by sharing with us their extensive knowledge, without which a fuller understanding of the importance of the Russian collections would not be possible.

Last, but far from least, we would like to thank the National Academy of Sciences of the United States and the Academy of Sciences of the USSR for allowing Hudson to study the Russian collections as part of an interacademy exchange program, and the Wenner-Gren Foundation for Anthropological Research, whose 1983, 1984, and 1985 grants allowed Hudson to examine additional Russian-acquired objects curated in Frankfurt and Munich, as well as California Indian material housed in some 32 European museums located in 14 countries. Appreciation is also extended to the National Endowment for the Humanities, whose *Travel to Collections* program also aided Hudson during the 1985 survey work in Helsinki.

* * *

The editors have also benefited greatly from the expertise, assistance, and enthusiastic support of numerous individuals during the lengthy process of preparing this book for publication, and we are most grateful to each and every one. Glenn Farris, in particular, was invaluable in providing useful references, correcting inevitable errors, suggesting necessary modifications, and significantly updating the text, as was Randall Milliken in supplying information on the identification and distribution of the various native groups that the Russians and other foreign visitors encountered in early California. We appreciate the kind assistance of the following individuals in obtaining various digital images used in this volume: Elena Prasolova and Nadezhda Stanulevich of the Russian Academy of Fine Arts, St. Petersburg; Kathy Arndt and Charles Hilton of the Elmer E. Rasmusom Library, University of Alaska, Fairbanks; Nuria Moreu Toloba, Departamento de Documentación, Museo de América, Madrid; Barbara Beroza, Acting Chief Curator, Yosemite National Park Museum; Robin Wellman, State Park Interpreter at Fort Ross State Historic Park; the staff of the Special Collections Department at the Honold Library, Claremont; and Brian Bibby, who permitted us to use photographs taken during his own visit to study collections at the Museum of Anthropology and Ethnography, St. Petersburg. We are also grateful to the University of Oklahoma Press for permission to reprint numerous excerpts from James R. Gibson's recent volume, *California Through Russian Eyes, 1806–1848*. Fred Schaeffer played an especially critical role at the Santa Barbara Museum of Natural History in locating, selecting, and assembling images, obtaining and improving digital scans, and obtaining necessary permissions from various institutions. He was assisted in this by Jan Timbrook, Ray Corbett, Katherine Bradford, Naomi Buffington, Brian Holguin, Danisha Figueroa, and Susan Morris. Finally, Pat Mikkelsen at Far Western Anthropological Research Group kindly volunteered to produce the map, ably assisted by Paul Brandy, with advice from Randall Milliken. Thank you one and all.

Chapter 1

Introduction

The Kunstkamera's California Collection

For Spain's Minister to Russia, the Conde de Lacey, the year 1772 was filled with anxiety. Rumors were circulating in St. Petersburg of further Russian expansion into the North Pacific, rumors similar to those which only three years before had prompted the beginnings of a chain of missions and presidios along the Alta California coast to protect that area from Russian expansion (Watson 1934:19–22). Suspicions of continued Russian interest in the North Pacific found alarming support in the discovery of a printed Russian map. For de Lacey, the situation called for a notification of Madrid at once in the hope that there might still be enough time for Spain to extend and reestablish her claims to the coast above Monterey, which was also vaguely considered to be Alta California. Orders went out from the Spanish court to outfit an expedition to the North Pacific to investigate Russian activities and to reaffirm Madrid's claim. Through the viceroy of New Spain, the task was assigned to Juan Josef Perez Hernandez, whose vessel *Santiago* sailed into the waters off what is now western Canada two years later (Wagner 1937:172–173); however, the voyage was already too late.

The riches to be gained from the fur trade had already come to the attention of St. Petersburg, and as a consequence, the Russians were sailing the waters of the North Pacific in search of sea otters and fur seals. The hunters, called *promyshlenniks*, were originally sent out by merchants and investors representing a number of trading companies, but by 1799 the number of parties involved had been reduced to one—the Russian-American Company. Its presence in the North Pacific created even more difficulties for Spanish claims through the establishment of permanent settlements in the land of "Russian America" (Zagumlennyi 1964).

Treasures from Native California: The Legacy of Russian Exploration, Travis Hudson and Craig D. Bates, Edited by Thomas Blackburn and John R. Johnson, 23–28.

a. 

Figure 1.1. Fort Ross as depicted by two early visitors: (a) Auguste Duhaut-Cilly, 1828;

Russian fur trading companies differed somewhat from their British and American counterparts; they not only traded directly with the natives, they also conscripted them. Aleut and Kodiak Islanders, for example, became serfs, with their compulsory labor paid in clothing, tobacco, and food (Gibson 1978:363). This system resulted in a number of colonies becoming permanent outposts and settlements from which the Russians could then operate. Moreover, because excessive hunting eventually created a need to scour new regions for "soft gold," the Russian presence and influence in the area quickly spread (Gibson 1978:359; Wagner 1937:156–157), and—to the detriment of Spanish interests—the general direction that expansion took was southward along the coast. Madrid countered with its own colonial expansion, which moved northward along the coast of Alta California and established a series of missions and presidios. It was now only a matter of time before a Russian sailor or hunter would encounter a Spanish soldier or priest somewhere north of San Francisco along the rugged California coast.

Although the initial contact between Russians and Spaniards in California took place in San Francisco during the 1806 visit of Nikolai Rezanov, actual Russian settlement occurred some 50 miles further north, at a place the Spanish called Bodega Bay and that the Russians called Port Rumiantsev. Here, a shallow bay afforded Russian vessels from as far away as Kamchatka and Alaska a place to unload their cargo and pick up furs and other produce bound for the north. By 1812, Count Rezanov's 1806 dream of a Russian settlement had become a reality (Figure 1.1). The new colony would soon include not only Port Rumiantsev, but also a stockade (Fort Ross) and some intervening farms as well, all of which were expected to provide a base of operations for both the sea mammal hunters that were exploiting California's soft gold and for the agricultural activities whose products could be exported to Russian colonies in the far north (Essig 1933:151). The Russians hoped that the malnutrition, scurvy, and other hardships that afflicted Sitka, Kodiak, and the other northern settlements would be alleviated by importing fresh fruits and vegetables from California to grace their tables; the profits to be made from furs were a welcome bonus (Petrov 1977; Rokitiansky 1977).

Fort Ross became a way station, and among its many visitors were a few military men and

b.

(b) Il'ia Voznesenskii, 1841. *Courtesy of Ft. Ross State Historic Park.*

scientists who took a keen interest in the natural history and ethnography of the region that the Russians were to call "New Albion," and of adjacent portions of Alta California.[1] Many ethnographic objects were taken back to Russia (and other European countries) by these men as curios, collectibles, and souvenirs, and these items often ended up in the various "cabinets of curiosities" and "chambers of rarities" that were so popular at the time (Bates 1983; Blackburn and Hudson 1991; Hudson 1984). At first these small, private "museums" merely represented the natural history and "artificial" interests of their princely or gentleman-scholar owners; however, in time they were to be accessioned into much larger, public-oriented collections which constituted the nucleus for many of Europe's finest ethnographic museums. The cabinet of Tsar Peter the Great, for example, later formed the basis for St. Petersburg's Kunstkamera Museum, known today as the Museum of Anthropology and Ethnography and named after Peter the Great (Anonymous 1970).

The Kunstkamera has the distinction of being Russia's first scientific institution. Begun in 1718 on the banks of the Neva, the building was completed two decades later and became the museum for the Imperial Academy of Sciences. The museum, which is now nearly 300 years old, is still operating, and is presently administered by the St. Petersburg Division of the Russian Academy of Sciences. The Kunstkamera is not only Russia's oldest scientific institution, it has the additional distinction of housing the largest collection of pre-1850 California ethnographic materials to be found anywhere in the world.

Most Californians—and indeed, most Americans—would probably be astonished to learn that such a large collection was housed in Russia rather than in a prominent American institution such as the Smithsonian, the Museum of the American Indian, or the Autry Museum. How, they might wonder, could it have ever gotten there? The answer is simple. Before the Smithsonian Institution was established in 1846, such collections were taken to museums in various European cities, and no such museum was as involved with or as interested in California as the Kunstkamera. It became the repository for the many minor collections from Russian America that were assembled by navigators, explorers, and naturalists; it also came to house the incredible collection acquired by Il'ia Voznesenskii in 1840 and 1841. Voznesenskii, whose natural history and ethnographic specimens numbered in the thousands, was active during the final months of Russian involvement with California (Bates 1983) and just before the 1849 Gold Rush was to destroy many aspects of traditional California Indian culture.

Despite the uniqueness of the Kunstkamera collections—particularly those portions assembled by Voznesenskii—they were fated to languish for decades in almost total obscurity. There were many reasons for this neglect, although problems of communication stemming from geographical distance, language differences, and national politics were particularly critical. Russian scholars were faced with such difficulties as the absence of comparative collections, a lack of training in California ethnography and archaeology, and limited access to both published and unpublished data, while American scholars were generally unaware of the scope of the Russian collections and had no idea as to who might be consulted for specific information.

The importance of the Kunstkamera collections, of course, is a result of the fact that they are unique, and that they represent a period of California Indian life that is otherwise known only from skimpy historical descriptions and from limited archaeological collections. Rapid changes in material culture took place after the arrival of Europeans in California, as newly introduced tools, materials, processes, and ideas displaced traditional ones. Within the span of eight decades—from Spanish settlement in 1769 until territorial annexation under the Americans—tribe after tribe succumbed to foreign influences, until in many places traditional ways of life existed only in memory.

The loss of many individuals through murder, warfare, and disease (Cook 1943) also contributed to the diminished populations of native peoples, and the near annihilation of many groups. When these changes occurred, any opportunity for the few fledgling American museums, then extant in the east, to acquire examples of traditional material culture items was difficult at best, and in some cases impossible. A few pre-1850 objects, of course, did make it into American collections—such as the 1841 materials acquired by the Wilkes expedition (Viola and Margolis 1985), which were eventually deposited with the Smithsonian (and some of which were later exchanged with other museums)—but for the most part such objects were taken to Europe.[2]

Although the single largest collection of early California items is to be found in the Kunstkamera, other much smaller collections have been found in the most surprising places, probably as a result of various types of transactions: objects were given as presents, sold to museums and dealers, sold again at auction, passed on to relatives, and so on (Blackburn and Hudson 1991; Gunther 1972:ix). In Moscow, for example, the university's Museum of Anthropology has a small collection of 11 undocumented pieces from California. Similar California pieces are turning up in Germany because of their past association with Russified or Baltic Germans. In Frankfurt, for instance, the Museum für Völkerkunde houses eight pieces which were collected by Ferdinand von Wrangell, while the Staatliches Museum für Völkerkunde in Munich has seven California pieces, some of which were acquired by Georg von Langsdorff. The Staatliches Museum für Naturkunde und Vorgeschichte in Oldenburg houses a feather belt collected by Ivan Kuprianov. Helsinki's Suomen Kansallismuseo has 67 objects from California that were collected by Arvid Adolf Etholen and Uno Cygnaeus. A feather headdress and decorated bone ear ornament collected by Ferdinanad Deppe in San Jose in 1837 is present in the Christy collection at the British Museum's Museum of Mankind; they were obtained in an exchange with the Berlin Museum. Undocumented—or more correctly, unidentified—early California pieces are probably to be found in other European museums as well, like the recently discovered basket (SVZ 11788a) in Zurich which stylistically resembles others from Russian California, or the two similar baskets at the Estonian History Museum in Tallinn.

To small European museums, such unidentified pieces are often of little importance, and their lack of provenance tends to foster a lack of appreciation. Moreover, such objects, which were collected "just yesterday" (that is, in the eighteenth or early nineteenth century), might seem to local museum personnel to lack the glamorous antiquity of paleolithic tools or the beauty of ancient Egyptian or Greek sculptures and ceramics (Gunther 1972:ix). As a consequence, most of the interest in these smaller collections has tended to come from American scholars. Our own interest in the collections from Russian California began as a result of correspondence with our Russian counterparts in the Kunstkamera (or as it is actually known today, the Museum of Anthropology and Ethnography or MAE). Additional information, although unfortunately very limited in scope, was obtained from papers by such Russian scholars as Efimov and Tokarev (1959), Liapunova (1967), Kojean (1979), and Okladnikova (1981). None of these sources, however, was a satisfactory substitute for an examination of the actual specimens; fortunately, Hudson was given the opportunity to study the entire collection in person in March 1983.

After being selected to take part in a scientific exchange program between the National Academy of Sciences of the United States and the Academy of Sciences of the USSR, Hudson was able to devote three weeks to studying the California collections in St. Petersburg. A portion of that time was devoted to working with the curator assigned to the collections, Elena Okladnikova, who has since published additional descriptive information on these objects (Okladnikova 1984). The scientific exchange program also allowed Hudson to briefly see the collections at Moscow State University's Museum of Anthropology.

Additional support provided by a grant from the Wenner-Gren Foundation enabled Hudson to visit 32 other museums in 14 countries while he was in Europe, including Finnish and German institutions that were known to hold early California materials collected by the Russians. Subsequent correspondence with still other European museums has been added to the information in hand to expand our understanding of this little-known period in California Indian ethnohistory (Bates 1983; Blackburn and Hudson 1991; Hudson 1984).

After Hudson's sudden death in 1985, the manuscript for the present book languished unfinished for several years. However, in May, 1998, Bates had the opportunity for further research at the Kuntskamera. He accompanied a group of Native Americans from Northern California (Grindstone Reservation in Glenn County) who went to Russia to give a performance of traditional Nomlaki/Wintun/Pomo dances and to carry out research at the Kuntstkamera in St. Petersburg. The Grindstone group had been asked to participate in an annual international music festival and was the sole representative from the United States. There were nine performers from Grindstone Reservation, as well as Brian Bibby, Craig Bates, and David Roche. The eight-day event included three performances, an afternoon of cultural exchanges, a morning spent viewing the materials on exhibit, and two additional days of examining the collections in storage. The trip was funded by the Trust for Mutual Understanding (N.Y.) and Arts International as both a cultural exchange and an opportunity for further research.

Because we are placing particular emphasis on Russian interactions with native California peoples, we have chosen to look at Russian California from a cultural rather than from a political or geographical perspective (although most of the objects and many of the descriptions are directly related to that specific region). The objects which we will describe here were all collected by Russians, or by Russified Finns or Germans, within a broader California that included Spanish-Mexican Alta California to the south and the great central valley to the east; these collectors were the very same Russian visitors whose descriptions of California Indian people we will also cite. It is this broader, ethnographic California which will provide the setting for our study of Russian collecting activities.

Although a comprehensive description of the early Russian collections is not yet feasible, we still wish to share—in the form of detailed descriptions and commentary—some of the beauty and anthropological importance of these fascinating objects from an earlier California.

Chapter 2

Documenting a Collection

The Collectors and Their Objects

Although the great Russian collections represent the most comprehensive sampling available of the material culture of California Indian peoples of the first half of the nineteenth century, they do have one significant drawback—poor documentation. Documentation provides important information about an object's place in time and space, and thus gives us a reliable means by which to define or evaluate the item's function, technique, form, decorative style, and ethnic source. An absence of documentation requires that we make "educated guesses" or attributions, and base our statements upon what we have learned from documented pieces. Obviously, the more we know about the provenience of an object, the greater its scientific value, and—in the case of collections from Russian California—that scientific value ranges from slight to extremely high.

It may come as a surprise to some readers to learn that the best documented collections are not housed in Russian museums, but rather in German and Finnish institutions. The reasonably good provenience data associated with the items collected by Wrangell (in Frankfurt), by Langsdorff (in Munich), and by Etholen (in Helsinki) allow us to place them rather narrowly in time and space within native California. The opposite extreme—involving objects with no provenience data at all—is represented by the Moscow collection (and possibly by the Zurich basket, if we assume that it may also have had an earlier, Russified German connection). Since these two extremes in documentation are present in the Kunstkamera collection, and because its contents comprise the great majority of the materials upon which we have based our study, it is important to examine its documentation closely.

First, the Kunstkamera's catalog indicates that the museum staff initially thought the collection contained 305 objects from California; 296 of these were assigned the prefix number 570,

Treasures from Native California: The Legacy of Russian Exploration, Travis Hudson and Craig D. Bates, Edited by Thomas Blackburn and John R. Johnson, 29–46.

Table 2.1 California Items in European Museums Collected by Russians

Functional Category	(MAE) St. Petersburg	(MSU) Moscow	(MFV) Frankfurt	(SMM) Munich	(SNO) Oldenburg	(FNM) Helsinki	Totals
Hunting-Gathering							
Tule boat	1	-	-	-	-	-	1
Hair rope	1	-	-	-	-	-	1
Decoy headdress	2	-	-	-	-	-	2
Bow	9 (3)	-	-	-	-	3	12
Arrows	163 (34)	5	-	-	--	50 (2)	218
Quiver	1	-	-	-	-	1 (1)	2
Net bag	2	-	-	-	-	-	2
Seed beater	1	-	-	-	-	-	1
Burden basket	4	-	-	-	-	-	4
Carrying net	2	-	-	-	-	-	2
	186 (37)	5	0	0	0	54 (2)	245
Home-Hearth							
Winnowing tray	2	-	-	-	-	-	2
Sifting tray	1	-	-	-	-	-	1
Mortar/pestle	2	-	-	-	-	-	2
Hopper basket	1	-	-	-	-	-	1
Basket tray	2	-	-	-	-	-	2
Basket bowl	1	-	-	-	-	-	1
Seed cake	1	-	-	-	-	-	1
Firemaking kit	1	-	-	-	-	-	1
Woven mat	3 (3)	-	-	-	-	-	3
Feather blanket	2	-	1	-	-	-	3
Storage jar	1	-	-	-	-	-	1
	17 (3)	0	1	0	0	0	18
Apparel							
Woman's skirt	2	-	-	-	-	-	2
Flicker headband	5 (4)	-	-	1	-	1	7
Feather topknot	6	-	1	-	-	-	7
Hairnet	2	-	-	-	-	-	2
Hairpin	17 (9)	-	-	-	-	4 (1)	21
Feather cape	1	-	-	-	-	-	1
Kukshui cloak	1	-	-	-	-	-	1
Mollok cloak	1	-	-	-	-	-	1
Clamshell belt	1	-	-	-	-	-	1
Feather belt	4	-	1	-	1	1	7
Feather band	-	1	-	-	-	-	1
Ear rod	18 (2)	3	-	-	-	-	21

Functional Category	(MAE) St. Petersburg	(MSU) Moscow	(MFV) Frankfurt	(SMM) Munich	(SNO) Oldenburg	(FNM) Helsinki	Totals
Ear pendant	-	-	2	-	-	-	2
Necklace	5	-	-	2	-	-	7
Feather rope	1	-	-	-	-	-	1
	64 (15)	4	4	3	1	6	82
Ritual Gear							
Gourd rattle	-	-	-	1	-	-	1
Birdbone whistle	4 (2)	-	-	-	-	-	4
Ceremonial basket	6 (3)	-	-	-	-	1	7
Feast basket	2		1			5 (4)	8
Gift basket	19 (4)	2	2	3	0	1	28
Gaming bones	2	-	-	-	-	-	2
	33 (9)	2	3	4	-	7	49
Totals	**300 (64)**	**11**	**8**	**7**	**1**	**67**	**394**

Note: the number of missing items is in parentheses. Totals do not include two baskets at the Estonian History Museum in Tallinn.

and were attributed to I. G. Voznesenskii. Six of the remaining nine objects were given a prefix number not associated with Voznesenskii, while the remaining three items received no number at all! At some time in the remote past, the Kunstkamera museum staff reconsidered some of their identifications in the 570 series, and subsequently transferred three baskets (570-110, -111, and -112) to the Northwest Coast collections, and two whistles (570-60, -61) to the South American collections. During Hudson's 1983 visit, new identifications again changed these totals: two "California" baskets were considered by him to be Chinese, while two feather blankets attributed by the Russians to Polynesia were identified as Californian. The corrected total for the Kunstkamera collections as of March 1983 was, thus, 298 California objects, 290 of which were in the Voznesenskii series. In 1985, Kunstkamera visitors from Western Europe discovered that a buckskin object decorated with shell beads and identified as an Iroquois man's robe (1901-1) was actually a California woman's skirt (Feest 1985); in 1998, another such skirt (MAE 1-1061) was found in the Northwest Coast collection, bringing the total number of California pieces to 300. Table 2.1 provides a summary of the collection. (See Appendix for a detailed list.)

It is apparent from the catalog data that the bulk of the collection (98 percent) is assigned to Voznesenskii, but we suspect that that percentage is about twice what it should be; in other words, we question the attribution of all of these specimens to Voznesenskii, and we offer the following history of the St. Petersburg collection to show why.

Voznesenskii, who collected in California in 1840 and 1841, sent his natural history and ethnographic objects via ship to St. Petersburg, where they were delivered to the appropriate museum staff. The ethnographic materials were received at the Kunstkamera by curators Radlov and Russov, and their list was then compared with Voznesenskii's inventory. Nothing further was done with the material until 1892, when curator F. F. Russov hired ethnographer K. K. Gil'zen (1864–1918) to sort out the entire Russian American collections, including the California materials. Gil'zen, working with the original specimen lists prepared by Voznesenskii many years before (Liapunova 1967:5; Shur and Gibson 1973:55; Stepanova 1944:278), concluded that Voznesenskii's California collection included 152 objects, which Gil'zen believed fell into the following groupings: 68 hunting objects; 31 objects of clothing and ornamentation; 8 religious items; and 45 tools, utensils, and materials (Liapunova 1967:26).[1] In conclusion, although the 570 series now contains some 300 California pieces, only 152 are likely to have been actually collected by Voznesenskii.

Since Voznesenskii's original specimen lists were later used to arrive at the type and total number of objects collected, it seems logical that these very same lists, supported by the collector's field notes, could be used to sort the items he actually collected from those which he did not. Unfortunately, these materials remain unpublished, and as such are unavailable to non-Russian scholars. What precious little we do know about these manuscript materials suggests that they may be of little help. Five of Voznesenskii's 12 notebooks on Russian American ethnography were devoted to California Indian people. Although Gil'zen was also assigned the task of organizing these notes for publication, the work was never completed (Liapunova 1967:5; Stepanova 1944:278), and one Russian scholar described their condition as "poor; often descriptions are fragmentary and difficult to read. Also, his journals have little organization for the entries" (Lipshits 1950:416–417). Another Russian scholar described Voznesenskii's handwriting as "small, very hurried and illegible...the text often alternates with lists of zoological and ethnographical collections" (Shur and Gibson 1973:56).

One published Voznesenskii inventory concerns a list of various objects that he had acquired at Mission San Rafael and was sending back to the Kunstkamera, including a feather belt called a *kala* (Liapunova 1967:14). If the object was received by the Kunstkamera and survives in the collections to this day, then it must be one of the four feather belts which Hudson observed during his visit; three of them had 570-series numbers on them, while a fourth had no catalog number at all. Without additional information, it is impossible to determine which of the four is Voznesenskii's Mission San Rafael *kala*.

Another example of the problem of matching written records with actual specimens can be found in the St. Petersburg arrow collection. Liapunova (1967:26) mentions that Voznesenskii's original arrow inventory included 26 examples collected from 18 different—and specifically named—villages. This appears to be wonderful documentation, until one examines the actual arrow collection and finds that it contains 163 arrows, all attributed to Voznesenskii, and none of which carries any identification as to where it may have been collected; in addition, 34 arrows could not be located at all during Hudson's visit.

There are problems even when written documentation can be matched with actual museum specimens. The two feather cloaks (Figure 2.1), which represent the *kukshui* and *mollok* costumes worn by central Californians (Bates 1983), are good examples. Voznesenskii (with the help of John Sutter) was able to acquire these two specimens, which are now extremely rare, somewhere in central California. But from whom did he acquire them? Was it from the Southern Maidu (Nisenan) or Miwok? Since there is little comparative material available in

Figure 2.1. California exhibit at the MAE, St. Petersburg. The objects on display were collected by Voznesenskii in the vicinity of Sutter's Fort in 1841. The figure on the left is wearing a *mollok* cloak made of an entire condor skin, while that on the right is dressed in a *kukshui* cloak (a long, enveloping cloak made of crow feathers). *Photo courtesy of the MAE.*

American museums, and no information exists that tells us where Voznesenskii acquired the objects in central California, we are unable to attribute them to any particular region.

The overall integrity of the 570 series poses yet additional problems. It was noted above that the collection contained baskets attributed by Hudson to the Northwest Coast and China, as well as two bone whistles that were considered by the Russians to be South American.[2] Since California and South American bone whistles could be quite similar, Hudson made an effort to locate these items in order to verify the identification, but they could no longer be found. The same thing occurred in conjunction with the three Northwest Coast baskets. The 570-series catalog also listed one object (570-71) that was described only as "unknown." Hudson's request to see this specimen elicited the comment that the item had been destroyed during the German siege of Leningrad in World War II. How the Germans managed to destroy this particular "unknown" object alone was never explained. Another 64 missing objects were reported to be in conservation, although no list of these items had been made, and the conservator was unavailable for comment.

Some of the problems that exist concerning the integrity of the 570 series are also evident in the 2520 series. This series involves a collection of blankets, two of which are very beautiful examples of California feather work. The Kunstkamera catalog indicates that these two objects are documented; in fact, it states that the pieces were acquired during Captain James Cook's third voyage (1776–1780) and were collected on the Pacific Northwest Coast (Gunther 1972:208, 260–262; Rozina 1978). This obvious error shows the need to review any original documentation whenever possible; the complete story is worth summarizing here.

In the summer of 1779, Cook's vessels put into the Russian port of Petropavlovsk in great need of supplies. Their needs were met by the port commander, Major Behm, who received several ethnographic pieces in return as a token of British appreciation. Behm sent these objects on to the Tsar's museum in St. Petersburg, where years later they were catalogued in various numbered series, one of which was the 2520 grouping that included blankets.

The problematic identification of the two blankets in this group (2520-8 and -9) surfaced when a Polynesian scholar noted that the blankets could not be from that region of the world, or from the Northwest Coast, the two regions that had been visited by Cook. Kaeppler (1983), questioning the Cook-Behm "documentation" further, resorted to the original documentation—the list prepared by Behm himself of the objects which he sent from Petropavlovsk to St. Petersburg. The two blankets in question were not listed. When the catalog entries were examined, it became clear that the two objects had been added to the list (2520-1 to -7) of Behm's material, which suggests that someone at the museum had misidentified these objects and assumed them to be part of Cook's collection, and therefore had attributed them to Behm while neither checking the original lists nor identifying the provenience of the objects under consideration. Kaeppler (1983) continued working on the problem of identification and determined (with the assistance of William Sturtevant, later confirmed by us) that the two blankets were indeed from central California.

Figure 2.2. California objects in the (Kunstkamera) Museum of the Imperial Academy, St. Petersburg, in 1873. California items shown are a topknot headdress (570-4), two feather belts (570-11 and -12), and a feather blanket (2520-9). The photograph was found at the Musée de l'Homme in Paris. *Robert Heizer Collection, Santa Barbara Museum of Natural History.*

How these pieces became associated with Behm material is anyone's guess, but we can perhaps date the error as having taken place sometime after 1873, on the basis of a photograph of that date (Figure 2.2). A University of California, Berkeley, anthropologist, Robert Heizer (n.d.), discovered the photograph during his work at the Musée de l'Homme, Paris, in the 1950s; the picture shows four California pieces that are labeled as having come from Fort Ross, along with another object from Kodiak Island. A notation on the print states that the photograph was taken in 1873, and that the objects depicted were in the Museum of the Imperial Academy, St. Petersburg—which is, of course, the Kunstkamera.

Heizer must have been as puzzled by the photograph as we were, for such questions as who took it and why, and how it ended up in Paris, have just recently been answered. Since the chain of events that was involved nicely illustrates some of the detective work involved in ethnohistorical studies, as well as providing some insight into early foreign interest in the Russian collections, the reader will perhaps forgive us for digressing for a moment in an effort to reconstruct the picture's history.

A clue as to who took the picture, and why it was taken, appeared in a short footnote in a published Russian article that was later translated into English (Shur and Gibson 1973:38, 58, note 8). The note mentioned the fact that Hubert H. Bancroft, the pioneer California historian of the West, had hired a French scholar named Alphonse Pinart (1852–1911) to transcribe various Russian California documents housed in the archives in St. Petersburg and Moscow, and that the work was undertaken in 1874–1875. Since Pinart was also a Parisian, and one so interested in California Indian languages that he visited the state in the late 1870s (Heizer 1952), it seems to us that the photograph can reasonably be attributed to him; perhaps he intended to provide Bancroft with illustrative material on California Indian objects in Russia. Pinart was certainly in St. Petersburg at the time the photograph was taken, and (as we later learned) he was also interested in the descriptions of Choris and Kotzebue of California Indians (Pinart 1955:133–135), and was interested in studying the collections from Russian America (Parmenter 1966:7–9, 11).

Pinart's interest in artifacts was discovered when we contacted the Bancroft Library at the University of California, which houses both Bancroft's papers and many of the transcriptions made for him by Pinart (Morgan and Hammond 1963:176). We wondered if a file of correspondence between Pinart and Bancroft might contain a letter or note about the photograph. No such file was found, but we did encounter several folders of drawings made by Pinart of various Russian American artifacts from the Arctic and Northwest Coast (Pinart 1873). The drawings had been made in 1873 during Pinart's visit to a number of museums in Europe, including the St. Petersburg's Kunstkamera, Moscow's "Rumantzoff [Rumiantsev] Collection in the Public Museum," Dorpat's (=Tartu, Estonia) "Das Vaterlandische Museum," and others in Finland and Copenhagen. Unfortunately, whatever notes, drawings, or photographs of California materials that Pinart may have studied were not found in any of the folders, and we can only surmise that he must have separated them out for some special purpose. In addition to the mystery of the missing drawings, we wonder why Bancroft failed to even mention the name of Il'ia Voznesenskii in his Russian California sections, since his hired researcher, Pinart, had almost certainly come upon Voznesenskii's materials in St. Petersburg.

Whatever the story behind the photograph might be, it is clear that in 1873 the feather headdress (MAE 570-4), the feather belts (570-11 and -12), and the feather blanket (2520-9) were considered to be from California, and that the selection of these particular objects may have had something to do with a particular collector, although we can only guess. It would thus seem that after 1873 someone—and we suspect Gil'zen because it was his task to catalog the collection in the 1890s—assigned the feather blankets to Behm's collection. We might point out here that problems with documentation such as this are not unique to Russia, but can be found in museums throughout the world in which very early, poorly documented collections are curated.[3]

We suspect that a sorting of objects by material (as occurred in the example of the 2520 series) might explain some of the mixing in the 570 series as well: additional items were added to the Voznesenskii list just as they were added to Behm's, thus doubling the apparent size of the collection. Such a sorting is evident within the 570 series, for all of the headdresses have been grouped together, as have all of the bows, all of the ornaments, all of the arrows, and so on. Curators, in grouping items by type rather than by collector—perhaps the old records were not available, or a mixing of Voznesenskii's materials with other early Russian collections had already occurred prior to the 1880s—created a situation in which a large number of objects became associated with a few collectors, and whatever information that might have existed on their provenience was lost. This hypothesis would not only explain why little or no information exists for many of the objects, but would also resolve the question of what became of some of the early collections which are known to have been deposited at the Kunstkamera: they were simply absorbed into a large, generic "California" collection that was attributed solely to Voznesenskii. The following review of some of these collections supports our inference.

Let us begin with the collection of Georg von Langsdorff, a Russified German medical doctor and naturalist who in 1821 was elected to the Imperial Academy of Science (Golovnin 1979:31, note 23). Langsdorff had visited San Francisco in 1806, where he had collected a number of ethnographic objects; these were later divided between Munich—where some items were presented about 1825 as a gift to Maximilian I, King of Bavaria (Müller 1980:21)—and St. Petersburg, which also received some objects which had belonged to Admiral Johan von Krusenstern (Anonymous 1970:1). Certainly some of Langsdorff's collection went directly into the Kunstkamera. Liapunova (1967:7–8) states that Krusenstern had received written orders to collect for the museum, and that upon the expedition's return a collection was sent to the Admiralty Museum (St. Petersburg), as well as to the Kunstkamera. It is not known what happened to this collection, but we firmly believe that at least some of the California objects in it were at some point in the past resorted, catalogued into the 570 series, and erroneously attributed to Voznesenskii.

Figure 2.3 California and Alaskan items collected by Georg von Langsdorff in 1806, as illustrated in his account (1814) of his travels. *Courtesy of the Honold Library.*

Figure 2.4. Munich shell necklace (SMV 213) matching one illustrated in Figure 2.3.

Langsdorff (1814:II:55–60) mentions his California collection, and states that "among other curiosities that I procured" were flicker headbands, bows, arrows, baskets, clam shell money, and feather blankets. He apparently had someone illustrate his collection upon his return to Europe, for drawings of a number of these objects were prepared for his book (Figure 2.3). What is important in all of this is that one of the necklaces that is depicted (Langsdorff 1814) matches perfectly one of the necklaces (570-23) in the Kunstkamera's collections (Figure 7.29). The second necklace (Figure 2.4) has turned up in the Langsdorff materials in the Staatliche Museum für Völkerkunde, Munich (SMV 213). It would seem that Langsdorff's collection was distributed between these two great museums, and that the Kunstkamera probably received more than just a necklace. Other illustrated pieces are suggestive, but without details we can only speculate.

It is virtually a certainty that the Kunstkamera received other ethnographic collections from Russian visitors to California. From its very conception, the Russian-American Company supported such activities, as Dmitry Zavalishin, a naval officer and visitor to Russian America and Mexican California in 1824, noted:

> In a scholarly sense the company's activity is no less significant. It sends out scientific expeditions and makes reports on both sides of the Pacific; its ships make discoveries at sea, and it publishes maps, has established a magnetic observatory, produces geological investigations, and promotes research and the assembling of collections in natural history, etc. (Zavalishin, quoted in Liapunova 1967:11)

Zavalishin himself may have been a contributor to the Kunstkamera collections. As a member of Mikhail Lazarev's crew, which circumnavigated the globe on the frigate *Cruiser*, the young man spent the winter of 1823–24 in California, visiting various missions and the Presidio of San Francisco, and upon one occasion was presented with a feather belt (Gibson 1973:369, 382). A year later, Zavalishin was in St. Petersburg, hoping to convince the Tsar to annex California; unfortunately, his membership in a secret society (whose members were later called Decembrists and who had staged an abortive revolt in 1825) led to his arrest and a sentence of 13 years of hard labor in Siberia (Gibson 1973:372). Since it would be unreasonable to assume that Zavalishin's feather belt went with him to Siberia, it is possible that he, or one of his family or friends in St. Petersburg, may have placed it in the Kunstkamera.

It is also possible that some members of Otto von Kotzebue's two expeditions to California (in 1816 and 1824) contributed ethnographic objects to the Kunstkamera. Kotzebue, a Russified German, was accompanied on his first voyage by naturalists Adelbert von Chamisso and Johann Friedrich Eschscholtz, whose plant and animal collections were taken back to St. Petersburg (Chamisso 1986; Kotzebue 1830; Mahr 1932). Artist Louis Choris, whose drawings of California Indian people we shall see later in this work, was also a member of this expedition, and like the others may also have picked up ethnographic objects during his travels. Unfortunately, if such collecting did take place, we have no record of it, although some of the objects in the Kunstkamera collections do generally resemble some of Choris's illustrations of California Indian "weapons and

Figure 2.5. California artifacts as depicted by Louis Choris. Entitled "Weapons and Utensils of California," the 1822 lithograph is based upon a lost 1816 watercolor.
Courtesy of the Honold Library.

utensils" (Figure 2.5). However, such similarities are to be expected, since Choris visited tribes where objects were known to have been collected by other visitors. It is interesting that American anthropologist Roland Dixon (1907:438) was of the opinion that a large bundle of unlabelled bows in the Kunstkamera had been collected by Kotzebue. The basis for Dixon's conclusion is unknown, although he may have been in communication with Gil'zen; however, the reasons for Gil'zen making such an attribution will probably remain a mystery.

Eschscholtz was present again, along with two other naturalists, during Kotzebue's second California visit. Their collecting activities centered about San Francisco Bay, with visits to missions Santa Clara and San Rafael, Fort Ross, and Point Reyes (Essig 1933:207–208). Again, it is not known whether ethnographic objects were acquired at this time, but it would appear that Kotzebue himself had such a collection. Portions of his Northwest Coast materials were housed at the family estate in Reval (=Tallinn), Estonia, until 1929, at which time they were purchased in part by the British Museum (Coe 1976:149, item 342). What became of the rest of the collection is a mystery, although there is a possibility that some of it may eventually surface in an Estonian museum or perhaps in a private collection someplace in Europe.[4]

Russia's next significant visitor to California, Vasilii Golovnin, should definitely be considered a contributor to the Kunstkamera's collections. Golovnin's 1818 expedition visited Fort Ross and Monterey, where Golovnin and artist Mikhail Tikhanov set about describing California Indian people (Shur 1974), specifically those encountered at Bodega Bay (Farris 1998). Golovnin (Figure 2.6), like Kotzebue, was a collector; upon his return to St. Petersburg he mentioned that "in my collection of curiosities [from California] I have many items made by them, such as baskets" (Golovnin 1979:149). One would suspect that some of these objects were an assortment of gifts "consisting of various parts of their regalia, arrows, and household items" which had been presented to Golovnin by a Port Rumiantsev [probably Coast Miwok] chief referred to as Valenila (Farris 1998; Golovnin 1979:165). Some of these objects may well have been illustrated by Tikhanov, whose drawings will appear later in this book. There are some rather interesting correspondences; for example, some of the Kunstkamera regalia—a beaded hairnet, a topknot headdress, and a banded feather rope—appear in one of Tikhanov's drawings, as do bows, arrows, and quivers. But as we noted earlier regarding Choris's sketches of material culture, such correspondences are to be expected. The eventual fate of Golovnin's collection is unknown, but it probably went to the Kunstkamera. Golovnin is known to have been actively involved with this museum and to have been a member of the Imperial Academy of Sciences at the time of his death in St. Petersburg (Golovnin 1979:xxvi).

One collection which is known to have ended up in the Kunstkamera is that assembled by Kiril Khlebnikov, an officer in the Russian-American Company—and the collection is also known to have disappeared there. Khlebnikov's collection from America, which was sent to the Kunstkamera sometime shortly after 1825, almost certainly included California objects (Dmtryshyn and Crownhart-Vaughan 1976:iii–iv). During his long involvement with California, which included visits to Monterey, San Francisco, and Santa Barbara (Farris 2013; Khlebnikov 1990; Shur and Gibson 1973:45), he is likely to have assembled a collection from south-central California. He is the only Russian collector known to have visited the Chumash area (around Santa Barbara), and it is probably significant that the Kunstkamera collections were found by Hudson (1983a,b) to contain three Chumash baskets, two of which had 570 series numbers. One south-central California basket in the collections might well have been collected by Khlebnikov as well, as might have other central California examples. During Khlebnikov's 16-year span of visits to California (1817–1833), Russian expeditions from Fort Ross did venture into the interior.

Another official of the Russian-American Company who is known to have been a collector was Admiral and Governor Ferdinand von Wrangell. He was in California on at least three occasions: in 1818 as a member of Golovnin's staff; in 1833 when he toured Fort Ross and inland areas along the Russian (Slavianka) River as part of an inspection tour; and in 1835 while enroute to Russia via Mexico (Dufour 1933:243; Gibson 1969:213–214; Pierce 1972b:40, 44–45). It can not be determined during which of these years his small but dazzling collection of California ethnographic pieces was assembled, although his official visit in 1833 seems the most likely candidate because he recounts an expedition he made up the Russian River to the Santa Rosa Plain on that trip (Wrangell 1980:34–40). He was greatly impressed by the artistry of the Native Californians, and

Figure 2.6. Some prominent Russian visitors to early California: (a) Otto von Kotzebue (from Kotzebue 1948, *courtesy of the Rasmuson Library*); (b) Vasili Golovnin (from Golovnin 1864, *courtesy of the Rasmuson Library*); (c) Ferdinand von Wrangell (from Nordenskiöld 1881, *courtesy of the Rasmuson Library*); (d) Il'ia G. Voznesenskii, *courtesy of Nicholas Rokitiansky.*

in 1833 wrote a description of them which mentioned a headdress, belts, and earrings as being among the objects which exhibited their inventiveness (Wrangell 1974:4); these were probably the very same objects which were later donated by his father-in-law, Baron Wilhelm von Rossillon, the councillor at Reval, to the Senchenburg Naturalists Society in Frankfurt.[5] The date of the gift was July, 1854, according to museum catalog records. In 1877, the Society transferred the collection to the Historical Museum; in 1904, that museum passed it on to the Municipal Ethnographic Museum (Vatter 1925:75, 77–78). The items are presently curated at the Museum für Völkerkunde, Frankfurt.[6] The Deutsches Leder- und Schuh Museum in Offenbach has two of the Wrangell pieces on exhibit at this time. We can only hope that if other Wrangell pieces are extant in Eastern Europe (for example, in Estonia), they will eventually surface.

Still another official of the Russian-American Company who was known to have been a collector was Admiral and Governor Ivan Kuprianov, who served in Sitka between 1835 and 1840 (Dufour 1933:243–244; Essig 1933:209, note 64; Pierce 1972a). Kuprianov is known to have had a collection of ethnographic objects which had been brought to him as presents, and it would seem that one of these objects was a California feather belt (SNO 335) resembling Wrangell's, which is now housed in a museum in Oldenburg (Feest 1984:71). Kuprianov may have collected the belt himself during his brief visit to San Francisco on his homeward journey to Russia (Pierce 1972a:24). However it was acquired, Christian Feest (1984) notes that Kuprianov's collection of 89 numbered objects—with only the belt being from California—was sent to Oldenburg when a Russian princess married the Duke of Oldenburg, sometime after 1840. It is possible that some of the Kuprianov material remained in St. Peterburg and perhaps ended up in the Kunstkamera before his death in 1857; we will probably never know for sure. Liapunova (1967:12) mentions that Kuprianov's collection of ethnographic materials was arranged, catalogued, and packed for shipment to St. Petersburg by Il'ia Voznesenskii during his May to July 1840 visit to Sitka; the task helped to acquaint the young scholar with the sorts of ethnographic objects he would later see in Russian California.

Admiral Arvid Adolf Etholen, who was Kuprianov's replacement as governor (1840–1845), also assembled an ethnographic collection from Russian America. Etholen, who was born in Helsingfors (= Helsinki) at a time when Finland was a part of the Russian Empire, joined the Russian-American Company and arrived in Sitka in 1818. He served for several years as the commander of various company ships involved in trade, transport, and exploration. In 1824, in company with Khlebnikov, he visited California; this visit was followed by a return to European Russia and a departure from service (Pierce 1972b:19). He rejoined the company less than a year later, and again commanded various ships, some of which visited California in 1828, 1829, 1832, and 1833, travelling as far south as San Diego (Farris 2013:21). In 1837 he paid a short visit to Helsinki; he then returned to Sitka in 1838 and was eventually appointed as governor (Pierce 1972b:20–21).

During his first visit home (1825–1826), he donated some ethnographic objects to the Turku Academy. The academy's minutes for 1825 list a number of such objects, including a feather-beaded basket and two feather-beaded belts from California; the minutes for 1826 list additional objects, such as a head decoration (flicker band?), stone ax (?), and stone arrow point. None of these objects had tribal identifications. A year later, the entire collection was destroyed by fire (Varjola 1981; personal communication 1985).

Etholen compensated the Academy for its losses sometime between 1827 and 1847; the additional objects included six "northern Cali-fornia" baskets (marked with the number 63 followed by Russian letters), four hairpins, a feather belt, two bows, one quiver, two large bundles of arrows, and a basket (marked with the number 39), all of which came from the Rio Sacramento village of *Siuamni* (Varjola 1981; personal communication 1985).

Siuamni corresponds to the Plains Miwok village of *Seuamne*, which was located in the Sierran foothills southeast of Sutter's Fort (Bennyhoff 1977:113, 165). Since the region had only been visited by a handful of Spanish explorers and American and Hudson's Bay Company fur trappers prior to Etholen's California tours, it seems doubtful that he had somehow found his way to *Seuamne*. A more logical hypothesis involves a Russian ethnographic collector who did—Il'ia Voznesenskii. In 1841, less than two years after Captain John Sutter had established his fort, Voznesenskii arrived in California and was aided by Sutter in collecting a number of ethnographic objects from various villages in the locality; among these items were a number of arrows that were collected at *Seuamne* (Liapunova 1967:26). In 1841, Voznesenskii left California for Sitka, where he would have had the opportunity to provide Governor Etholen with a small ethnographic collection from *Seuamne*, assembled either by him or received as a gift from Sutter. One obvious way to test such a connection between Etholen's materials and those of Voznesenskii involves the arrow collection, which is presently housed in the Finnish National Museum with the rest of Etholen's materials. It is reasonable to assume that if Voznesenskii had given Etholen examples of *Seuamne* arrows, he might either purposefully or unwittingly have failed to select specimens from the same quiver sets—sets in which all of the arrows were identical in terms of their riband markings, materials, and (usually) dimensions and arrow point type as well. To find out if this had occurred, we compared the Helsinki arrows against those in St. Petersburg; the results confirmed the fact that there was indeed a connection. Four of the Helsinki arrows perfectly matched three in St. Petersburg, which suggests that they had originally been part of the same quiver set and had been divided after being collected. Alternatively, of course, the arrows with the same riband markings could be the work of a single arrow maker; thus if the arrows were collected at *Seuamne*—by either Voznesenskii or Etholen—they would appear the same. Therefore, while it is tempting to conclude that the arrows were from the same quiver set, it can not be stated unequivocally that they were collected by the same individual and later separated. We can only suggest that Etholen very probably received all of his *Seuamne* and "Rio Sacramento" objects from Voznesenskii in 1842, and then presented them to the Turku Academy sometime between 1845 and 1847.

Another Finnish collection in Helsinki which has an Etholen connection involves Finland's most respected educator, Uno Cygnaeus. Cygnaeus, a Lutheran pastor, traveled with Etholen from Finland to Sitka in 1838, and remained there to establish a chapel; he returned to Finland in 1845 in the company of Etholen (Pierce 1972b:21). In 1913 his descendants presented the Finnish National Museum with various ethnographic objects, among which were a bow and several arrows that they believed were from California. There is no information which links this collection directly with Etholen, but the similarities are so striking that one cannot help but wonder if Cygnaeus received the objects from either Etholen or Voznesenskii. We compared the arrows in this collection with those in St. Petersburg and found no exact matches, although most of the arrows shared enough features to indicate that they had a common source, which perhaps was *Seuamne* or its environs.

Other Russian American Company employees who may have collected objects that eventually reached the Kunstkamera were Georgii Chernykh, an overseer of a ranch not far from Port Rumiantsev (Chernykh 1967; Essig 1933:209), and Petr Kostromitinov, an agent of the company during the final days of Fort Ross and the author of an ethnographic account about California Indian people (Kostromitinov 1974).

The small collection curated at Moscow (Lomonosov) State University's Museum of Anthropology may well have come from any of the sources mentioned above, but since they are without documentation we will probably never know for sure. Perhaps the collection once formed part of what Pinart called the "Rumantzoff Collection" in the Public Museum of Moscow, which in 1873 housed several Northwest Coast pieces. Russian collectors who are known to have been associated with Moscow include two physicians of the Russian-American Company, Eduard L. Blaschke and Friedrich Fischer (both of whom are known to have acquired natural history specimens which they deposited in St. Peterburg and Moscow), and Adelbert von Chamisso, the member of Kotzebue's 1816 expedition who was mentioned earlier (Chamisso 1986; Essig 1933:207–209). Since Chamisso's natural history collection is known to have been donated to the Imperial Museum in Moscow, it is possible that he may have also provided the ethnographic pieces that Pinart found in the Rumantzoff Collection, which was the rubric applied to the items acquired by the exploring party led by von Kotzebue. Chamisso (1986:245) comments: "Among many of them [California Indians] the weapons are the bow and arrow. Among some of them these are of extraordinary elegance, the bow light and strong, the outer arch covered with animal sinews."

Although it is possible that California materials are presently housed in Estonia's ancient Dorpat, our efforts to communicate with contemporary staff to verify our suspicions have been unsuccessful. We can only surmise that California pieces were (and perhaps still are) there, since Pinart described the original collection as containing objects from the Northwest Coast.[7]

None of the other collections mentioned so far, of course, can compare in either quality or quantity with that found in the Kunstkamera, nor can any other contemporary collector's achievements match those of one Russian visitor to California, Il'ia G. Voznesenskii, who was largely responsible for assembling that collection.

Chapter 3

A Superb Collector Visits California

Il'ia G. Voznesenskii

For a man responsible for nearly half of the California objects housed in the Kunstkamera, Il'ia Gavrilovich Voznesenskii had a rather humble origin. Born in St. Petersburg on July 19, 1816, he was the son of a retired junior officer on disability from the Academy of Sciences, and as a consequence received only an elementary education. At the age of five he was a student in the academy's print shop, where he remained until the age of 11. A transfer to the Zoological Museum, probably due to the boy's interest in science, set the stage for Voznesenskii's training as a naturalist, for he worked as a conservator under the direction of E. P. Menetrie. As his interests continued to develop, he took part in various collecting trips to the Caucasus region and to the shores of the Caspian Sea (Gil'zen 1916:2–3; Liapunova 1967:6).

In 1839, his destiny was determined forever when academicians of the academy recommended that he be sent as a naturalist to Russian America to collect zoological and botanical materials for the academy's several museums. After his appointment was approved, Voznesenskii was given instruction in specimen collection by curator F. F. Brandt. Fortunately for California Indian studies, the scope of his activities was broadened to include the collection of ethnographic materials for the Kunstkamera, and curator E. I. Schroeder provided the young assistant preparator with instructions on the collection of such specimens. By August 20, 1839, the 23-year old adventurer had left St. Petersburg and was well on his way to the New World and the start of a distinguished career (Gil'zen 1916:3–4; Stepanova 1944:277).

Voznesenskii arrived in Port Rumiantsev on July 20, 1840, where he devoted the next 10 days exclusively to collecting botanical and ornithological material. The three-masted vessel *Helena* served not only to bring him to Russian California, but also to give him shelter during this period.

Treasures from Native California: The Legacy of Russian Exploration, Travis Hudson and Craig D. Bates, Edited by Thomas Blackburn and John R. Johnson, 47–50.

Then, after brief visits to ranches run by fellow Russians Igor Chernykh and Efim Munin, the young naturalist headed the short distance northward to Fort Ross (Alekseev 1977:33; 1987; Blomkvist 1972:105).

Aleksandr Rotchev, the manager of Fort Ross, was there to greet him, and although the tiny colony was in a hectic state of activity in preparation for the abandonment of the fort, Rotchev nevertheless found time to support the young man's endeavors. After receiving an orientation to Russian California, Voznesenskii resumed his collecting activities, venturing on one occasion as far north as Cape Mendocino (Alekseev 1977:35; 1987; Lipshits 1950:416–417).

By mid-October 1840, Voznesenskii had decided that it would be wise to prepare the large number of specimens he had acquired during his three months in Russian California for shipment to the St. Petersburg museums. The collection, which was packed into 13 boxes and two kegs, included two boxes whose contents were listed as being ethnographic in nature: Box 2 contained costumes, while Box 14 was listed as containing "weapons and other items" (Liapunova 1967:16). These materials were transferred to San Francisco, where they were loaded aboard the *Nicholas I* for the long journey back to Russia (Liapunova 1967:16). However many objects there may have been in these two boxes, we can conclude that the material most likely consisted of bows, arrows, and feather regalia from the Kashaya and Southern Pomo peoples, and perhaps from the Coast Miwok as well.

With these Russian California materials on their way, Voznesenskii now decided to devote his attention to collecting in adjacent Mexican California. He devoted the next four months to this project, spending much of the time in the San Francisco Bay region. Using Yerba Buena (modern San Francisco) as a base of operations, he made frequent collecting trips along the shores of the immense bay: in the south, to Mission Santa Clara and the pueblo of San Jose; in the east, to San Leandro, San Antonio, San Pablo, and Pinole; in the north, to Napa, Petaluma, and Sonoma; and in the west, to Mission San Francisco, Cape Drake, Sausalito, and to various islands within the bay (Alekseev 1977:37, 39; 1987; Liapunova 1967:14).

The second shipment of objects for St. Petersburg was prepared on February 16, 1841, and included only one container (Box 21) of ethnographic objects. In a letter to Schroeder, Voznesenskii described the material as coming from the Suisun Indians, and stated that it included a belt, or *kala*, which was a gift from Padre Tijos[1] of Mission San Rafael; a hairpin, or *sipek*; earrings, or *alok*; and a headband, or *uaglku*. The letter also stated that during his entire time in the bay area, he was unable to "barter with the Indians" (Liapunova 1967:16). From this we might conclude that he collected relatively few items in Mexican California, and those probably consisted only of the items named above, some or all of which were from Mission San Rafael.

Having shipped the Mexican California collections back to St. Petersburg, Voznesenskii now turned his attention to a third region, that surrounding Sutter's "New Helvetia" property, located in what would later become Sacramento. The area presented him with an exceptional opportunity to "find there...some dwellings of Indian tribes" and have "a favorable opportunity to barter with the Indians" (Voznesenskii, quoted in Liapunova 1967:16). It would seem that disturbances to traditional lifeways in Russian and Mexican California had reached such a point that by the time of Voznesenskii's visit only New Helvetia offered the opportunity to visit and collect in a more traditional cultural setting. Sutter was extremely helpful, and directed the young man's attention to a number of villages where he was extremely successful in acquiring "some rather rare items in the area of ethnography" (Liapunova 1967:15). Two of these objects were the now famous Kuksui and Mollok costumes (Alekseev 1977:40–41, 1987) that were mentioned earlier (see Figure 2.1); there was also a collection of arrows from some 26 different villages, the names of which Voznesenskii recorded in his notebook (Liapunova 1967:26). Randall Milliken, by using mission records, was able to identify many of the villages listed by Voznesenskii: they included Seku, which was apparently a Southern Maidu village that the Plains Miwok referred to as Sekumne, and Yalesumne, as well as the Plains Miwok villages of Sonolomne, Uaypeymne (Guaypem), Siusumne, Chucumne, Noipume, Seuamne, Tihuechemne, Ssicomne, Lelamne, Macheme, Yakhumyamne, Sakayakumne, Lopotstimne, Locolome, and Tuseale. These villages represented a wide array of Plains Miwok triblets that extended eastward to the Sierra Nevada foothills. Perhaps Voznesenskii's route took him down into the Delta, up the Mokelumne River, overland north to the American River, and then back to Sutter's Fort. It is also possible that he only visited some of the villages named, and met native peoples from others either at the fort or at some of the villages that he visited. At any rate, those villages which can be located with some degree of certainty are shown on the map (see Frontispiece).

Voznesenskii arrived back at Yerba Buena on April 2; after a few days visiting, he proceeded on to Fort Ross, where he began preparing the New Helvetia materials for shipment back to Russia (Alekseev 1977:40–41, 1987; Liapunova 1967:15). Since Russian scholars have not yet published an inventory of his California collection, we can only infer that the scope of this final ethnographic assemblage must have been considerable when compared to the number of objects that Voznesenskii had already shipped home from Russian California and Mexican Alta California.

Between April and August 1841, Voznesenskii returned to the exploration of New Albion, with small excursions to visit Mission San Rafael and climb to the 4,343-foot summit of Mt. St. Helena in Napa County. During the final two months of his visit Fort Ross ceased to exist as a Russian colony (although title to the fort was not legally transferred to Sutter until January 1, 1842). Port Rumiantsev was now the scene of a new and final phase of Russian activity in California as the colonists prepared to depart. What ethnographic materials (if any) may have been collected during these final days we do not know. On September 5, 1841—after being in California for slightly over a year—Voznesenskii departed with the former Ross residents for Sitka (Alekseev 1977:42; 1987).

Alaska, Kamchatka, and the Aleutian Islands became the sites for Voznesenskii's collecting activities over the next several years, as academicians in St. Petersburg continued to extend his fieldwork. A large number of natural history and ethnographic specimens were collected as a result. However, in 1848 Voznesenskii's prolific collecting came to an end; with his health deteriorating, he returned to St. Petersburg on June 23, 1849, thus concluding 10 years of intensive fieldwork in Russian America and Siberia (Alekseev 1977:43, 1987; Gil'zen 1916:5–6).

For Voznesenskii, the time had come to focus upon the curatorial needs of his collection. The position of conservator was proposed, with the suggestion that he replace Schroeder. However, in tsarist Russia, this position was considered to be class-dependent, and Voznesenskii was not therefore qualified; he was instead given the title of Acting Conservator, with the full rank of collegiate registrar. Although he lacked the title, the young man had essentially replaced Schroeder and assumed the latter's responsibilities for maintaining the acquisitions inventory and the technical laboratory (Gil'zen 1916:12–13). These duties seem to have occupied much of his time, for Voznesenskii failed to publish the results of his important work.

The extreme importance of Voznesenskii's collections and notes can to some extent be measured in terms of their scope and range. The natural history collections alone, for example, include over 9,000 objects; about 6,000 of these are zoological, 2,000 are botanical, and about 750 consist of fossils and minerals (Gil'zen 1916:10–11), some of which represent life forms that are now extinct. Voznesenskii's various journals, notebooks, and pencil and watercolor sketches also serve as important sources of information on the natural history and anthropology of Russian America; today, these documents are widely scattered throughout the various museums and archives of the Russian Academy of Sciences (Blomkvist 1972; Lipshits 1950:416–417; Stepanova 1944:278).

The more than 1,071 ethnographic pieces that he collected (Liapunova 1967:26)—many of which are not duplicated in the collections of any of the world's other great museums (Gil'zen 1916:12; Stepanova 1944:277)—represent yet another significant contribution. Voznesenskii certainly recognized the importance of his California collections, for he wrote that "the great wealth of my acquisitions in all branches of science and ethnography was made upon my move to Ross" (Lipshits 1950:416).

Recognition of Voznesenskii"s accomplishments came within his lifetime; not only did he achieve advancement within the museum, he also was awarded memberships in various distinguished organizations. In 1852, for example, he was elected to the Imperial Geographic Society, followed a few years later by charter membership in the Russian Entomological Society. Tsar Alexander II also awarded him recognition. However, despite his position, honors, and awards, he was never financially secure. He passed away, a widower, at the age of 55 on May 17, 1871, survived by his 13-year-old daughter, who was left without any means of support (Gil'zen 1916:8–9, 13–14). Il'ia G. Voznesenskii was buried in Smolensky Orthodox Cemetery in St. Petersburg.

Perhaps the best tribute to Voznesenskii's work came from an academician at the Imperial Academy of Sciences, who wrote just after his death that Voznesenskii had

> unswervingly and with rare energy, overcoming all obstacles, frequently experiencing personal privations, carried out his mission with tireless labors. Museums of the Academy have been enriched by enormous collections of natural and ethnographic objects from the furthest reaches of our possessions. In a scientific sense, Voznesenskii's rich collections have served as a basis for new academic endeavors of Messrs. Academicians Behr, Brandt, Middendorf, Schrenk, and Schtrauch;[2] and there is not any learned publication about Eastern Siberia and our former North American colonies in which the name Voznesenskii is not gratefully mentioned. (Gil'zen 1916:9)

Indeed, that list is still growing, as we (and others) begin to appreciate the richness and complexity of the world's greatest collection of early California ethnographic material and learn more about the man responsible for creating it.

Chapter 4

Describing a People

The Russians as Ethnographers

One visitor to San Francisco Bay in 1816, Adelbert von Chamisso, was most unusual. As a member of Kotzebue's staff on board the *Rurik,* Chamisso served as the expedition's naturalist and collected information on California's varied plant and animal forms. However, it was not these intellectual activities that made him a bit unusual for his time, but rather his emphasis on the need to learn as much as possible about California's Indian people. He wrote:

> Every fragment of the history of man is of importance. We must leave it to our successors, as our predecessors have done to us, to collect more satisfactory information respecting the natives of California and their languages. (Mahr 1932:85)

Spanish attitudes, for the most part, were quite different, and certainly the Spanish administrators, priests, military men, and other officials—who had the greatest possible opportunity to take note of California Indian peoples—actually took the least interest. As Robert Heizer commented in a discussion on the history of anthropological research in California:

> The Franciscan missionaries were not concerned with recording the "heathenish customs" of their "gentile" (that is, unbaptized) wards, whom they generally classed as ignorant and stupid savages.... Because there is so little fact recorded during the Spanish-Mexican period (1542–1846) on Native Californians in either their "wild" or "domesticated" (missionized) situations, the journals of Spanish, French, German, Russian, and English voyagers who visited the California coast...are ethnohistorically important. (Heizer 1978a:6)

Chamisso himself expressed an opinion as to why the Franciscan missionaries were not interested in native peoples:

Treasures from Native California: The Legacy of Russian Exploration, Travis Hudson and Craig D. Bates, Edited by Thomas Blackburn and John R. Johnson, 51–59.

> The contempt which the missionaries have for the people, to whom they are sent, seems a very unfortunate circumstance. None of them appear to have troubled themselves about their history, customs, religions, or languages: "They are irrational savages, and nothing more can be said of them. Who would trouble himself with their stupidity? Who would spend his time upon it?" (Mahr 1932:83)

Given the severe treatment that the Aleuts and Kodiak Islanders had earlier received at the hands of the Russians (Gibson 1978:363), it seems hypocritical for them to have commented upon Spanish attitudes toward the California Indians. Yet Russian descriptions of the negative attitude that the Spanish had toward native peoples were written not so much in ignorance of their own treatment of the Aleut and Kodiak Islanders, but rather in light of their later treatment of the Tlingit and other Indian people. While harshness was found to be effective in controlling the Aleut and Kodiak Islanders, the Russians soon realized that it could not be applied to the Northwest Coast tribes. As Gibson (1978:380) has noted, the eastern drive from Siberia to Alaska had been too undermanned and too overextended to allow the Russians to effectively subjugate and pacify the far more populated, densely clustered, and socio-politically complex native peoples they were beginning to encounter. The Tlingit, for example, hated the Russians for having seized their ancestral lands and abusing them; their response was to completely destroy Sitka and Yakutat in 1802 and 1805, respectively. The Russians learned from this experience that Tlingit support of their activities was essential; as a consequence, they treated these people with care and respect (Gibson 1978:365, 368). There is little doubt that this "Tlingit policy" was deliberately put into practice at Fort Ross—Russian America's most remote colony—so that the mistakes that had been made at Sitka would not be repeated.

In 1811, Aleksandr Baranov dispatched Ivan Kuskov to select a site for what later would become Fort Ross. The selected site, called *mé-ti'ni* (meaning "unknown") by the Kashaya (McLendon and Oswalt 1978:279), measured about one by two miles in extent and was paid for with three blankets, three breeches, two axes, three hoes, and some beads;[1] the Kashaya were apparently "delighted" to have the Russians come as "allies and protectors" (Bancroft 1885:297).

Spain, however, did not recognize the Russian ownership of Ross as valid and began to apply pressure for the outpost's removal. As a consequence, Baranov brought about a renewal and extension of the old cession by native chieftains by sending Captain Leontii Hagemeister in 1817 to formalize their title by treaty (Dmytryshin, Crownhart-Vaughn, and Vaughn1989:296–298). The result was a treaty which is the only document known to have been executed between Europeans and a California Indian people (O'Brien 1980:11; Spencer-Hancock and Pritchard 1981).[2]

The Russians and Aleuts, who were known to the Kashaya as *'ahqha yow 'bakhe ya'* or "persons from in the water" (McLendon and Oswalt 1978:278), began interacting with the Indian people as "hired laborers" rather than through conscription reinforced by harsh punishment. The local Kashaya became employees of the Russian-American Company, and as such they received an acceptable wage, lodging, and articles of clothing (Fedorova 1973; O'Brien 1980:11). This rather interesting tricultural system existed throughout the lifetime of the settlement and was vividly described by Auguste DuHaut-Cilly (1946:10–11, 1997) during his 1828 visit to Fort Ross. The Russians apparently took considerable care to maintain good relations with Indian people even in areas outside the settlement.[3]

Zavalishin attributed such good relations with California Indians to a Russian acceptance of other cultural systems:

> Whoever has studied the Russian national character knows very well that Russians, if they have not been aroused by some special external circumstance, are very good-natured and well-disposed to everyone, despite differences in religion, nationality, and social status. A Russian disdains neither a savage nor a heterodox.... "Such is their custom," a sailor would say, and without disdain or mockery he would watch the strangest things and perhaps sometimes merely add "wonderful people, really wonderful!" No wonder that the [California] Indians liked the good-natured Russian sailors, especially the generous and affectionate officers. (Gibson 1973:385)

One obvious difference between the Russian and Spanish attitudes toward the California Indians concerned their intelligence. Geiger and Meighan probably summed up the Spanish attitude best when they wrote: "One reason the missionaries held the Indians as simple and backward was the fact that they were not farmers and were failing to make 'proper' use of the excellent agricultur al land they possessed" (Geiger and Meighan 1976:165, note 35).

Moreover, leaving aside the accomplishments of civilized Europe, the Spanish could not help but make comparisons between the California Indians and the Aztec of Mexico, with their monumental architecture, metal work, calendrical system, class society, and so on.

The Russians, on the other hand, did not seem to correlate intelligence with the use of agriculture as opposed to hunting-and-gathering, perhaps because their primary interest was in utilizing the particular abilities involved in the latter lifestyle—a dependence upon natural resources and great skill in hunting animals, particularly for pelts and food—for their own benefit. Of all European visitors to California, the Russians seem to have been the least inclined to consider the Indian people "stupid." Golovnin, for example, whose visit came two years after that of Kotzebue, took exception to some of the earlier comments about the "dull mindedness" of California Indians that had been made by an English explorer, George Vancouver (1792),[4] and by a French explorer, Jean Galaup de la Pérouse (1798). Golovnin (1979:148) reasoned that the simplicity seen in California Indian technology was not a reflection of their intelligence, but a reflection of their environment, since the Indians had to cope with such an abundance of natural wealth in their country.[5] Khlebnikov reached a similar, environmentally deterministic, conclusion:

> Since the native in his primitive condition readily finds his chief needs, food and shelter, everywhere, there is consequently no reason for exerting his intellectual capacities in improving his state; he thinks that of all the inhabitants of the entire world, those of neighboring territories or territories rumored of, he is the happiest. Perhaps it is this mode of life that is responsible for his deep ignorance. (1940:332–333)

Khlebnikov went on to note that in spite of these technological limitations, "one cannot deny a certain degree of intelligence in the Indians.... Their bows...are made very ingeniously." Their arrowpoints are "skillfully" mounted; their basketry is "neatly and firmly woven," and their feather decorations are "beautifully done." In addition, he commented that the Indians who live in the missions comprise artists and craftsmen of all kinds, even though not skilled ones; but that is, perhaps, because they have had neither systematic training nor the chance to observe. Many of them understand the Spanish language and learn to read and write. (1940:333)

Wrangell shared a similar opinion: "Their headdresses, belts, earrings, etc., mostly made of feathers, betray not only their inventiveness, but also a certain penchant for beauty" (Wrangell 1974:5).

Zavalishin also raved about their technology:

> Even in the wild state they displayed remarkable abilities in many respects. They made many artistic and very durable items. Their root baskets and hats were waterproof and combined unusual lightness and durability with resilience; head ornaments, belts, the outsides of baskets, and other articles, which were minutely decorated with the various and multicolored feathers of local birds, were splendid examples of art and patience. (Gibson 1973:382)

However, although the Russians were able to discuss the native environment and technology without comparing them with aspects of European civilization, they were truly unable to be objective about the physical and emotional characteristics of California Indian people at all. As members of the family of mankind, Indian people (Figures 4.1–4.4) could not escape comparison with Europeans. Golovnin, for example, stated that in general the California Indians

> are small of stature and appear to have a weak and flabby build; they are dark skinned, have a somewhat flat facial structure, with straight, very black, coarse hair, and regular white teeth; many have beards, although some pluck out their facial hair in youth by means of bivalve shells. (1979:148)

Kotzebue wrote the following description:

> The physiognomy of these Indians is ugly, stupid, and savage, otherwise they are well formed, tolerably tall, and of a dark brown complexion: the women are short, and very ugly; they have much of the negro in their countenance, only that a negro head may be called handsome in comparison with theirs; they are principally distinguished from the negroes by their very long, smooth, and coal-black hair. (Mahr 1932:61)

The observant Chamisso was as much interested in the similarities as the differences among the native people:

> In their general appearance, they resemble each other, except the Tcholovonians, whom we soon learnt to distinguish by their marked physiognomy, which the fathers [mission priests] could not do. They have all a very savage look, and are of a very dark colour. Their flat, broad countenance, with large staring eyes, is shaded by black, thick, long, and smooth hair. The gradations of colour, the languages, which are radically different from each other; the mode of life, arts, arms, in some of them various lines tattooed about the chin and neck, the way in which they paint themselves for war and for the dance, distinguish the different tribes.[6] (Mahr 1932:83,85)

Kostromitinov, whose residence for a time among California Indian people probably provided him with opportunities for greater insight into their character, wrote this comment:

> The Indians are of medium stature, but one also finds tall individuals among them; they are rather well-proportioned, the color of their skin is brownish...; eyes and hair are black.... The physiognomy of the Indians in general bears an expression of good nature rather than savagery, and one often encounters charming

Figure 4.1. Native Californians as depicted by Louis Choris in 1822 lithograph. Groups represented are *(left to right)* the Ululato, Numpali (probably Olompali), Suysum (Suisun), Olumpali, and Tcholovoni (Cholvon). *Courtesy of Honold Library.*

Figure 4.2. Additional Native Californians depicted by Louis Choris in 1822 lithograph. Groups represented are *(left to right)* the Guymen (Huimen), Utschim (Huchiun), Guymen, and two Saclan. *Courtesy of the Honold Library.*

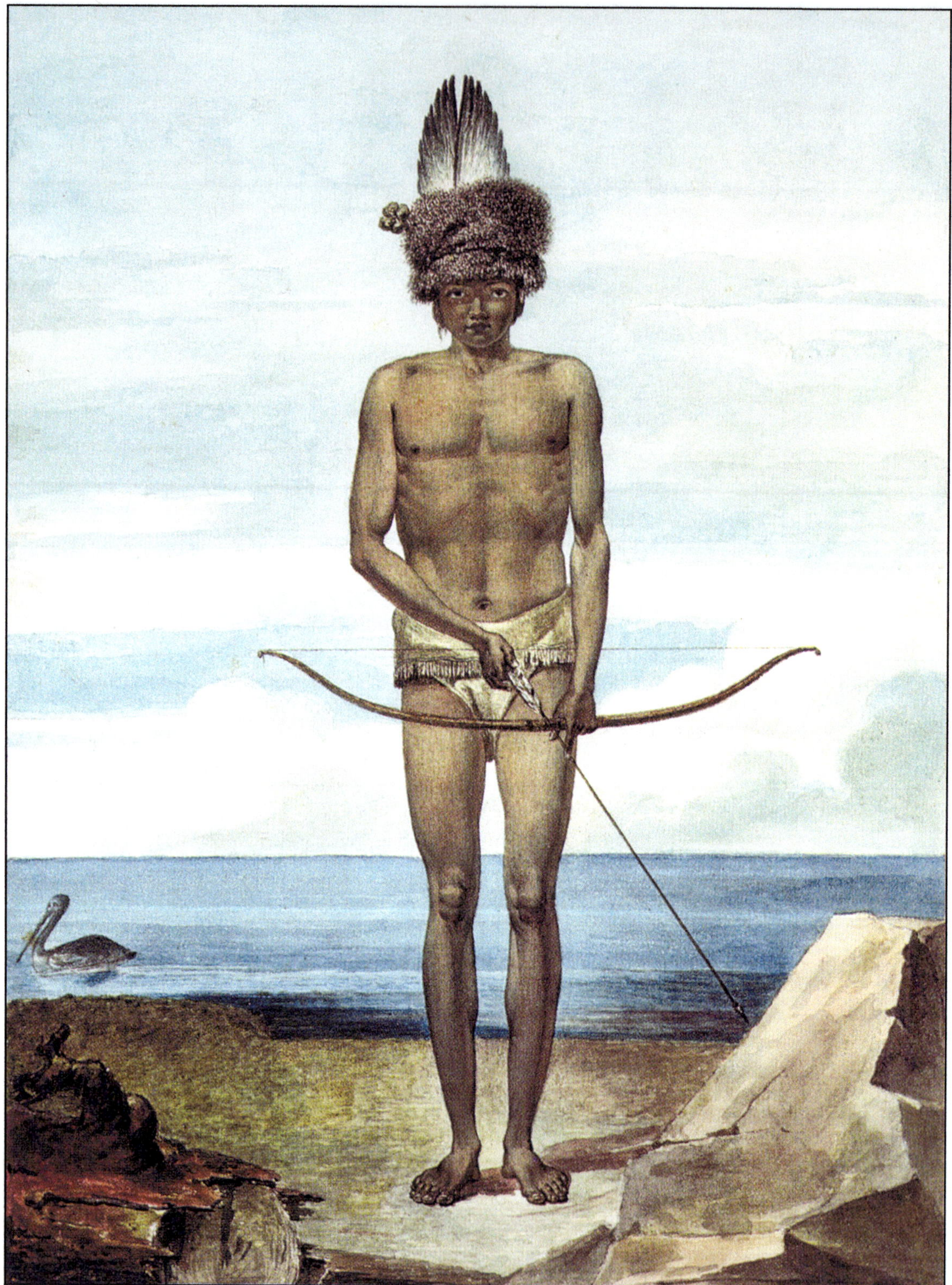

Figure 4.3. A Coast Miwok man at Bodega Bay as depicted by Mikhail Tikhanov in 1818. The watercolor is entitled "An Inhabitant of California by the Name of Valthazar." *Courtesy of the Scientific Research Museum of the Russian Academy of Fine Arts, St. Petersburg.*

Figure 4.4. A Coast Miwok woman at Bodega Bay as depicted by Mikhail Tikhanov in 1818. The watercolor is entitled "An Inhabitant of Rumyantsev Bay in New Albion." *Courtesy of the Scientific Research Museum of the Russian Academy of Fine Arts, St. Petersburg.*

faces, among males as well as females. They are gentle and peaceful and very clever, especially in the comprehension of material objects. They give the impression of great stupidity only because of their excessive indolence and light-heartedness; but they only need to see once some not too difficult or complex task, and they are able immediately to imitate it. (Kostromitinov 1974:7)

Karl Gillsen was also left with a reasonably favorable impression of the native peoples:

> The Californians are of medium height, broad shouldered, and muscular; they are dark chestnut in color, and their features, although somewhat sullen, are not at all unpleasant.... The disposition of the savages seemed gentle to us; but the Spaniards asserted that they are crafty and vicious. Among the women, who dress like the men, we saw several young ones whose appearance was rather agreeable. (Gibson 2013:163)

Language and tribal identity were also descriptive aspects of California Indian life that were of interest to the Russians, but as Golovnin (1979:167) noted, most Europeans were unable to pick out minor differences in customs, manner, and language among these people. Language was given the greatest emphasis in Russian attempts to classify various groups of people into "tribes." In 1806, Langsdorff (1814:II:55, 104) reported that the tribes in and about Mission San Francisco were the Estero, Tuiban, and Tabin, while inland were the Tscholban (= Chamisso's Tchalabones) and the Tamkan;[7] he listed two tribes, a Coast group and an Inland group, near Mission San Jose. Ten years later, Choris and Chamisso expanded the number of tribes in the region to about 15, on the basis of information undoubtedly provided to them by the priests at Mission San Francisco. In 1821, Vasilyev also named a number of native groups in the area (Gibson 2013:203). Many of these "tribes" were probably single villages. In modern terms, these names represent people that we now identify as Coast Miwok, Ohlone, Patwin, and Chulamni Yokuts. Such were the tribes in the northern regions of Alta California.

In Russian California, Wrangell (1974:4) reported that the people living near Port Rumiantsev (that is, Bodega Bay Coast Miwok) could not understand the people (Southern Pomo) living on the plains of the Slavianka (Russian) River, nor those living north of the fort (Central Pomo?). Kostromitinov (1974:7) mentioned several tribes as being present in the vicinity of Fort Ross; they included the Bodega Bay (Olamentko), Steppe-Indians (Kainama = Southern Pomo), Northern (Chwachamaju), and the Marginal groups.[8] The latter, Kostromitinov continued, "are subdivided into a large number of tribes, but their number and relationships are not known in the Ross colony." McLendon and Oswalt (1978:278) noted that the present day Kashaya Pomo were unable to recognize the Russian designations given by Kostromitinov. Some of these tribal designations may have originated with the Eskimo or Aleut; one example of this might be the modern place-name Gualala, which refers to a place that is situated on the coast just north of Fort Ross. McLendon and Oswalt (1978:278) have pointed out that although the place-name was derived from a Central Pomo word relating to water, the name appears as Wallalakh in an 1813 letter from Kuskov to Alexandr Baranov; the *-kh* ending appears to be an Eskimo or Aleut absolutive case suffix, which suggests that the sea hunters had altered a Pomo place-name for their own use. The terms Erio (for the Kashaya people at the mouth of the Russian River) and Erussi (for those at Fort Ross) are corruptions of the Spanish terms *el rio* and *el ruso*, respectively (McLendon and Oswalt 1978:278).

Voznesenskii apparently recorded a number of "tribal" designations and place-names in his notes, but these data unfortunately are still unpublished.[9] Liapunova (1967:26) has stated that Voznesenskii identified the Coast Miwok Indian people as Khukiyuzme, and the Valley Nisenan as Tsuellesk; in addition, Stepanova (1944:278) has mentioned that among Voznesenskii's notes is a manuscript which lists the clans and tribes of the Northern Maidu. Hopefully, when these materials are published, they will not only help to untangle the confusion over ethnic designations, but also help us determine which particular people Voznesenskii was in contact with. Such information is extremely critical to any future understanding of the weapons and clothing, the baskets and utensils, and the host of other objects collected by the Russians to which we now turn our attention.

Chapter 5

Objects of the Quest

Hunting and Gathering Equipment

Hunting devices were among the most prominent possessions of California Indian men, and as such were popular items for foreign visitors to take home as mementos of their trip to North America. We are fortunate that a number of such items in the Russian collections—particularly bows and arrows—survive in European museums, even though nearly all extant examples lack specific collection data concerning which people made or used the item, or in which region in particular the piece was collected. In addition to weapons, the Russian collections are especially noteworthy in that they contain such other items as deer decoy headpieces, a rope, and a model tule boat. These items help to round out our picture of what hunting equipment was like in early California and also document the changes that were taking place in hunting equipment at the turn of the century, when American ethnographers began to seriously study native peoples and collect materials for American museums.

However, while hunting was indeed an important economic activity in Native California, gathering was even more significant. Throughout the state a host of wild plant materials—from roots, bulbs, stems, and leaves to seeds, nuts, and fruits—served as major food sources. The task of efficiently selecting, gathering, and transporting such resources was the responsibility of the women, as was the simple but time-consuming task of processing them for storage or consumption. Such actions required a considerable understanding of botany, but they also required a considerable amount of work. The acorn, for example, required sorting, hulling, drying, pounding, sifting, leaching, and finally cooking; many other types of seeds and nuts also required such extensive processing.

Treasures from Native California: The Legacy of Russian Exploration, Travis Hudson and Craig D. Bates, Edited by Thomas Blackburn and John R. Johnson, 61–93.

The technology most associated with gathering involved basketry. A host of basketry items were manufactured, some by twining and others by coiling, and fashioned from various materials into shapes which over a period of thousands of years had been found to be the most effective. Baskets most closely identified with food preparation will be described later (see Chapter 6); those concerned with gathering are treated here. They include the seed beater and the conical burden basket, which together formed a tool set, as well as the often associated large-meshed net into which the burden basket was placed for carrying. Smaller-meshed net bags, which were used to carry a variety of objects, have been grouped together with hunting devices, since they were more often associated with men and could be used to transport small game.

Hunting Equipment

Model Tule Boat

One of the more significant items in the Kunstkamera's fine collections is a toy or model tule boat (MAE 570-114), no other examples of which are known (Figure 5.1). While this particular example could perhaps have been made for a child or as a model for a European visitor, it undoubtedly reflects the features, in miniature, of a much larger watercraft, one which probably plied central coastal or Bay Region waters. Langsdorff saw such a craft in 1806 and wrote:

> When [communication by water is needed] they make a kind of boat of straw, reeds, and rushes, bound so compactly that it is watertight, and in this they manage to go very well from one shore to the other. It is called by the Spaniards "balsa." The oar used is a long, narrow pole, somewhat wider at the ends, with which they row, sometimes on one side, and sometimes on the other. (1814:II:93–94)

A sketch was made of one of these canoes during this visit; it is reproduced in Figure 5.2 and shows an upturned prow, while the gunwale-sheer line is straight. The stern is nothing more than the termination of the bundles.

Like Langsdorff, Choris and Chamisso wrote about the tule balsa:

> The Indians build their canoes when they are about to undertake an expedition on the water; they are made of reeds. When they get into them they become half filled with water so that the occupant, when seated, is in water up to the calves of his legs. They propel them by means of long paddles having pointed blades at both ends. (Choris in Mahr 1932:101)

> They do not possess...canoes of any kind; they only know how to fasten together bundles of rushes, which carry them over the water by their comparative lightness. (Chamisso in Mahr 1932:85)

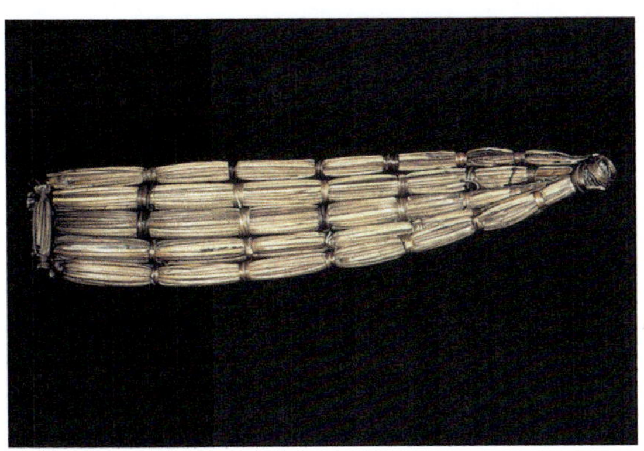

a.

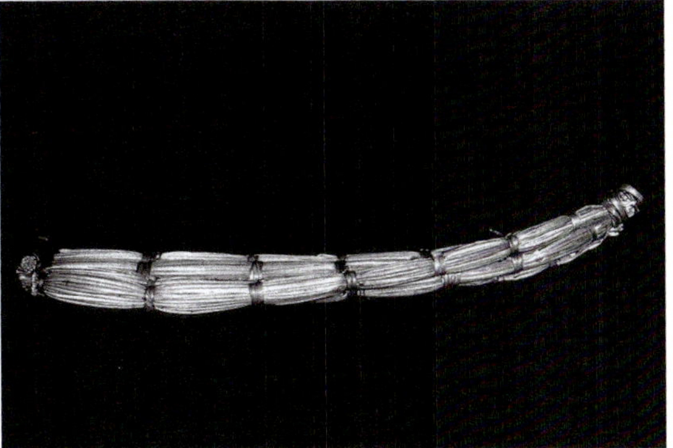

b.

Figure 5.1. Two views (a, b) of a model balsa canoe (570-114).

Figure 5.2. Balsa passing the Presidio of San Francisco in 1806. The lithograph is based upon a sketch by W. G. T. von Tilenau (Langsdorff 1814). *Courtesy of the Honold Library.*

Figure 5.3. Choris lithograph of a balsa on San Francisco Bay (Choris 1822). *Courtesy of the Honold Library.*

Choris also depicted a Bay area tule balsa (Figure 5.3).

Golovnin provided a more detailed account of this type of watercraft:

> These rafts are made of several bundles of long grass or reeds, closely and tightly tied together; one of these, about a sagene [seven feet] and a half long, is placed in the center; the others, somewhat shorter, are placed on each side of the long bundle, but each one is gradually tapered at the ends. Several such bundles, tightly tied together, constitute a grass raft of the above-mentioned length and about half a sagene wide in the middle, becoming somewhat narrow at the ends. The rowing is done with a paddle with two blades. The person sitting on the raft is frequently in the water up to his waist. (1979:148)

Shishmaryov, who visited California in 1820–1821, was also impressed by native boats:

> The Indian boats merit much attention. They are made from several bunches of reeds, which are tied together very tightly to resemble a boat. [The Indians] kneel in them by twos or threes and propel them with paddles 1 1/2 arshins [2 1/3 feet] long; they cannot, of course, move as well as wooden boats, and they sit very high in the water. So it can be supposed that [the Indians] cannot navigate very far, for these boats on their own accord age very rapidly and become unusable. (Gibson 2013:139)

Vasilyev made a similar observation:

> The coastal [Indians] make boats by tying several bunches of reeds together, and they kneel in them and hold in both hands a long paddle with two blades, and they stroke two, three, or four times on each side in calm weather only and until the reeds are waterlogged. They catch fish with nets. (Gibson 2013:175)

Another Russian account of the balsa, this one by Zavalishin, provides some additional information, although it may be describing a more makeshift, expedient craft:

> In only one occupation were the Indians completely unskillful...the California Indians had not devised any other means of navigation than two bundles of rushes tied end to end. Parting the middle, a man squeezed between them, keeping the lower part of his body below water, and navigated with a paddle or short oar like a spade. These rush bundles supported him in the water and were his boat or raft. (Gibson 1973:383)

Khlebnikov had a comment concerning the use of such craft by non-Indians:

> There [San Francisco, or the bays of Great and Little Bodega] when the natives sail across, they use cane woven together in the form of a skiff or canvas, in which they speedily move during stormy weather, while in San Francisco soldiers are frequently transported in them to the missions. (1940:333)

Voznesenskii also observed these balsas in use, and in one of the few published accounts written by him on California Indians, a sketch from one of his notebooks of a balsa is accompanied by the caption, "A reed boat, called a shaka. The oars are called vyvak" (see Lipshits 1950:417). The Indian people of San Francisco Bay apparently often carried as many as seven people in these boats, and on December 12, 1840, Voznesenskii observed one of the craft crossing the Bay. He wrote:

> At a glance it looks like a bundle of reed, bound together by the same material. The front end of the raft is pointed, and could be likened to a prow. The Indians row two by two and one by one in each boat. The paddles are made from a relatively long stick. On the end of the stick a smaller reed stick has been bound crosswise that is shaped like a spade (not like an oar). (Voznesenskii, quoted in Lipshits 1950:417)

Ethnographic accounts of these balsas, coupled with extant specimens, are rare for most of the central California peoples with whom the Russians were in contact. Only the Pomo seem to be an exception. As far as the Ohlone and Nisenan—who are known to have used such boats—are concerned, details regarding the shape, size, and configuration of their craft are lacking (Broadbent 1972:64; Harrington 1942:11; A. Kroeber 1929:261); however, those of the Patwin are known to have had the prow elevated and the stern flat (A. Kroeber 1932:283). These boats were probably similar to Pomo examples.

Pomo tule balsas were of three distinct types: (1) a waterfowl-hunting balsa which carried two men and was the smallest, narrowest, and most manageable of the types made; (2) a fishing balsa which carried four or five men and was about 18 to 20 feet in length; and (3) a cargo balsa that was used to carry heavy loads and was up to six feet in the beam. All of these boats had bindings of native grapevines and were built on the same general plan: four bundles of tules, each carefully bound as an individual unit, were bound to their adjacent neighbor; the center or "keel" bundle was the longest (Barrett 1952:I:163–166; McLendon 1977:35). By the 1980s, the knowledge needed to construct these boats, passed on by oral tradition, barely survived; one man, Kenny Fred (Pomo), occasionally constructed models for sale, as well as retained the knowledge of how to build the full-sized craft, even though the need for such boats vanished long ago. Since 1970, a few non-Indians have also constructed life-size tule balsas in conjunction with cultural recreations at such locales as Coyote Hills Regional Park in Fremont.

The Kunstkamera example (570-114) measures 44 cm in length by 9 cm in width, and is composed of five bundles of small tules (or perhaps immature tules), each of equal size and about 2.5 cm in maximum diameter. Each bundle is individually tied, apparently with the same material, and these bundles are bound together at the prow and stern. The prow is slightly upturned, while the stern remains straight with a small bundle tied at the transom. Whether this was made as a toy for a small child or as a more easily transported model for one of the Russian travelers, we do not know, nor are we able at this time to correlate its form with a particular function; that is, the waterfowl hunting balsa, the fishing balsa, the cargo balsa, or possibly none of these. What we can say is that the tiny specimen represents the sole extant example of a California tule boat dating from the early part of the nineteenth century.

Hair Rope

Although it is rather mundane in appearance, a hank of rope in the Kunstkamera collections (MAE 570-74) may have been used for procuring small game by functioning as a snare. The rope, which is made from what appears to be human hair, consists of two-ply, S-twist cordage whose length is probably greater than 15.3 m; this is an estimate, since the fragile nature of the piece would not permit unraveling some 18 loops, each about 85 cm in length, of what appeared to be one continuous cord. The loops had twisted about themselves in such a manner as to make separation impossible without damage to the rope.

Although one's first impression might be that the various loops were made to create a belt of some sort, no comparable examples could be found in American collections. Two Maidu belts (AMNH 50/5250; BKM 08.316) that are made from cordage are very different in their construction, being manufactured from simple loops of native cordage wrapped several times at one end, and without the "twisting" so evident in the Russian specimen.

The piece seems instead to be more comparable to those in American collections that served as snares of various sorts. Similar bundles with twisting strands of native hemp, though shorter in length, have been collected from the Patwin (OPM 16-2775, -2776, -2794, -2795, -2796, -2797), and one specimen carries the catalog notation "for catching rabbits" (OPM 16-2802). Supportive ethnographic accounts also exist for various Sierran peoples, such as the Maidu at Berry Creek, who are known to have caught mountain quail in lasso-like snares of human hair cordage (Hudson n.d. b), and the Sierra Miwok, who likewise made similar snares of horsehair cordage (Barrett and Gifford 1933:183; Fuentes n.d.); the horsehair probably replaced an earlier use of human hair. Alfred Kroeber (1929:265) reported that Valley Nisenan women "kept their combings to use in what they manufactured," which (although we are not told what the manufactured items may have been) could well have been cordage. In short, we suspect that the use of human hair cordage for snares may well have been widespread.

Deer Decoy Headdresses

Many different methods were employed in the taking of large animals; one of the most widespread in Native California involved the use of a decoy headdress, particularly in hunting deer and antelope. Some of these headpieces also included a skin cape, and the whole ensemble was intended to disguise the hunter and—in conjunction with movements that mimicked those of his prey—allow him to get closer to the animal. Such practices did not go unnoticed by the Russians; as Langsdorff observed while at Mission San Jose:

> The Indians fasten the horns of a deer on their heads, and throw a portion of the skin over their shoulders. Thus disguised, they lurk in the high grass, where the stags and the does come to feed. (1814:101)

A British visitor to the Ohlones, Captain Frederick Beechey, also wrote a description of the decoy headdress of these people:

> The artifice of deceiving the deer by placing a head of the animal upon their shoulders is very successfully practiced by them. To do this, they fit the head and horns of a deer upon the head of a hunstman, the rest of his body being painted to resemble the colour of a deer. (1831:II:74)

A French sea captain, Cyrille Laplace, who left an account of a visit to Fort Ross in 1839, also describes local native methods of hunting deer:

> One among them, disguised in the skin of a deer, horns on the head and hide on his back, moves toward the poor beasts grazing peacefully on the plain, until he finds himself near enough to that which he wishes to make his first prey, to be able to shoot it with a killing arrow. A second is taken the same way, then a third, and the massacre continues thus here and there until the rest of the herd, finally taking alarm, disperses afar in the high grass or nearby woods. (2006:45)

Descriptions of such practices among various California peoples are widespread. At least some of the Ohlones used the general style, keeping the antlers and stuffing the head with grass (Broadbent 1972:59). The Coast Miwok, Valley Nisenan, and River Patwin also used such decoys, although details of their construction are lacking (Kelly n.d.:401; A. Kroeber 1929:262, 1932:280). The Sierra Miwok made use of them as well, replacing the heavy antlers with lighter imitations made from manzanita or oak branches, often darkened by charring, and sometimes with pieces of male mallard duck scalps covering the eye openings (Barrett and Gifford 1933:180; Clark 1904:33). The Chumash also made deer decoy headdresses, employing a wooden hoop about the neck and stuffing the head with grass (Hudson and Blackburn 1982:74–77).

Perhaps the most data currently exist for Pomoan examples, which are described as having the antlers replaced by wood copies, and having pieces of flint placed in the eye openings; in some cases pine pitch mixed with charcoal and modeled in the round to look natural was fitted into the eye openings. The nostrils were painted red, and the lower jaw was discarded (Barrett 1952:I:126–127; Essene 1942:3, 54, item 26). One of the few extant deer decoy headdresses comes from the Yana; it consists simply of a head without

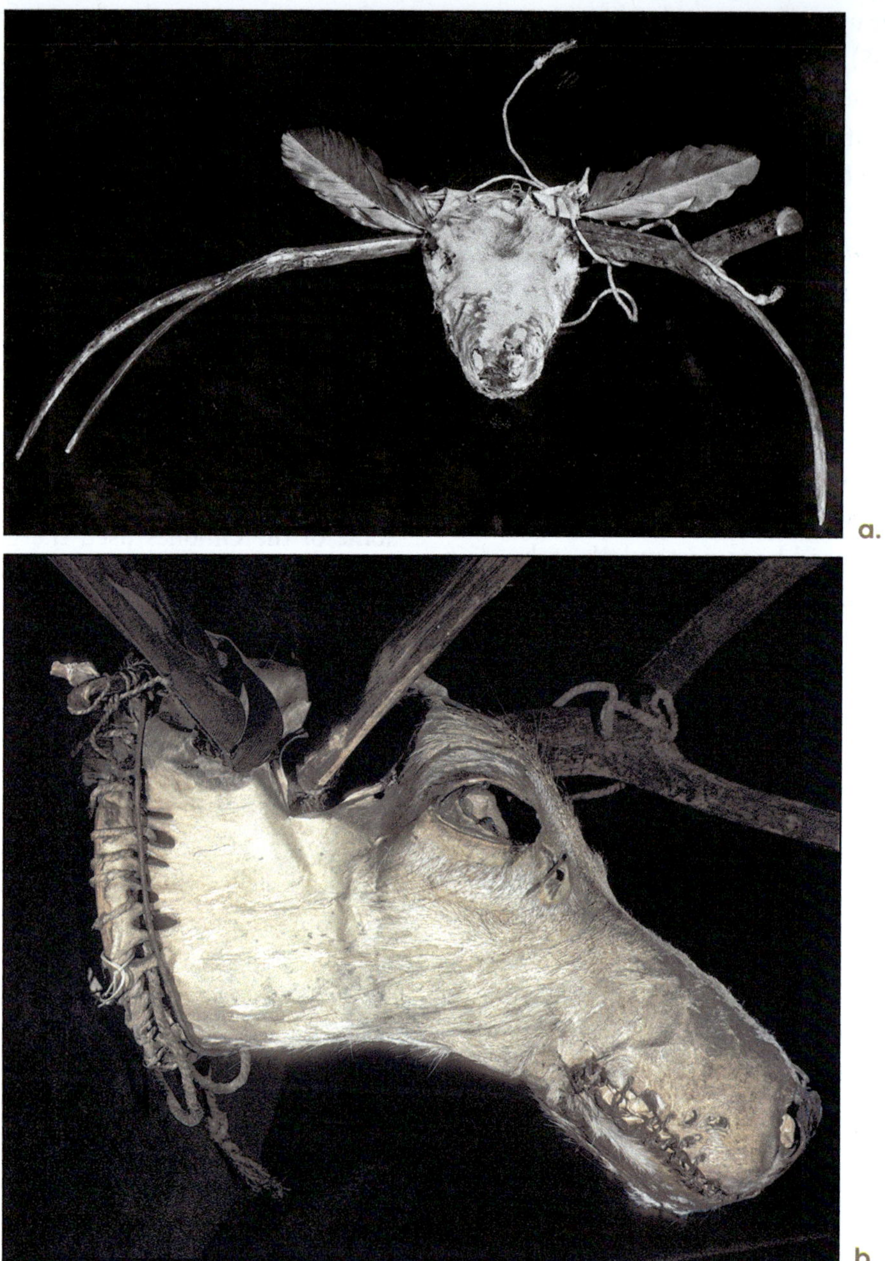

Figure 5.4. Front (a) and side views (b) of a decoy headdress (570-122).

antlers, stuffed with leaves and twigs, and with the lips sewn shut (T. Kroeber 1961:195; Pope 1918:128, pl. 34).

Thus, with only one extant specimen present in an American museum, and little specific detail available in either historical or ethnographic accounts, the two decoy headdresses in the Russian collections are of more than passing interest. Both are constructed in a similar fashion, and while both are also on exhibition, one (570-122) was made available for closer inspection (Figure 5.4). The entire skin of the head is untanned, and the ears have been removed. It was apparently stuffed with some sort of material to provide support while the skin was drying hard, but the stuffing was later removed to leave a light and hollow head form. The lips are sewn shut with two-ply cordage, while the base of the neck is attached to a wooden ring by twine sewing. The ring, made from an unidentified shoot, is 13 cm in diameter and about 8 mm in thickness.

As was noted in ethnographic accounts, the antlers on 570-122 were removed and replaced by two forked wooden sticks. These antler sticks are connected to one another inside the head by simple wrappings of cordage about their ends; they are somewhat lens-shaped in cross-section. Substituting for the ears are two large, trimmed black feathers approximately 22 cm in length by 8 cm in width; they appear to be from a condor. Such large feathers, which were free to twitch in the slightest breeze, would make effective imitations of a live deer's ears. Had the original ears been left on the decoy, they would have dried hard and stiff, and would have lacked the flexibility and lifelike movements provided by their feather substitutes. The entire decoy measures about 64 cm from antler tip to antler tip.

The second decoy headdress, MAE 570-123, was mounted on a life-size human figure on exhibit and could not be removed for inspection. Superficially, it seems to have been made in the same fashion as 570-122; the wood antlers (which are round in cross-section on this example) have been covered with thin rawhide, which has been sewn in place using a fine, two-ply cordage, apparently of sinew. The mouth has been sewn shut with native cordage, probably of native hemp, using a buttonhole stitch. A large elk skin, draped over the mannequin, was apparently added decades ago by museum staff, and is not part of this outfit.

Although we might infer that both decoy headdresses had a similar origin because of their similar construction, we are unable to attribute either headdress to any specific group or region.

Bows

Bows and arrows have probably attracted the attention of European visitors more than any other artifact, and therefore historical descriptions are abundant. The earliest of these stem from the 1579 visit of Francis Drake to what must have been Coast Miwok territory. A member of the party, Francis Fletcher, wrote this description:

> Their bowes and arrowes (their only weapons, and almost all their wealth) they use very skillfully, but yet not to do any great harme with them, being by reason of their weakenesse, more fit for children then for men, sending the arrow neither farre off, nor with any great force. (1947:290)

Fletcher's description, however, is somewhat at odds with other accounts concerning the strength and accuracy of native California archery equipment. The French explorer La Pérouse, for example, described the bows of the Ohlone people at Carmel in 1786 quite differently:

> [Their] bows are very superior to those of the inhabitants of Port des Français; the arrows are flint tipped. (Heizer 1974:88)

An English traveler, Captain Beechey, was similarly impressed by the central California bows he saw in the late 1820s:

> Their bows are elegantly and ingeniously constructed [and backed with sinew which] embraces the ends, where they are turned back to receive the string. (1831:II:77–78)

Descriptions of such reflexed, sinew-backed bows are common in other accounts as well; for example, Langsdorff described some he had seen near San Francisco:

> Their weapons consist of the bow and arrow, and as these contribute essentially to the acquisition of many of the necessaries of life,

their construction seems a principal object of their skill and industry. The shape of the bow is pleasing in appearance. It is made of wood, is from three to four and a half feet long, neatly constructed, and drawn together very ingeniously with tendons of the deer. By this means the wood is kept in place securely, and the bow has such elasticity that very little strength and dexterity are required to draw the arrow. Both the bow and the arrow are very neatly made, and the arrows are pointed with vitrified lava, or obsidian. (1814:II:57–58)

On a visit to San Francisco Bay in late 1820 and early 1821, Captain-Lieutenant Mikhail Nikolayevich Vasilyev, who commanded the sloop *Otkrytie*, made some observations on the Indian construction and use of bows and arrows:

> They have one weapon—a bow with arrows of very good workmanship. The bow is made from animal sinew, tightly strung to one side of [a haft of] hard wood or, rather, from [a haft of] flexible wood affixed to sinew. A three-foot bowstring is made from sinew, and the arrows are made from reeds [or rushes] about half an inch in circumference, (soft) inside, and up to three feet long, and an arrowhead of transparent flint [obsidian?] is fashioned with the very same stone and affixed to one end, and feathers are tied to the other end. Others have sharpened arrows of wood only without arrowheads. They always hold the bow to bend against the wooden haft, and when they have to shoot an arrow they draw the bow very dexterously on the inside of the wooden [haft] and shoot very accurately without aiming at all. It is said that in battle they do so with a cry. I was unable to learn reliably whether they imbue the arrows with poison, but it seemed to me more likely that they do not do so.... To their bowstrings they tie the skins of young birds so that in shooting arrows their hand does not become sore and the shot cannot be heard, for without the skin the bowstring twangs. (Gibson 2013:173–175)

Zavalishin likewise noted these weapons:

> Concerning weapons, their bow, strung with sinew, was usually so taut that the strongest among us could not pull it without practice and skill. Their arrows were made of rushes with stone heads daubed with poison; wounds from them, regardless of the poison, were very dangerous, for they had a rough finish and a jagged edge. (Gibson 1973:383)

Kotzebue similarly noted that the bows and arrows which he saw were of "extraordinary elegance" (Mahr 1932:48). Both Chamisso and Choris were more descriptive; Chamisso wrote:

> Among many of them their arms consist of bows and arrows; some of these are of extraordinary elegance, the bows light and strong, and covered with the sinews of animals on the convex side; among others it is merely of wood, and rudely made. (Mahr 1932:85)

Choris added this description:

> They [the Tcholovoni = Northern Valley Yokuts] make beautiful weapons, such as bows and arrows. The tips of the latter are furnished with pieces of flint fashioned with great skill. (Mahr 1932:99)

English Lieutenant Edward Belcher, who came to California aboard the *Blossom*, visited Mission Santa Cruz in 1827 and was quite impressed with the bows[1] and arrows of non-Christian Indians who lived near the mission:

> The only manufacture carried on by this set [the non-Christian Indians] is that of bows and arrows, which they certainly make very

strong, light, neat as well as handsome. They are also serviceable, and are principally made use of by the Indians in taking deer, birds, etc. Wishing to ascertain their power as well as the precision of shooting, I made one of them fire at a bird about the size of a small blackbird, little dreaming that his arrow would go the distance. I was much surprised to see it fall close to its legs, and with another person paced the distance which amounted to 152 paces or fairly 150 yards. Their arrows for deer are pointed with stone, very neatly, and vary in length from three feet to four feet four inches. Those used for birds are merely wood. (Farris, Hodgson, and David 2004:61)

Khlebnikov had this to say:

All their weapons consist of bows and arrows made quite skillfully.... Their bows tied with deer thongs are made very ingeniously. In their arrows they place lances made of obsidian, jasper or flint, skillfully set in. (1940:333)

Kostromitinov wrote this description of the sinew-backed bow:

Their weapons consist of bow and arrow and a spear; all this is made mainly of young fir. The points of arrows and spears consist of sharp, artfully shaped stones and their bow strings come from sinews of wild goats. (1974:10)

Descriptions of bows in the ethnographic literature are often incomplete; those of the Ohlones and Valley Nisenan are described simply as being sinew-backed (Broadbent 1972:64; A. Kroeber 1929:26), while those of the River Patwin were imported from the north (A. Kroeber 1932:280). Although unbacked bows were widespread, especially those used by young boys, more detailed descriptions regarding their form and decoration—as well as extant examples in museum collections—are unavailable for most central California groups.

Data on the sinew-backed bow are unfortunately meager, but some data do exist for certain groups. Among the Pomo, it appears that two sinew-backed bow styles were known: (1) an elaborately decorated bow with painted designs and woodpecker scalps; and (2) a bow of better quality made from California yew and obtained through trade. While the latter bows often came with painted designs, they were stripped of everything ornamental and then re-ornamented according to Pomoan aesthetic conventions. This type of bow apparently came from the Yuki, or possibly even farther away in the northwest corner of California (Barrett 1952:I:127, 184–185; Essene 1942:15, 58, items 570–573; Hudson 1899; Kroeber 1925:299). It appears that these broad bows, which were lens-shaped in cross section, had recurved ends, and often sported painted decorations in a limited range of colors, were characteristic of the northern half of California, ranging at least as far south as Colfax in the Sierra Nevada among the Southern Maidu (Nisenan; FM 58341), and as far south as the Coast Miwok in the Coast Range (HMA 1-67279)—and possibly as far south as the Ohlone people of the San Francisco Bay area, if we can judge from a bow fragment that was recovered archaeologically (HMA 1-174972). Northward, the area in which such bows were used included the entire Klamath River drainage (so the bow was therefore present among the Yurok, Karok, Hupa, and Tolowa), extended northeastward to perhaps include the Klamath (BKM 9377) and Modoc (BM 1959 Amx 1 114; LBNM n/n), and reached south to include the Atsugewi (LVNP 2492). It is possible, if one considers the information that is available on trade routes, that these groups made and supplied fine, sinew-backed bows to their southern neighbors—the Maiduan, Pomoan, and Patwin peoples—who probably also occasionally made fine bows of the same type.

Figure 5.5. José Cardero depiction of a Monterey Indian hunter in 1791. Note the recurved bow and the animal skin quiver. *Courtesy of Museo de América, Madrid (Inventory No. 02283).*

Another style of reflex bow, with a thicker and narrower biconvex cross section and nocks consisting of "hooks" built up from layers of sinew that extend beyond the margin of the wood structure of the bow stave, was produced primarily by the Sierra Miwok people. It appears that this bow type extended to the south among the Western Mono people, and to the west probably as far as San Francisco Bay, with a range that included the intervening northern Valley Yokuts (Bates 1978; see Figures 5.5 and 5.6).[2]

Nine bows are listed in the Kunstkamera catalog, but only six could be located for study; one of these six is a self-bow, while the remaining five are sinew-backed. Before describing them, we should note that all of the bows that were examined which were strung were done so for storage and not as they would normally have been strung for actual use. Normally, the bowstring pulls along the non-sinewed face or "belly" of the bow, while the sinew-backed surface or "back" faces away from the archer.

MAE 570-124 is the only self bow among the examples seen. It is 133 cm in length from nock to nock along the bowstring, and is 2.5 cm wide by 2.0 cm thick at the grip. No buckskin wrapping is present on the grip, nor are there any traces of decoration or coloring. The nocks are of the simple "pin" type (Figure 5.7a), although the bowstring is somewhat unusual (if the identification is correct) in being two-ply rawhide. Bows of such a length, made of plain wood without sinew backing, remind one of the split elderberry or laurel-wood bows used among the southern Valley Yokuts (Latta 1977:285), and it is possible that the northern Valley Yokuts with whom the Russians came in contact used this type of bow as well.

Figure 5.6. Two "Cholovoni" (Chulamni Yokuts) hunters near San Francisco Bay (Choris 1822). *Courtesy of the Honold Library.*

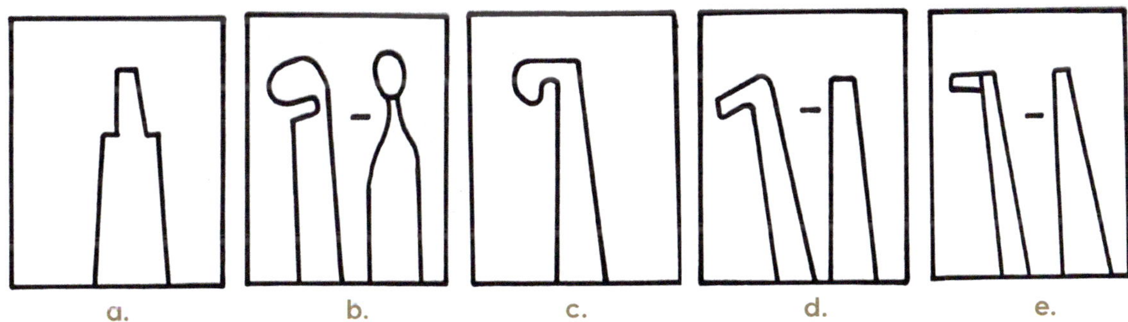

Figure 5.7. Sketches showing different types of bow nocks: (a) 570-124; (b) 570-127; (c) 570-132; (d) 570-129; (e) 570-130.

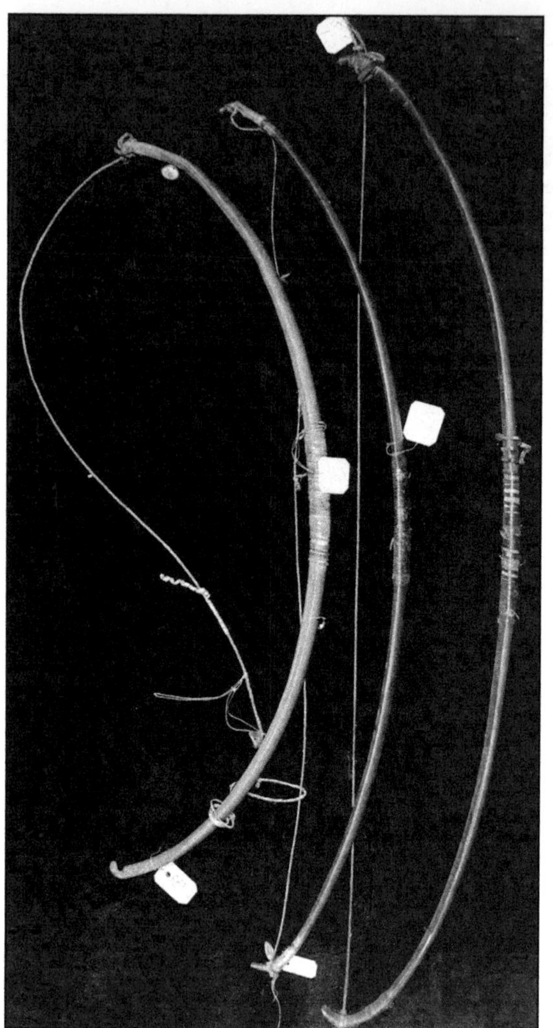

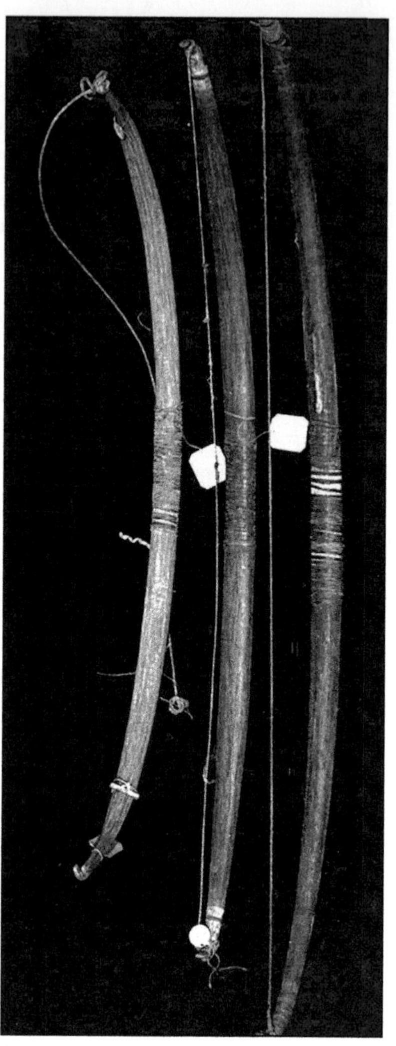

a. b.

Figure 5.8. Two views (a, b) of bows (570-127, 570-130, and 570-129).

MAE 570-127 (Figure 5.8) measures 79.5 cm from nock to nock in a straight line. The bow, which is made of a light-colored wood—possibly incense cedar, *Calocedrus deccurens*—is thick, biconvex in cross section, and is 3.1 cm wide by 1.9 cm thick at the grip. These dimensions are reduced to 1 cm and 1.3 cm, respectively, at the nocks. The bow is thickly backed with sinew, which has been brought up and around the ends to form hook-shaped nocks (Figure 5.9) that are as dense and as hard as the wood itself. Because of the construction of these hook-like nocks, the final 3 cm of the bow wood on the belly is covered with sinew, as is that on the back. The grip is formed by a 3 mm thick wrapping of buckskin thong, covering an area 13 cm in length.

MAE 570-128 (Figure 5.10) is similar in construction. It measures 97 cm in a straight line from nock to nock, and is 3.5 cm and 3 cm in width and thickness, respectively, at the grip, which is also wrapped with a buckskin thong. However, the sinew wrapping, which lies at a right angle to the backing, extends 5 cm down both faces of the bow. The bowstring is missing.

MAE 570-132 is similar to the above two examples, although the nocks are somewhat

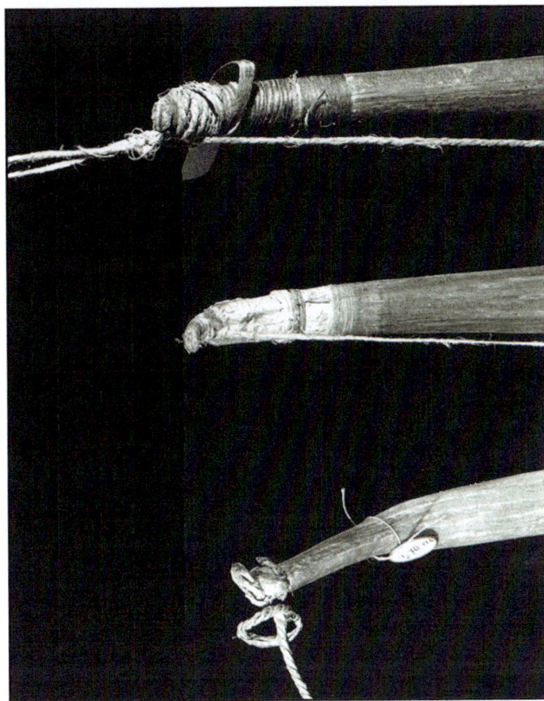

Figure 5.9. Nocks (*top to bottom*) of bows (570-129, -130, and -127). The top bow is strung.

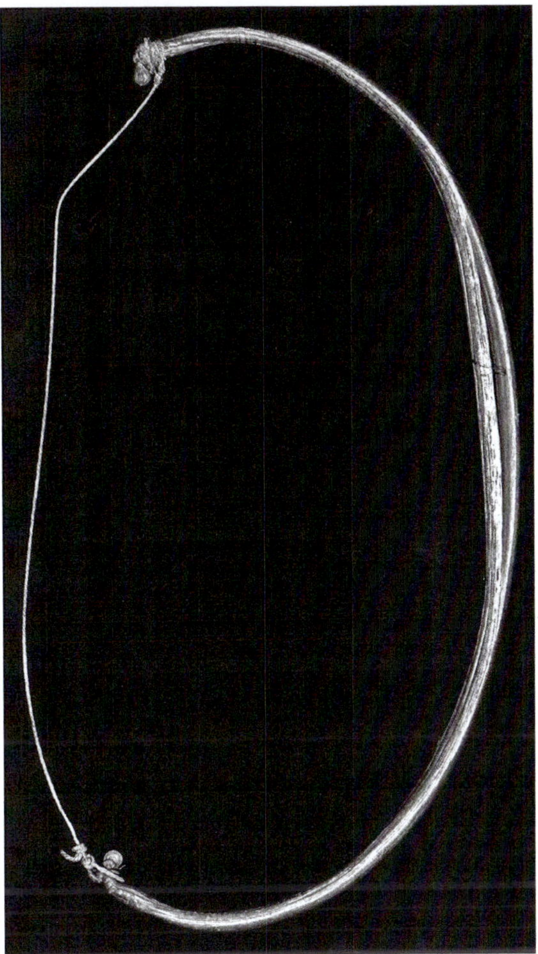

Figure 5.11. Bow (570-132).

Figure 5.10. Bow (570-128).

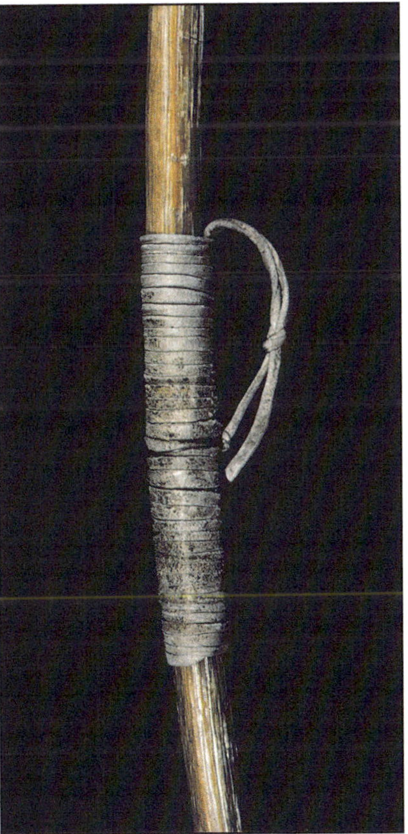

more elongated where the indentation for the hook to receive the bowstring is located (Figure 5.11). This bow is 68 cm in length in a straight line from nock to nock, and is 3.5 cm in width by 1.5 cm in thickness. A two-ply, twisted sinew bowstring remains with the bow. The sinew backing has separated from the wood along the middle portion of the bow; such a separation occasionally occurs in old bows that have been subjected to extremes in temperature, and especially to excessive heat and dryness. Such conditions result in the sinew becoming tauter, thus pulling the bow into a more and more C-shaped configuration, as seen in this example. If allowed to continue, such extreme stresses—which pull the bow into a shape not intended by its maker—will continue to separate the sinew from the bow wood and ultimately completely shatter the bow.

These three bows, MAE 570-127, 570-128, and 570-132, are most similar to those used by the historic Sierra Miwok people, and they may well represent a bow type once important in trade between these people and those along the coast (Bates 1978). Therefore, they could well have been collected by Russians along the coast—Langsdorff made a drawing of one that he collected in the San Francisco region (see Figure 2.3)—or among the lowland peoples of the San Joaquin Valley, or even in one of the various Sacramento Valley villages visited by Voznesenskii.

MAE 570-129 (Figure 5.8, right) is made from a wood that appears similar to that used in making 570-127, although the bow itself is quite different. It measures 101 cm in length from nock to nock in a straight line, and is 3.7 cm in width and 2 cm in thickness at the grip. The cross section is biconvex. The grip itself is some 15 cm in length and is wrapped with a buckskin thong dyed black. The wooden nocks (Figure 5.7d) are angled toward the back of the bow, covered with sinew, and then wrapped for a distance of 7 cm from the tip down to the body of the bow with a strip of coarse, rather than finely split, sinew. The bow measures 1.2 cm in width and 7 mm in thickness at the nocks. The bowstring is of two-ply twisted sinew, with a loop made from a buckskin thong attached to the bowstring at the nock. "Sacramento River" was handwritten in Russian in ink on the belly of the bow, apparently by a former curator (Gil'zen?) about 1900 (Okladnikova, personal communication 1983). If this bow actually came from the Sacramento River area, it may well have been collected by Voznsenskii, although we have no information as to how the curator determined the bow's provenience.

MAE 570-130 is the last bow in this group (Figure 5.8 center). It is some 93 cm in length from nock to nock, while at the grip it is 3.7 cm in width and 1.2 cm in thickness. Biconvex in cross section, the wood of the bow is yellowish-orange in color, and like the other examples it is sinew-backed. The pin type nocks (Figure 5.7e) measure 2.2 cm in length and are bent nearly at right angles toward the back of the bow; the pin itself is sinew-wrapped and dyed red. The same reddened sinew wrapping is present at 3.5 cm and 5 cm below the shoulders of the pin and served, we would guess, both as decoration and as a means of securing the paper-thin covering of what is apparently pecardium or bladder, which was a common feature on the nock areas of bows made by the Wintun (LM 1-4484) and other northern California peoples. The pin form of these Wintun examples was also similar. The grip on 570-130 consists of a wrapping of thin strips of buckskin 12 cm in length, with the ends of the grip wrapped with a 1 cm wide band of deer sinew, dyed red like those mentioned previously for the decorated bands at the nocks. The bowstring, like the others, consists of two-ply, twisted sinew.

Bows 570-129 and 570-130 are not unlike those collected in the northern half of California, among such diverse peoples as the Yurok in the northwest and the Maidu in the east. It seems likely that this bow style was once popular. Thus bow 570-129—with its aged, handwritten reference to the Sacramento River—may well have been collected where the "documentation" suggests.

There are three bows in the Helsinki collections; two of these were donated by Etholen (VK- 336 and VK-337) and were identified as coming from the village of Seuamne near modern Sacramento, while a third was donated by Uno Cygnaeus and was attributed to California (Figure 5.12). Both of the Etholen

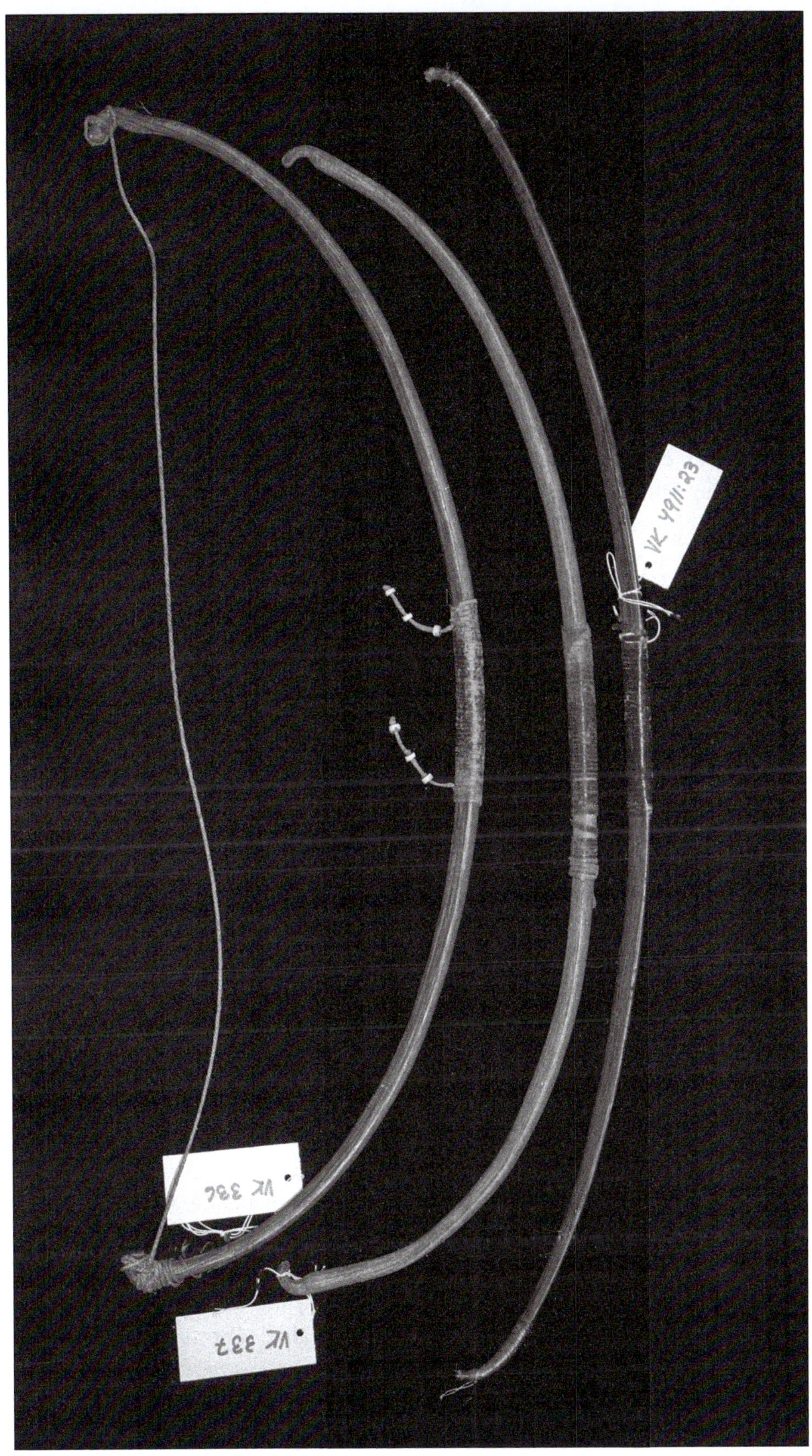

Figure 5.12. Bows in Helsinki collected by Etholen and Cygnaeus (FNM VK-336, VK-337, and 4911:23).

bows are made in the Sierra Miwok style of reflexed, sinew-backed bows. The first is 88 cm in length along the cord, 4 cm in width and 1.5 cm in thickness at the grip, which is wrapped with a brain-tanned deerskin thong. The upper and lower ends of this thong serve to fasten a small piece of deerskin, which is decorated with three clam shell disk beads, to the bow. The other bow, which lacks such ornamentation, is 87 cm in length along the cord, and 3.5 cm wide and 2 cm thick at the grip, which is also wrapped with a strip of rawhide. Both bowstrings are made of vegetable fiber cord. The fact that these bows came from Seuamne suggests that they were probably collected by Voznesenskii; some of the Etholen arrows may have been directly associated with them (see the next section, "Arrows"). We therefore surmise that both of these bows originated among the Plains Miwok, or their neighbors.

The Cygnaeus bow (VK-4911:23), unlike these Sierra Miwok examples, has a pin-type nock that is similar to that of MAE 570-130, described earlier (see Figure 5.9). It is also sinew-backed and has a deerskin wrapping around the grip. The pins, however, are wrapped with a vegetable material. The bow is 101 cm in length along the cord, 3.5 cm in width and 1.5 cm in thickness at the grip. Like MAE 570-130, it was probably collected in central California, possibly by Voznesenskii. The arrows in the Cygnaeus collection associated with it compare with those in the Etholen collection, which are documented as coming from Seuamne (see the next section, "Arrows"). Perhaps this bow was secured by Voznesenskii at Sutter's Fort or elsewhere and represents a more northerly Sacramento Valley or north-central California type.

Arrows

The arrows in the Russian collections comprise the largest extant sample of such items (though smaller collections are in other European museums) from the early to middle nineteenth century. American museums have few examples, with the meager bulk of those coming from the lower Klamath River area—that is, from the Yurok, Karok, and Hupa; they generally do not date much before 1900, and later examples commonly appear to be reproductions of former styles that were made for collectors or anthropologists. Therefore, there is little comparative information in American collections to draw upon.

We do know from ethnographic accounts that a variety of woods was used in the manufacture of arrows in most of central California: mock orange, California rose, willow, snowberry, spicebush, and others. Since these plant resources are widely distributed, wood identification alone cannot help in attribution, as is also true for much of the lithic material used in manufacturing the associated projectile points.[3] Similarly, the feathering and attachment of points, done with sinew, are nondescript, as is also the case for the style of projectile point. Indeed, our only clues seem primarily to involve very detailed features in construction, such as the length of foreshaft compared to length of mainshaft, the length of feathering, the coloring and pattern of riband markings, and to some extent the form of the nock which receives the bowstring (Figure 5.13).

Some 34 of the 163 arrows listed in the Kunstkamera catalog could not be located during the 1983 study, leaving 129 specimens available for examination. Five additional arrows, curated in Moscow, were also unavailable for study, although very generalized verbal descriptions were provided. Helsinki's collection of 48 arrows (two additional ones were missing) was

Arrow type	Point type	Mainshaft		Foreshaft		Fletching		Nock type
		L	D	L	D	L	Form	
A Comp.		67–96	1	5–12	0.7	7–9		
B Self		85	0.9	(none)		8	?	
C Comp.		68	0.9	13	0.5	8	?	
D Comp.		85–90	0.9	14	0.5	15		
E Comp.		80	1	7	0.8	9		
F Comp. & Self		80–86	1	11		8–11		

Figure 5.13. Characteristics of arrow types. All measurements are in centimeters.

briefly examined and will be discussed here.

The task of examining the 129 arrows that were available in St. Petersburg was not without major difficulties, mostly due to time constraints and to the way in which the arrows were made available for study. The collection was presented piecemeal, as stored, in the form of arbitrary bundles of arrows; each bundle contained from 12 to as many as 22 arrows, none of which were numbered in sequence nor arranged by function, characteristics, or other features representing some sort of logical order. Instead, each bundle (of which there were eight in all) contained a haphazard mixture of types (Figures 5.14–5.17). Since each bundle was brought out separately, cross-bundle comparisons could not be made. Such comparisons would not have been very helpful anyway, due to restrictions against mixing arrows between bundles, and the lack of available space in which to spread the entire collection out for comparative study. Moreover, given the size of the collection and the need to examine all possible objects in St. Petersburg, only about 15 minutes were available in which to examine, photograph, measure, and take notes on each bundle. Thus our discussion treats the Kunstkamera arrows within the framework of a more generalized context.

a.

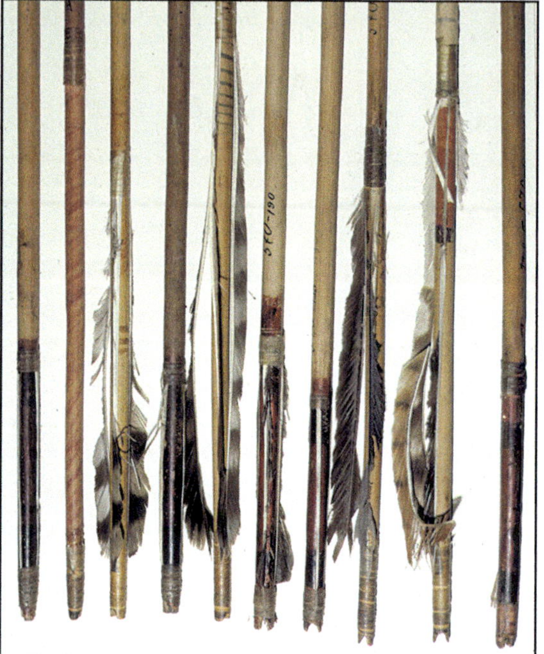
b.

Figure 5.14. Assorted arrows in Bundle IV, showing (a) point and (b) nock ends.

Working from notes and photographs, an analysis of each complete arrow was undertaken in an effort to determine whether or not identical counterparts were present, either within its member bundle or between bundles, so that the arrows could be regrouped by "quiver set." We use the term "quiver set" to designate those arrows (and in our sample, those with projectile points) which share identical or nearly identical features with other arrows in the collection. These features are mainshaft and foreshaft lengths (if they are compound arrows, and shaft length if they are self arrows), shape of nock, method of hafting the projectile point, type of projectile point used, style and length of fletching, and (most importantly) the coloring and patterning of the riband markings. The sample used involved 64 complete arrows; we were able to define 39 quiver sets (discussed later in this chapter) within that sample that allow us to describe and attribute the arrows to more specific regions and groups. We should note here, however, that these 64 arrows comprise only 40 percent (64/129) of the total Kunstkamera collection, and it is therefore quite likely that the actual number of arrows per quiver set may be larger than we estimate. Moreover, there is

a.

b.

Figure 5.15. Assorted arrows in Bundle VII, showing (a) point and (b) nock ends.

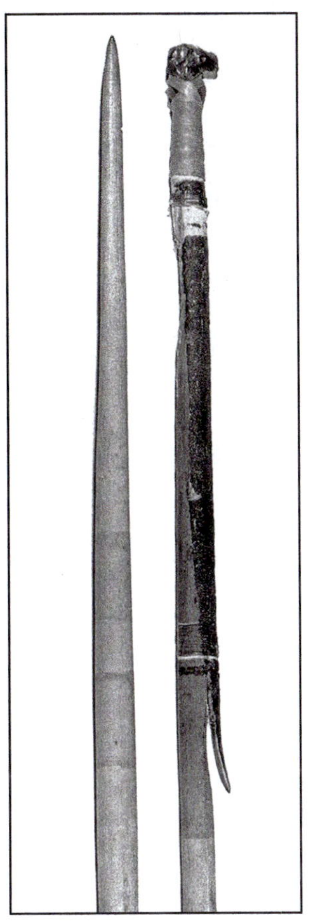

Figure 5.17. Barbed and self arrows from Bundle VIII.

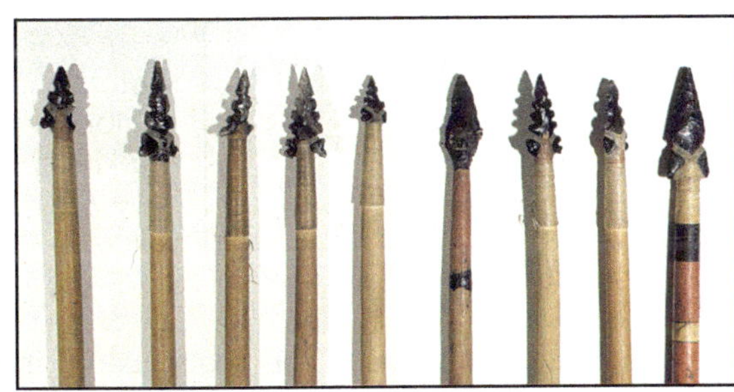
a.

b.

Figure 5.16. Assorted arrows in Bundle VIII, showing (a) point and (b) nock ends.

also the possibility that additional arrow types could be defined among the arrows that were incomplete or that could not be located. It goes without saying that the sample discussed may reflect not the total range in variation present in the Kunstkamera arrows, but rather the range in variation present in the complete specimens that were shown to us.

Our six arrow types (see Figure 5.13), which are lettered A–F, are described here, along with a generalized summary of the various features which, in most cases, serve to define them. However, there are some arrow features common to all types that crosscut our groupings. We should mention that the selection of woods and feathering used in manufacturing was common to all. The mainshafts were all made from a pithy-centered wood, quite probably mock orange

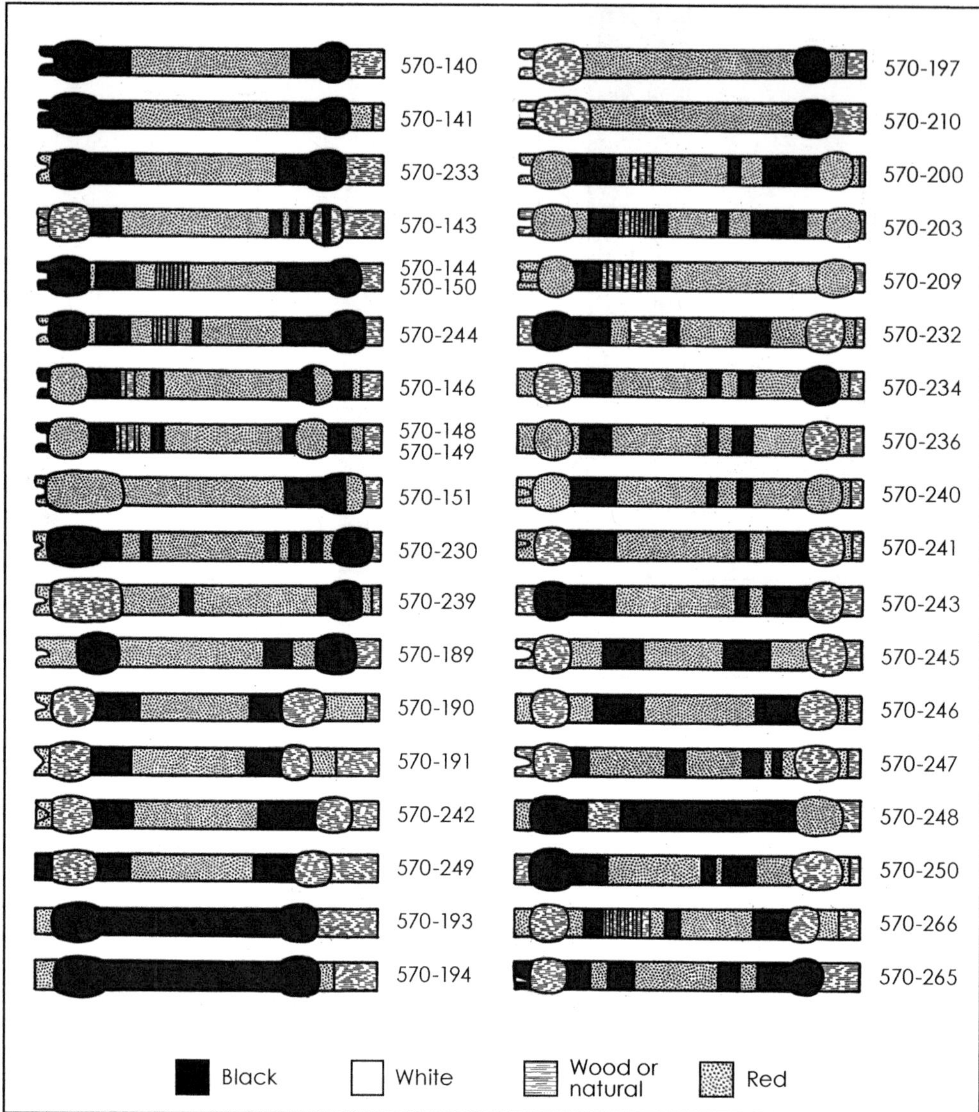

Figure 5.18. Sketch of riband markings, Type A arrows.

(*Philadelphus lewisii*), with a hardwood foreshaft. The fletching typically utilized hawk feathers, although other birds—especially eagles and turkey vultures—appear to be represented as well. Riband markings are illustrated in Figures 5.18 and 5.19.

Unfortunately, there are no clues in the Kunstkamera catalog that might help us to attribute any of our identified arrow clusters to a particular geographic region or ethnic group. However, it is important to note that at least one (if not more) of these clusters should reflect Voznesenskii's arrow collecting activities in the Sacramento Valley. This conclusion is based upon Liapunova's (1967:26) statement that Voznesenskii had collected some 26 arrows from 18 different villages during his central California work (see Chapter 3). One would expect, therefore, that the arrow collection should contain representative specimens from at least 18 different quiver sets (one for each village); given the rather large number of sets involved, the only arrow grouping which can accommodate this is Type A, since nearly 59 percent (23/39) of the total number of quiver sets are in this group.

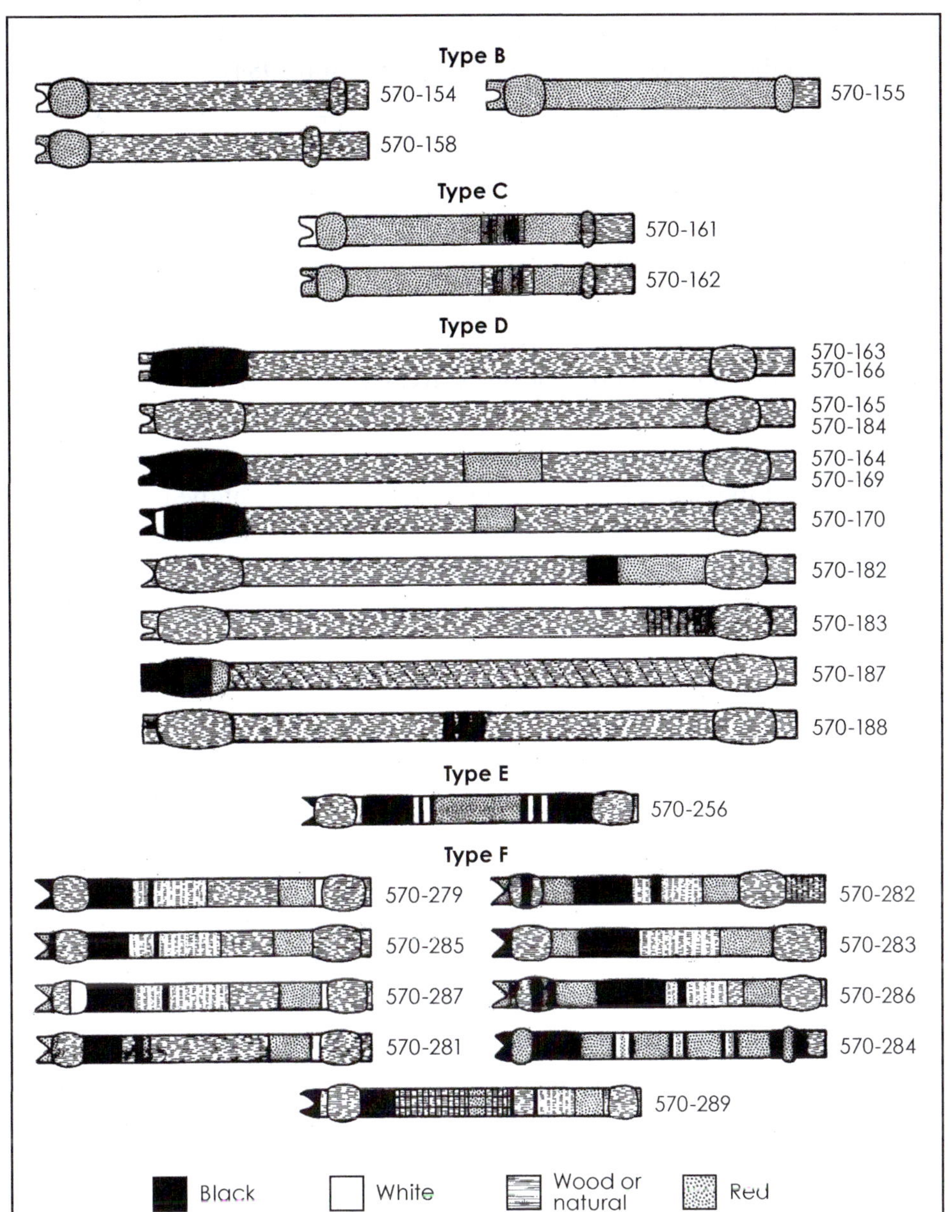

Figure 5.19. Sketch of riband markings on arrows of types B–F.

Although the Kunstkamera catalog is of little direct help, some clues can be obtained from the study of arrows in another museum collection. The 38 arrows in Finland, which were donated by Etholen, had a demonstrable connection with both Voznesenskii and the village of Seuamne, as we noted earlier. This village was one of the 18 named communities where Voznesenskii is stated to have collected arrows; therefore, those arrows in Finland which are known to have come from this village and which have counterparts in Russia should help identify the arrows in the Kunstkamera collections that are also likely to have come from Seuamne or its environs. Therefore, it is necessary at this point to describe both the Etholen collection and that of his Finnish associate, Uno Cygnaeus. We will then integrate the Kunstkamera and Helsinki collections in our descriptions of each arrow type.

The Etholen collection consists of two bundles: VK-339 (the catalog indicates that the bundle contains 20 arrows numbered 1 to 20, although VK-339:18 is missing), and VK-340 (which contains 18 arrows numbered 1 to 18, with VK-340:2 missing). The Cygnaeus collection consists of 10 complete arrows (VK-4911:38 to 47), and two stone-tipped hardwood foreshafts (VK-4911:77 and 78). Alhough all 48 arrows share the same general features as the Kunstkamera examples, only two of the six types of arrows, A and F, are represented in the collection. Type A is represented by all of the Cygnaeus examples (represented by five quiver sets) and some of the Etholen specimens (16 arrows represented by three quiver sets), while Type F is represented only in the Etholen examples (20 arrows represented by six quiver sets).

Type A

The Type A arrows are compound in form, with "U-shaped" nocks and short fletchings with associated riband markings, usually in red and black. The projectile points are either leaf-shaped or corner notched with barbs. The points in the St. Petersburg collection are made of obsidian (63 percent), chert (26 percent), or glass (11 percent), while those in the Helsinki collection are made mostly from obsidian, with a few made from glass. The flaked glass points are not surprising in this context, since some of the arrows from the 1841 Wilkes Expedition, which are now curated at the Smithsonian Institution, are tipped with points made from green glass. They have also been found in archaeological contexts throughout much of California; for example, at the Farmington Reservoir sites 20 miles east of Stockton (Treganza 1952:18) and at the Camanche Reservoir (J. Johnson 1967:37, 82, 141, 174, 277). The archaeological distribution of the corner-notched and leaf-shaped projectile point is equally widespread (Fredrickson 1984).

Most of the Type A arrows have relatively short foreshaft lengths (usually between 5 and 6 cm in length by 1 cm in diameter) when they are associated with corner-notched points; two quiver sets in Helsinki, however, have much longer foreshafts (11 to 12 cm) and are associated with leaf-shaped points. Mainshaft lengths average 70 to 75 cm. Typically, the foreshaft and mainshaft are joined in a stepped manner rather than being tapered. The sinew wrapping about the base of the point tends to be somewhat bulbous, and all the arrows have a somewhat stocky appearance because of the workmanship.

Riband markings (Figure 5.18) take the form of either black or red bands, in simple patterns, with most consisting of solid, bold lines. A few (five quiver sets in the Russian collection, and a few sets in the Helsinki collection) have an interesting pattern consisting of thin, linear lines done in black. These sets are so similar to one another that they may well have been collected from the same village, or from villages that were very close to one another.

We are reasonably certain that Type A arrows were collected in the lower Sacramento River region, probably by Voznesenskii. We base this conclusion on both the fact that Type A is the only group large enough to accommodate the 18 or more different quiver sets collected by Voznesenskii, and upon the results of our comparison of Etholen's Seuamne arrows (VK-339 and 340) with those at the Kunstkamera. All of the Helsinki arrows classed as Type A (sets 38 to 46) are very similar to sets 1 to 23 in the Russian collection, and in one case the similarities are so striking that the arrows in both museums might have originated in the same quiver; the only difference between Helsinki's Set 38 and the Kunstkamera's Set 9 is an absence of red paint under one of the sinew wrappings. There are other sets which have close correspondences as well—enough so that the arrows probably came from the same village or regional source.

Type B

Type B is represented by three self arrows. Their projectile points (which are of obsidian) are leaf-shaped, and two of the three have a shallow notching near their convex base. The nocks are similar to those found in Type A. The form of the fletching can not be determined, but judging from the sinew wrapping which remains, it was about 8 cm in length, and thus was somewhat similar to that used on Type A. Riband markings (Figure 5.19) consist of only one color, red, and there was no effort to arrange the bands in anything but very simple patterns.

Type C

There are only two examples of Type C arrows; both are compound and are hafted to leaf-shaped points with rounded bases and with serrations along the lower half of the point edges. This type of point was previously known only in archaeological contexts; some were recovered at sites near Red Bluff dated to ca. 1800–1850 (Treganza 1954:Fig. 2j), while others were found at Camanche Reservoir in Miwok territory (J. Johnson 1967:Figs. 45u, v).

While the Type C sets resemble those in Type A in having a heavy, bulbous sinew wrapping about the base of the point, a "stepped-junction" where mainshaft and foreshaft meet, and similar fletching lengths and nock forms, there is one very noticeable difference between them—the foreshafts on Type C arrows are nearly twice the length as those on Type A arrows, and the riband markings (Figure 5.19) are distinctive in their use of red in large, bold areas that are separated by unpainted bands filled in with very thin, linear red lines. While this painting is not reminiscent of any extant arrows known to the authors, the lengthy foreshafts and long projectile points are very similiar to some extant Patwin arrows collected in Colusa County (FM 79816.1, -.2, and -.3).

Type D

Type D arrows, in their overall form, are very distinct from types A–C. The 11 examples of this type are compound in form, with the mainshaft nicely tapered down to meet a long foreshaft; all have Desert Side-notch points, 73 percent of which are made of chert, and the remainder of obsidian. These points fit in style with both the Delta and basic forms reported in California. The style is widespread over much of the central part of the state: in various locales in Marin County (Moratto, Riley, and Wilson 1974:71, Fig. VI-2); from El Dorado and Placer counties (Heizer and Elsasser 1953:42); from a site in Tehama County near Red Bluff (Treganza 1954:Fig. 2g); from Redding (Clewett and Sundahl 1981:48); from a site at Pinole (Davis 1960:Fig. 4); from Yosemite National Park (YPM various); and from a site in Amador County (Palumbo 1967:Pl. 2). It is not known whether or not the point type occurred at Sutter's Fort, since the recovered artifacts have not been described (Gebhardt 1958:12), but clearly the archaeological distribution is extensive. Ethnographically, the point type is found on arrows collected from the Northwestern Maidu (AMNH 50/284a,b,c) and the Sierra Miwok (SDM J.126–129).

In addition to the differences between the Type D and the types A–C arrows just mentioned, the hafting technique also varies in that an "X-wrap" is used and kept very tight and close to the foreshaft in Type D arrows to eliminate any bulbousness, a feature identical to that used on the Maidu and Sierra Miwok arrows just mentioned. The nock and fletching on Type D arrows are also different. The nock is shallower, pointed on the butt edges, and has been nicely worked into a V shape. The fletching is about twice the length of that on types A–C arrows, and the feathering has a different pattern in that the feathers, rather than being cut into a simple convex curve, are cut rounder on the nock-facing end, so that the upper edge becomes only a simple taper.

Riband markings (Figure 5.19) include painting on both the mainshaft and the foreshaft, with red and black being the colors used. The mainshaft decoration involves simple bands that are usually very bold in form, although three Type D arrows have thin, linear lines. Such a combination of features, including the spiraling lines on one (570-187), the presence of considerable painting, and the length of the feathering, would seem to argue for a northerly affiliation for these arrows, especially in view of the similarities that we have already noted with Maidu examples.

Type E

Since only one complete arrow representative of Type E exists, any discussion of variation is impossible. The arrow is compound in form, with the mainshaft nicely tapering to meet the foreshaft; the point is distinctive with its rounded shoulder barbs. The material used to make the point is glass. The nock and arrow fletching is different from that found in any of the other types, in that the nock is formed by a very deep, sharp V shape, with a portion of the base of the nock being covered by sinew wrapping, making the base of the nock artificially wider. The fletching pattern is unique in the way in which the nock-facing edge has been trimmed; rather than being rounded as in the other types, the edge has been cut straight to produce a parallelogram. The riband decoration (Figure 5.19) is very complex and covers both mainshaft and foreshaft with bold and narrow bands done in red, black, and white. The sinew hafting on the point is somewhat similar to that found on Type A arrows, although there is some variation in that their basal corners have not been sinew wrapped.

Type F

Like Type B arrows, Type F arrows are not compound but are self arrows; however, the similarity ends there. Most of the Type F arrows have leaf-shaped obsidian points with serrations along both edges all the way to the point tip (rather than only part of the way, as was described for Type C points). This fully serrated type of point is found in the archaeological record only in Marin County; examples have been reported by Jackson (1974:73, Figs. 22, 26) and Slaymaker (1977:233, Fig. 28). Although this would seem to suggest that Type F arrows must, therefore, be Coast Miwok in origin, we hasten to add that we do not have enough distributional data to eliminate such other regions as the Delta or the Sacramento Valley. Two other projectile point forms, one side-notched and one leaf-shaped, are also present in this group.

The Type F nocks also differ from all but Type E nocks in being well formed. In fact, Type F arrows have the most carefully shaped nocks of any in the collection, with a medium deep V shape form and a slight corner rounding on the sides. The fletching, in form, is much like that found on Type D arrows, although the length is slightly less, falling between the length of the shorter Type A, B, C and E fletched arrows and the longer ones of Type D.

Riband markings (Figure 5.19) are very complex, and (as is the case with Type E arrows) involve the use of red, black, and white. Simple narrow bold bands are present, as well as some very finely made encircling striations, or grooves, that are located along the shaft under the fletching. Such grooves were apparently produced by holding a small section of the stem of a horsetail rush (*Equisitum* sp.) around the shaft and sanding the grooves into the wood. This practice was followed by a number of groups in central California, such as the Southern Miwok (where the grooving was called *su-tai-gus*; see J. Hudson n.d.b:38), and was practiced as far south as the Chumash area (Hudson 1974:Pl. 2). The practice also appears to have been employed on arrows in northwestern California, judging by museum specimens of arrows attributed to the Hupa, Yurok, and Karok (LM 1-2356, 1-14611).

The arrowshaft is also highly decorated with either red or black at the hafting tip where the projectile point is inserted. An X-pattern of wrapping is used for hafting the point. The fletching is usually lengthy, and is somewhat similar to that on Type D arrows.

Both Desert Side-notched and serrated triangular-shaped points are present; the latter are most typically found on the self arrows in this group, while compound arrows tend to have the former. Obsidian is used for both. Foreshaft lengths average about 10 cm.

We believe that the arrows comprising Type F, like the Type A arrows, were also collected by Voznesenskii in or near the Sacramento River area. The strongest evidence for this comes from comparisons between the Helsinki arrows and those in Russia; although very close correspondences are evident (for example, Set 46 with Set 37, arrow 282; Set 47 with Set 39, arrow 289; Set 48 with Set 37, arrow 283; and so on) throughout the two groups of arrows, definite matches occur as well. For example, the Helsinki and St. Petersburg arrows in sets 49 and 35 obviously came from the same quiver, for they are identical in riband markings, materials, and point type. We might also note that explaining the differences between types A and F, which we believe were collected in the same general region, will require a great deal more study than is possible here with our limited data.

Two additional arrows (Figure 5.17), which we did not place within any of the arrow types described, deserve separate treatment. One of these arrows (MAE 570-288) was once stone-tipped, but its point is missing, probably as a result of damage received after collection. What makes this arrow unique is the presence of a barb which has been cut into its wooden shaft. The other distinctive arrow (MAE 570-280) is a compound arrow with a wooden self point that was made by trimming and smoothing the hardwood; it is decorated with two broad ribands. Such arrows were very common and were used throughout California for hunting small game. It is most surprising that the Kunstkamera and Helsinki collections should have only one example between them.[4]

Figure 5.20. Arrow quiver (570-133). Portion of animal's face cropped in view.

Arrow Quiver?

Another object of interest in the Kunstkamera collections (570-133) is a skin which may or may not have served as an arrow quiver. It is just over 1 m in length by 33 cm in width at the widest point. Although somewhat worn, features of the face, claws, and fur suggest that it comes from a coyote or perhaps a native dog. The animal was skinned in a manner that involved cutting lengthwise down the belly and then removing the entire pelt, leaving the forefeet (and some claws) and face. The skin was tanned with the hair on; the mouth and belly were then sewn up, leaving the rectal area open. A few pieces of green cloth were used to patch some small holes in the skin, while a fiber cord was sewn about the opening (probably for decoration) by being passed in and out through a series of perforations along the edges of the hide, including the outlines of the hind legs (Figure 5.20).

This item could well have been an arrow quiver, but when it is compared with sketches made by various European explorers of California Indian quivers, some sharp distinctions become apparent. The quiver illustrated by Cardero (Figure 5.5) was held at the waist, and the arrows appear to have extended from the mouth of what seems to have been a complete fox skin; Choris's drawings, which apparently relate to the Chulamni Yokuts, show three quivers made from small animal hides in which the arrows passed completely through, from mouth to rectum (Figures 2.5 and 5.6).[5] Similar quivers were used in historic times by the Sierra Miwok (Barrett and Gifford 1933:319; YPM negs. Rl-14,033, -034, -036, -157), and certainly by others as well. The style survives to this day in the specific form of a dancing quiver carried by one performer in the Hesi ceremony of the Patwin, Pomo, and Nomlaki people, and it undoubtedly was also used by their neighbors who were participating in this dance at the turn of the century.

Quivers with the mouth area covered with tanned hide, or simply with the mouth and eye openings sewn shut, have been recorded for a number of groups, including the Yahi (Pope 1918:118–119, Pl. 23, Fig. 5), the Atsugewi (LVNP 667), the Modoc (LBNM n/n), and the Maidu (AMNH 50/282), although in the latter two examples the pelts have been turned fur side in.

The Kunstkamera skin (570-133) may also have been used as a skin sack. The Central Sierra Miwok used wildcat skins with the head openings sewn shut to store beeds and other valuables (FM 70272, 70273), while the Patwin used the skins to store tobacco (A. Kroeber 1932:292, 297).

Net Bag

Net bags, which were once common among many central California Indian people, were typically used by men to carry a host of objects, including small game. The Kunstkamera catalog indicates that they have two such bags, 570-69 (Figure 5.21) and 570-70 (which could not be located).

MAE 570-69 is 26 cm in length by 23 cm in width; it was produced by using a knotless netting technique in which the loops of one row hook into those of the previous row. It appears to be made from two-ply milkweed or native hemp-fiber cordage. The soiled condition of the bag makes positive identification uncertain at best. Bags similar to this specimen were widely used in central California, and a number of examples exist in various collections from such groups as the Maidu (OPM 16-2371, 16-2292, 16-2348, 16-2293, 16-2283; USM 131,099; AMNH 50/6446); Wailaki (LM 1-10592); Northeastern Pomo (OPM 16-2913); and other Pomoan groups (BKM 7949, 8351). Other groups that are reported to have had these bags, but for which extant examples appear to be lacking, include the Sierra Miwok (Barrett and Gifford 1933:247), the River Patwin (S. Kroeber 1932:284), and the Valley Nisenan (A. Kroeber 1929:263).

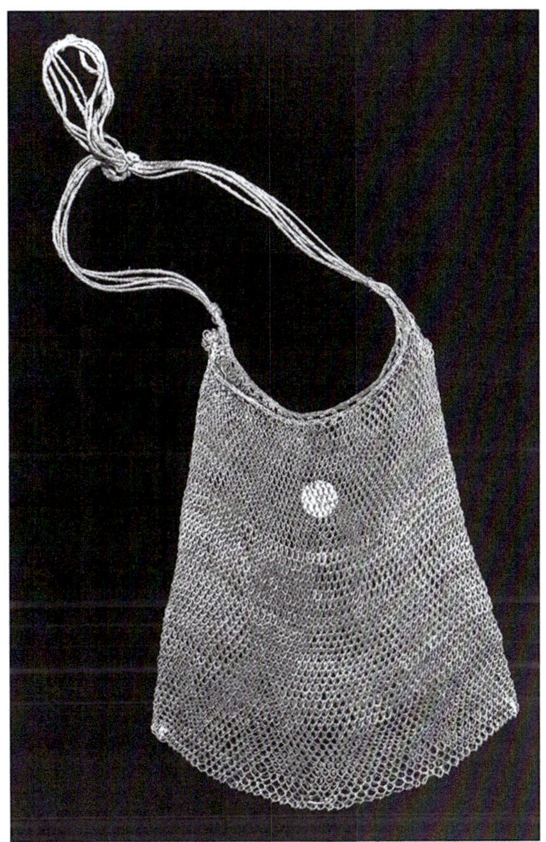

Figure 5.21. Net bag (570-69).

Gathering Equipment

Seed Beater

The Kunstkamera collections contain a seed beater (570-109; see Figure 5.22), which is not unlike many Pomoan examples collected at the turn of the century. This handled basket has a basin which measures 33 cm in diameter and is 9 cm deep; the attached handle is some 20 cm long and 4 cm in diameter. The manufacturing technique employed was wickerwork, using whole, peeled shoots, possibly from willow or hazel. The rim binding is of split grapevine, a tough material that would hold up to rough use. The device was used to knock seeds from plants into a tightly woven, conical burden basket. Such seed beaters were favored by Pomoan peoples, and examples similar to this one have been collected from villages such as *Yokiah* (just north of the town of Ukiah) at the turn of the century (SC Sheedy Coll. 6026; see also BM 06.331.8197).

Figure 5.22. Seed beater (570-109).

Burden Baskets

There are four examples of the conical burden basket (mentioned above) in the Kunstkamera collections (Figure 5.23); unfortunately, three of them (570-75, -76- and -77) were mounted high above a display case and were not available for inspection, while the fourth (without a catalog number) was placed in a carrying net on a mannequin and could not be removed from the exhibit for study. Nevertheless, some comments can be made about these pieces. All four baskets are Pomoan in style and are made from diagonally-twined split sedge root and redbud shoots. The rim sticks on all of the baskets are bound with split grapevines.

The three burden baskets with diagonal patterns are excellent examples of the type made by Pomo people living along the Russian River. The superb weaving and complex patterns in the baskets place them among the finest examples of their type.

The remaining basket is unique. The use of a horizontally-banded pattern on a diagonally twined burden basket is unusual. Documented examples collected from the Pomo all use plain twining. Similar, though different, burden baskets produced with diagonal twining with horizontal bands were made by the Koncow Maidu at Chico. In addition, the rim of this example is bound with split redbud shoots as well as split grapevines.

Figure 5.23. Conical burden basket, probably Pomo (MAE n/n).

Figure 5.24. Headband of carrying net (570-72) displayed on mannequin.

Carrying Nets

The carrying net was in common use throughout much of California for transporting the burden basket, as well as being used separately for carrying a variety of other objects. Such nets were in use among the Coast Miwok (Kelly n.d.:252), the Hill Patwin (A. Kroeber 1932:284), the Ohlones (Harrington 1942:20), and the Pomoan peoples (Barrett 1952:I:168–169)—examples collected from the latter group have survived in the greatest numbers (OPM 16-1344; MAI 3-9318).

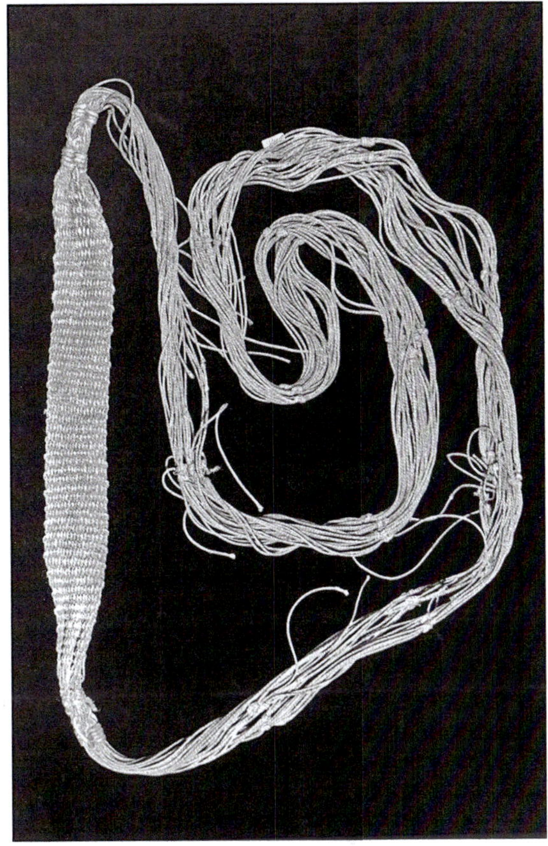

Figure 5.25. Carrying net (570-73).

There are two examples in St. Petersburg (570-72 and -73; see Figures 5.24 and 5.25). MAE 570-72, which was displayed on a female mannequin in 1984, is particularly noteworthy for the elaborate forehead band decorated with white glass beads; the beads are woven into it. White clamshell disk beads were used for decoration on these bands by the Pomo (for example, BM 06.331.8018), and no other example is known that employs glass beads. This particular carrying net is woven of finely made native hemp cordage, which is the most commonly used material in extant Pomo carrying nets. The undecorated headband of 570-73 is 41 cm long by 5 cm wide, and is woven into the net, which measures (in a half-folded position) 97 cm in length. The mesh squares of the net are 15 cm in length. The netting was done with double cords, a technique consistent with extant examples. The coloring of the cordage that was used to make this net suggests that the material is native hemp fiber. The net was made by carrying two strands of cordage on the netting shuttle, resulting in a double-cord net mesh.

Chapter 6

Objects of Home and Hearth

Food Preparation and Shelter

Throughout Native California the household was the focus of everyday existence, the hub around which family life revolved, and the place where family members engaged in a host of daily activities that were vital to the cultural, social, and psychological well-being of the community. Food preparation and consumption took place here, as did the manufacturing of tools and utensils from raw materials. But much more occurred here as well, for children also played, women gossiped, and old men recounted—in song and story—the events of a mythical past. Such a scene of rich and diverse domestic activities must have appeared rather exotic to the Russian visitors. In fact, artist Mikhail Tikhanov rendered a composite of such family activities in a drawing (Figure 6.1) done at Bodega Bay in 1818; it includes a woman pounding grain (identified as wild rye) in a hopper mortar, a young mother nursing her child with another child asleep in a baby basket in the background, a boiling basket being heated with hot rocks in the foreground, and a man holding a straight smoking pipe on the left (Farris 1998:4–6).

In 1824, Otto von Kotzebue visited Fort Ross and made the following comment about the diet of the local people:

> Apart from their daily work with the Russians, their sole occupation is hunting. They are very undemanding in their choice of food. They will eat any trash heartily, including various insects and worms, making an exception for venomous snakes only. In winter they stock acorns and the seeds of wild rye, which grows here abundantly. When the rye ripens, the Indians set fire to it. The straw is burned off, and the scorched kernels are left on the ground. They gather it in piles and mix it with acorns. In such form this dish is used as food. (Gibson 2013:305–306)

Treasures from Native California: The Legacy of Russian Exploration, Travis Hudson and Craig D. Bates, Edited by Thomas Blackburn and John R. Johnson, 95–108.

Figure 6.1. Tikhanov painting showing the interior of a Coast Miwok house near Bodega Bay in 1818. The watercolor is entitled "Inhabitants of Rumyantsev Bay in New Albion." It shows a variety of household activities, including a woman pounding wild rye kernels and a man smoking a pipe, with the Russian sloop *Kamchatka* visible in the background. *Courtesy of the Scientific Research Museum of the Russian Academy of Fine Arts, St. Petersburg.*

In Captain Cyrille Laplace's account of his trip to Fort Ross, there is a wonderful description of his visit to a nearby Indian village (*Métini*, probably). His observations reflect some of the changes already taking place in the culture, such as the use of beef:

> I could move freely in the huts and admit myself thus to the secrets of their interior.... The majority [of the women] were busy with the housekeeping, preparing meals for their husbands and children. Some were spreading out on the embers some pieces of beef given as rations, or shell-fish, or even fish which these unhappy creatures came to catch either at the nearby river or from the sea; while others heated the grain in a willow basket before grinding it between two stones. In the middle of this basket they shook constantly some live coals on which each grain passed rapidly by an ever more accelerated rotating movement until they were soon parched, without letting the inner side of the basket be burned by the fire. Some of these baskets, or more accurately, these deep baskets seemed to me true models of basket making, not only by their decoration but by the finishing touches of the work. They are made of shoots of straw or compact gorse so solidly held together by the thread [*sic*, coiling] that the fabric was water resistant, as efficiently as baked clay and earthenware. (2006:35–37)

Because of the presumed abundance and ready availability of various household tools and utensils in the various villages that were adjacent to Fort Ross or were located in regions such as the Sacramento area that were visited by the Russians, one might reasonably expect domestic items to be well represented in the Kunstkamera's collections; however, such is not the case. The reason why so few domestic objects were collected probably reflects the fact that the Russian visitors selected objects very much as most modern tourists do; that is, they seem to have preferred rare and fancy items over plain and common ones.

For sheer numbers, baskets head the list of common household objects that were collected. Each basket was made to perform a specific task: to stone boil acorn mush, to winnow acorns or grass seeds, to store food, to transport objects, to cradle infants, or to be presented as a gift. Basketry use in native California was thus multifaceted, and as would be expected, the materials, forms, and designs used in their creation were governed by traditionally accepted rules and ideas. Such rules established and defined what was "correct" in basket making; as a consequence, styles were slow to change as elderly female relatives passed on the time-honored skills to younger girls. By the age of 10, young basket makers were producing serviceable, well-made baskets characteristic of the traditional repertoire of their people.

The basketry examples in the Russian collections which reflect household activities provide us with a unique glimpse into this facet of the craft as it existed in the early nineteenth century. Although the number of examples is indeed small, the spotty collection does provide us with an opportunity to examine what appears to be an unbroken tradition in central California.

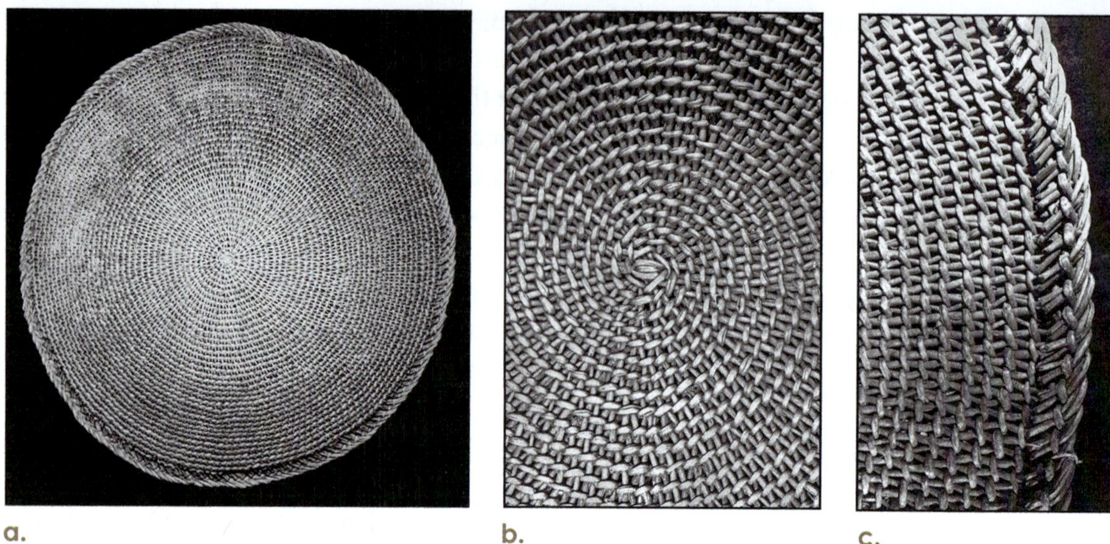

a. b. c.

Figure 6.2. (a) Winnowing tray (570-89); (b) starting knot; (c) rim detail.

Food Preparation and Serving

Winnowing Trays

There are two open-twined winnowing trays—both with a radial warp arrangement—in the Kunstkamera collection. One, MAE 570-89 (Figure 6.2a), is 32 cm in diameter and 11 cm in depth. This basket, which apparently was made with peeled willow or hazel shoots, was manufactured using a technique of diagonal twining with an up-to-the-right slant of turns of twining (Figure 6.2b). The selvage of the basket was accomplished by bending the warp rods over in pairs and then catching them with the last row of twining (Figure 6.2c). It is an unusual piece, and we have been unable to find any similar examples from elsewhere in California. Its general style suggests that it may conceivably be from California rather than elsewhere in the world; it may be the sole survivor of a type of peeled-shoot utilitarian basket that was once made in central California.

Another winnowing tray, MAE 570-88 (Figure 6.3), is similar in shape, although it was produced using lattice twining and is similar to other Pomo examples. It is made of peeled shoots, possibly willow, with sedge root (rhizome) wefts. The lattice rod is very even in diameter and is possibly made of willow root, although it is impossible to be certain due to the sedge wrapping. It is 32 cm in diameter and 12 cm in height.

Sifting Tray

MAE 570-87 is a sifting tray (Figure 6.4) that was produced by diagonal twining, with a down-to-the-right slant of turns of twining. The basket, which also has strengthening bands produced in lattice twining, is extremely soiled, apparently from native use. The materials are split sedge rhizomes, and the design is worked with split redbud shoots. This particular sifting tray, which is about 53 cm in diameter and 17 cm in height, appears to be similar to, but distinct from, those once popular among the Pomo. Every extant tray of this type known to the authors was produced by plain, rather than diagonal, twining.

Trays of this style were commonly used among the Pomoan peoples for both sifting acorn flour and receiving sifted acorn flour;

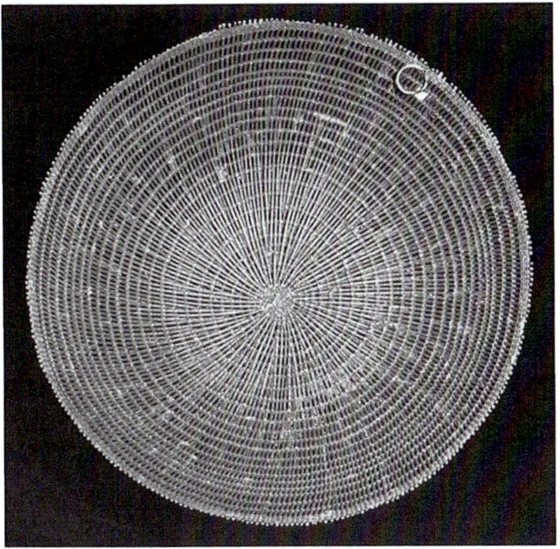

Figure 6.3. Winnowing tray (570-88).

Figure 6.4. Sifting tray (570-87).

this type of use can be documented in many early photographs of such activities (for example, see Bean and Theodoratus 1978:290, Fig. 1). Through comparison, one can see that the arrangement of designs and the positions of the rows of lattice twining are very similar. Trays of this form were therefore possibly made by the same Pomoan peoples whose other twined wares—such as burden baskets and large mush baskets—were also generally made using diagonal twining, or perhaps by a neighboring group such as the Coast Miwok.

a.

b.

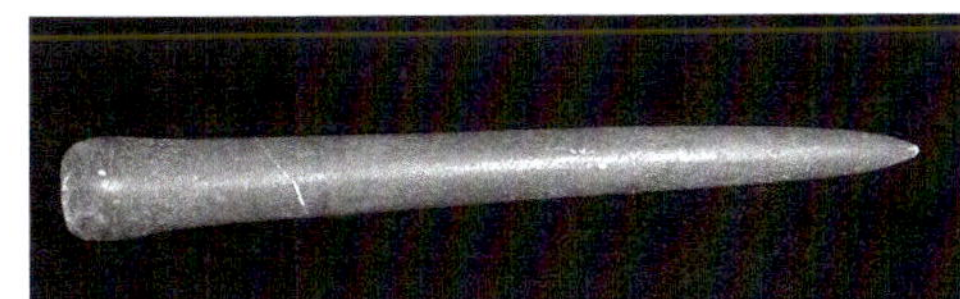

Figure 6.5. (a) Basket hopper mortar (MAE n/n) and (b) pestle (570-117).

Mortar and Pestle

A globular block of stone with a shallow basin-like depression is on exhibit in St. Petersburg; it almost certainly served as a mortar with an added hopper basket. Unfortunately, the mortar (Figure 6.5a) lacks a catalog number, so we can only speculate that it may originally have been attached to the hopper basket which rests upon it in the exhibit (MAE 570-84), or shared the same number as a pestle (MAE 570-117) that is described in the next paragraph. The mortar is 27 cm in diameter and 12 cm high, while the shallow depression is 17 cm in diameter but only 3 cm deep.

Mortars similar to this were usually accompanied by long, nicely shaped pestles like 570-117 (Figure 6.5b), which is also on exhibit. Such pestles, which were often made of black stone, were highly prized by the

Pomo (Allen 1972:66); they were also used by such neighboring groups as the Nomlaki and Patwin people (OPM 16-2081, 16-2066, 16-2490 to -2504, and so on). The Kunstkamera example is 58 cm in length and measures 6 cm in maximum width. Such pestles, which were made by pecking and abrading with a hammerstone, must have required a great deal of labor.

Hopper Basket

Another twined basket which appears to be of Pomoan origin is the hopper basket, 570-84 (Figure 6.6). The basket is 42 cm in diameter and 17 cm in height; it was made by plain twining with sedge root wefts and split redbud shoot patterning, and reinforcement bands of lattice twining and a rim sewn on with split grapevine are present.

Such baskets were used with rather flattish mortars (that is, perhaps the actual mortar whose number we lack), which were then embedded in the earth and the hopper basket held in place by the user's calves; the funnel-like shape of the bottomless basket kept materials such as acorn flour confined during the pounding process that reduced it to fine flour. This particular example is identical to other documented Pomo pieces, some of which were collected in Sonoma County (OPM 16-1279).

Basket Trays

It was surprising to discover Chumash baskets in the Russian collections, since the bulk of Russian collecting took place well to the north of Santa Barbara. Chumash basketry, which was renowned for its fineness and beauty, was frequently sought by various Spanish and English visitors to California (Hudson and Blackburn 1983); we now know that the Russians collected it as well. Although firm documentation is lacking, these items are likely to have been collected by Kiril Khlebnikov, an official of the Russian-American Company who visited Santa Barbara in the 1820s and had an ethnographic collection from Russian America which went to the Kunstkamera (Hudson 1983a, b). Although it is unclear just how far south Voznesneskii traveled, we do know that he reached the vicinity of San Jose and Santa Clara.

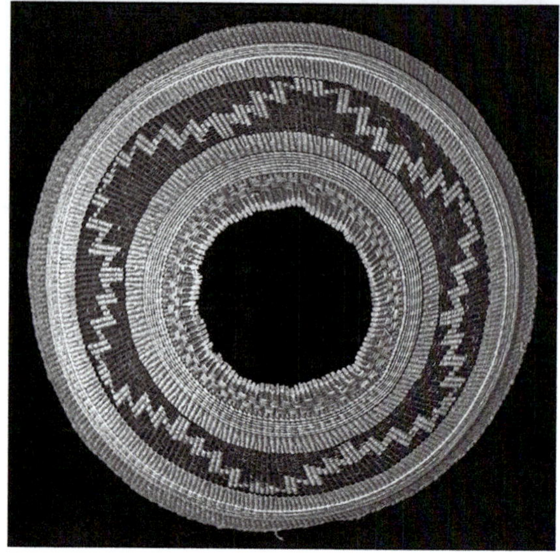

Figure 6.6. Basket hopper (570-84).

The collection plate and other baskets at the Carmel mission are Chumash. As the missions advanced, many of the Southern California Indians were brought along to 'colonize' the new mission sites until new recruits from the local area could be induced to join. They brought their personal baskets with them, as they were used in food production at the missions. The use of Indian baskets was an extension of Spanish agricultural basket use with an admixture of Native use as well. Many of the central California missions still have a few Southern California baskets in their collections (M. Mathewson, personal communication 2010).

In 1791, the Malaspina expedition arrived in Monterey, where members of the party were able to acquire a small but significant collection of 14 Chumash baskets. Fermín

Francisco de Lasuén, who held the office of president of the missions and whose headquarters were at Mission Carmel,

> bent every effort to help in the scientific inquiry.... He gave from his own sources of Indian artifacts, made interpreters available, and acted as an informant on the basis of his own personal knowledge and from mission records in his custody. More interesting was Lasuén's kindness in sending south to the Santa Barbara Channel missions a request that they send a collection of Chumash items for scientific study. The contents of this collection are part of the exhibit regularly displayed at the Museo de America in Madrid. (Cutter 1977:39)

Figure 6.7. Chumash serving tray (4296-6).

Figure 6.8. Serving tray (570-86).

Although Voznesenskii did not travel to Southern California, he might have easily acquired Chumash baskets in the central portion of the state.

One of the Chumash baskets in the Kunstkamera collections (MAE 4296-6) is a finely made basket tray (Figure 6.7), 45 cm in diameter and 12 cm in height. It was not cataloged with the Voznesenskii pieces, and unfortunately there is no associated documentation. Its construction involves a foundation of three-rod juncus coiled in a rightward direction. The sewing material is split juncus. It is possible that the background is of split sumac; the background color of the basket is very light, and it has not darkened to the extent that juncus usually does in older baskets. The designs are in red juncus, outlined in black dyed juncus, and stand out against the natural straw-colored background. The functions of such decorated basket trays among the Chumash varied, but they were usually employed in tasks involving food preparation and serving (Hudson and Blackburn 1983: 280–281).

Another basket of similar size is MAE 570-86 (Figure 6.8). It appears to be unfinished, and might well have been originally intended to become a basket bowl instead of a serving tray. This piece, which is 29.5 cm in diameter and 6.7 cm in height, is made on a grass-bundle foundation, with sedge rhizomes as the sewing material. The design work has been produced by using split redbud shoots for red and dyed bracken fern root for black. The interior of the basket was the work face, with the direction of coiling to the right; the fag ends of the sewing strands were cut on the work face.

The combination of these basketry features suggests that MAE 570-86 originated among the Yokuts; this conclusion is reinforced by the fact that the design style itself is similar to that of other pieces stemming from the southern San Joaquin Valley. It is interesting that this basket is nearly identical to one collected in Monterey in the 1860s (YPM 32474); both baskets were made using the same materials and constructional techniques, and they also share one of the design patterns. Since other Yokuts-type baskets are known to have been collected in Monterey prior to 1850 (MC; MAI 50/867), it is possible that some Yokuts basketry items were traded to the coast from inland regions, or were relics of Yokuts neophytes associated with coastal missions or trading expeditions. Nevertheless, it would appear that the most likely location for Russians to have collected MAE 570-86 would have been either at Monterey or in some part of the Sacramento region that was visited by Voznesenskii (assuming that villages in the latter area also traded with Yokuts groups). Sierra Miwok groups often obtained Yokuts baskets in trade, and it seems reasonable to assume that Plains Miwok people did as well. Indeed, one photograph taken of Plains Miwok people near Galt in the1800s (Moratto 1976:101) shows what appears to be a Yokuts basket nearly identical to one in the Yosemite Museum that was collected at Jackson from northern Miwok people (YPM 25524).

Basket Bowl

Another Chumash piece is a bowl-shaped basket, MAE 570-85 (Figure 6.9). The basket, which is 31 cm in diameter and 11.5 cm in height, is made with juncus sewing strands on a three-rod juncus foundation, coiled in a rightward direction on an inside work face. In contrast to the natural straw-colored background that was noted on the tray, this piece has a background that has been done in red juncus, with black dyed juncus designs outlined in white. This basket probably had many uses, but tasks associated with food preparation and serving were probably primary (Hudson and Blackburn 1983:221).

Figure 6.9. Chumash serving bowl (570-85).

Seed Cake

The last object associated with food preparation and consumption is a blackish-colored seedcake (MAE 570-116) about the size of a man's fist, which we surmise was probably collected by Voznesenskii. The cake, a food item, undoubtedly was a result of the widespread California Indian practice of grinding oil-laden grass seeds and then pressing them into balls or cakes for eating. This practice has been described among the Miwok by Barrett and Gifford (1933:152–153); the Miwok used the seeds of red maids (*Calandrinia caulescens*), but the practice was so commonly Californian that the source of the seedcake could have been any of several tribes.

Household Items

Fire-making Kit

When we turn our attention from objects that were associated primarily with food preparation to those that were used more generally within the household, we might begin by noting that no activity was more important than the ability to make fire. It is surprising, therefore, that the items associated with this activity, as well as the characteristics which might provide insight into regional or tribal patterns, have received relatively little attention in the literature. Numerous ethnographers, for example, mention the use of the fire drill among California peoples—the fire-making process in which rapid rotation produces heat by friction to ignite tinder—and discuss the type of wood used for the drill and hearth, but they usually overlook such details as the direction of the wood grain of the hearth, or whether it is made from a young shoot or old heartwood. However, it is just these sorts of details which we find to be highly significant. In light of such a lack of ethnographic information, it is easy to appreciate the value of documented museum specimens that can be used for making specific comparisons. However, even this approach is not without its problems. Many of the extant fire-making kits in museum collections show no signs of use, since they were made specifically for collectors at the turn of the century, at a time when the "old way" of making fire was no longer being used.

Therefore, the single fire-making kit (MAE 570-115a, b; see Figure 6.10) is of considerable interest. The hearth is made from an unidentified wood and is 90 cm in length and 1.5 cm in diameter; the associated drill is 76 cm in length and 1 cm in diameter. Since it was carefully debarked, the type of wood selected for the drill is also unknown, although the

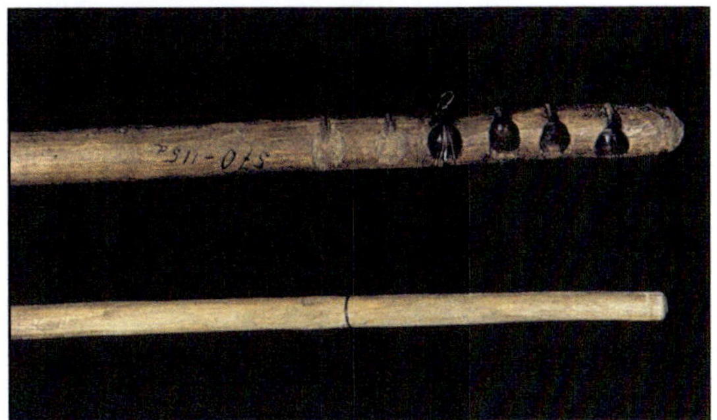

Figure 6.10. Fire-making kit (570-115 a–b).

presence of a large, pithy center suggests that it is either buckeye or elderberry. Both of these materials were favored by a number of groups for fire drills. The hearth block has four tapering holes at one end that show signs of use, with three additional, prepared holes which show no sign of use. Curiously, the drill for this particular fire-making kit exhibits signs of use on both ends of the shaft; the more common practice was for only one end (which was usually slightly larger in diameter than the other) to be used.

The hearth is also interesting in terms of its configuration, for it is extremely narrow in comparison with those collected at the turn of the century from among the Miwok (FM 70139, 70142, 70144; YPM 7577), Pomo (FM 61054, 61195), and Yokuts (FM 70438, 70440). All of the foregoing museum examples are two to five times wider than the Kunstkamera piece, and were manufactured from the heartwood of larger trees rather than being made from a shoot, as was 570-115.

The narrow configuration of the Russian example might have been intentional, in that it enabled the hearth to be carried in an arrow quiver; alternatively, the Russian example may represent an earlier form of fire drill. We offer the latter suggestion in light of the greater availability of heartwoods from large trees that occurred historically when lumbering became important; in earlier times, the lack of heavy woodworking tools among central California peoples made access to such materials difficult, so that the selection of smaller diameter saplings for hearths would have been a more logical choice.

Woven Matting

The Kunstkamera catalog states that three woven mats (570-64, -65, and -66) form part of the collections. No further information is provided, and the mats could not be located during Hudson's visit. Therefore, we can only note their reputed existence here and hope that someday they can be found and described.

Feather Blankets

Warm and luxuriant feather blankets were once widely used throughout much of California; their manufacture apparently ceased around 1850 when commercially-woven wool blankets became available in quantity. Today, there are only fourteen extant examples in museums worldwide; three of these are known to have been collected by the Russians.

As we noted in Chapter 2, Langsdorff was possibly the source for one, or perhaps both, of the Kunstkamera examples. He described them in the following way during a visit to Mission San Francisco in 1806:

> They also make for themselves garments of the feathers of several kinds of water-fowl, particularly ducks and geese. These they bind closely together in a string-like fashion, which strings are afterwards joined tight making a dress of a feather-fur appearance. Both sides are alike, and it is so warm that it would be an excellent protection against the cold of even a more northern clime. (1814:II:56)

He continued with a description of similar blankets that were made from sea otter skins:

> Sea otter skins are also cut by them in small strips, and these they twist together and join in the same manner as with the feathers just described, and also as with the feathers, both sides alike. These coverings are worn principally by the women, and but very rarely by the males. (1814:II:56)

Karl Gillsen described native dress in 1821 as follows:

> They clothe themselves in blankets interlaced with black and white feathers; across their shoulders as far as their knees they wear a kind of cloak. Around the middle of their body they wind bast-like matting of their own making, and the rest is bare. (Gibson 2013:163)

José Cardero, a member of the Malaspina Expedition which visited Monterey in 1791, sketched a California Indian woman wearing such a blanket about her shoulders (Iglesias 1980:197, Fig. 81); the sketch is reproduced here (Figure 6.11).

These blankets, which were usually made of waterfowl feathers, were produced by nearly all of the groups who occupied the heartland of central California's great valleys, where immense flocks of birds provided the feathers for the manufacture of such marks of affluence.[1] They were definitely produced by the Valley Nisenan, the Konkow, the Patwin, the Plains Miwok, and the Wappo (Azbill, personal communication, 1970; Barrett 1952:294; Chever 1870:133; Gifford 1917b:322, 327; McLendon 2001a; Phelps 1983:207), and perhaps by their neighbors as well. Extant examples are rare, but (in addition to those collected by the Russians) there is one specimen in Berlin (EMB IV B 182), one in Copenhagen (NMD Hd-37), one in Belfast (ULM 1910:188, Glover 1978:21,71), and one in Dresden (SMD 161). The Dresden example has an interesting history, in that it was presented by the Mexican Ambassador, José López Uraga, to the court of King Friedrich August II around 1852 (Uhle 1886:18–19;

Vatter 1925:100). (Wrangell may have originally given the blanket to the Mexican government as a gift, since he visited Mexico City in 1835 on his journey home to Russia.) Seven examples are known in American museums: three of these consist of blankets that were collected in 1841 by Captain William Phelps near Sutter's Fort; two are now at the Peabody Museum, Harvard (PM 98238, 98240), while a third is curated at the Denver Art Museum (DAM FMa-1-Ex). A third blanket at the Peabody Museum was collected early in the nineteenth century by William Gale (PMH 84680). Still another blanket, without provenience, is located at the American Museum of Natural History (AMNH50.1/7889); there is also a specimen in the Smithsonian's collections (USM 2119) that was procured during Captain Charles Wilkes's California expedition (Willoughby 1922). Still another blanket is curated at the Los Angeles County Museum of Natural History (LACMNH 3349.94-1).

Figure 6.11. Depiction by José Cardero of Monterey Indian woman wearing what appears to be a woven feather or fur blanket. *Courtesy of Museo de América, Madrid (Inventory No. 02284).*

The Frankfurt example is the best documented of the three feather blankets collected by the Russians. It was collected by Baron Ferdinand von Wrangell, probably in 1833 in Pomo territory; the blanket is 1.2 m in length and 1.42 m. in width. Both sides are identical, as is the case with all known examples. The end strips consist of very dark brown feathers, intermixed with blackish feathers, which have white stippling on them. The center section of the blanket consists of a single large field of light brown feathers, which (as is the case with the other blankets) probably came from an adult male mallard duck. The feathers of many birds were necessary to make a blanket.

One rather curious feature of the Frankfurt specimen involves two of the warp cords at the corners of the blanket. The cords, which were not trimmed and were perhaps left to serve as a tie for the blanket, are decorated with small glass beads.

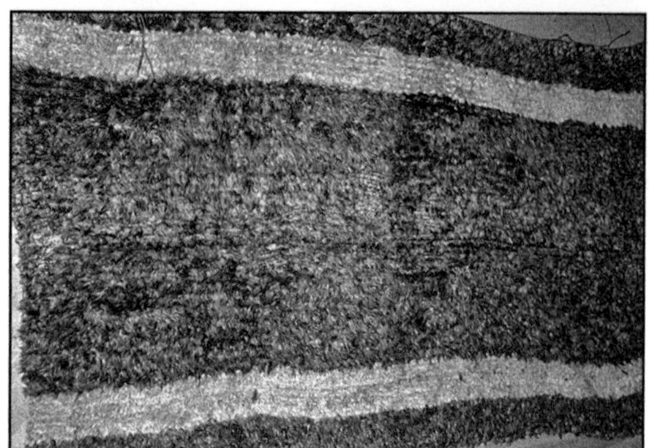

Figure 6.12. Feather blanket (2520-8). *Photo courtesy of Brian Bibby.*

Figure 6.13. Feather blanket (2520-9). *Photo courtesy of Brian Bibby.*

The two Kunstkamera feather blankets (MAE 2520-8 and -9) are identical in their construction, although their striping colors are different (Figures 6.12 and 6.13). The first, MAE 2520-8, is 1.26 m long and 1.78 m wide, with feathers that are of a dark brownish-black coloring in the center and on the edge bands. These areas are separated by a band done in white. The feathers are again probably from mallard ducks, although the MAE catalog states that this robe is made from "red-tail hawk feathers fixed on cordage." The starting cord of the blanket is a complex triangular braid, made from native hemp stained with ochre. The two-ply hemp weft pairs are anchored by simple looping over the start cord. The weft pairs are spaced about one "finger" apart along the start cord. As the twining of the weft pairs around the feathered warp cords progresses across the work, the wefts may be given a half turn, a full turn, or two turns between warps. This blanket displays superior workmanship.

The second blanket, MAE 2520-9, which was photographed (see Figure 2.2) as early as 1873, is 1.06 m. long and 1.26 m. wide, with similar striping, though the feathering used has a slightly more blackish-brown coloring. The construction techniques are the same as in MAE 2520-8 in the prior paragraph. The warp cords in both blankets are made by wrapping the split vanes of feathers around two native hemp strings as described in the next paragraph. The weft pairs on this blanket are mounted on the triangular start cord about 2.3 cm apart. The white bands are comprised of eight white feathered warp cords. Rozina (1978) included this item in the Polynesian collections, as noted in Chapter 2.

These blankets, which were highly valued by native Californians, were made from the feathers of literally hundreds of birds that were hunted for food. The warp was constructed of two parallel cords which were wrapped together using the stripped vanes of the wing feathers or (in some cases, apparently) the smaller body feathers, to produce a feather fur-like rope hundreds of feet in length. Among the Valley Nisenan, this warp was wrapped between two vertical poles which acted as the loom (A. Kroeber 1929:260–261). A curiously woven braid, apparently produced from two strands of cordage and triangular in cross-section, was then stretched on the one margin of the robe, parallel with the warp strands. The weft strands, of two-ply hemp cordage, were looped on to this braid, and the blanket's feather warps were then woven together by twining with these cords, in much the same way that a twined basket is made. Such wefts were generally about two inches apart.

Robes of this sort were highly prized not only by the Indian people themselves, but by Anglo visitors as well. Captain William Phelps secured three such blankets from Indian people working for Captain Sutter. He mentions the Sekumnes Indians, and it is likely that his description referred to the Valley Nisenan village of Seku:

> I saw a string of about 500 feet in length into which the feathers of the wild duck were closely worked, part of it white and part black. This was to form a blanket or at least the warp of one. The labour of making one of these blankets is immense. Captain Sutter presented me with one which he assumed occupied six females four months in the making. (1983:207)

It is little wonder, therefore, that these items are so rare in both European and American collections.

Figure 6.14. Chumash storage jar (570-113).

Storage Jar

The Kunstkamera collections contain a basket jar (MAE 570-113; Figures 6.14 and 6.15) which can be attributed to the Chumash. It is possible that this item was collected by Kiril Khlebnikov during his visit to Santa Barbara in 1820 (Hudson 1983b:99; Khlebnikov 1990:26, 89). The basket, which is typically Chumashan in design and construction, was made with dyed and natural juncus sewing strands on a three-rod juncus foundation, using a rightward coiling direction. The basket's red background is broken by white outlined designs done in black. In form, it is not unlike many Chumash basket jars with narrow necks that the Ventureño Chumash called *x'omoho* (Hudson and Blackburn 1983:410). Such baskets were used to store money and other small items.

While this basket shares a number of features with other Chumash basket jars, it is also unique in some ways. For example, it has a "skirt" or pedestal base, a typically introduced European feature that is found on some Chumash basket bowls and trays. Another odd

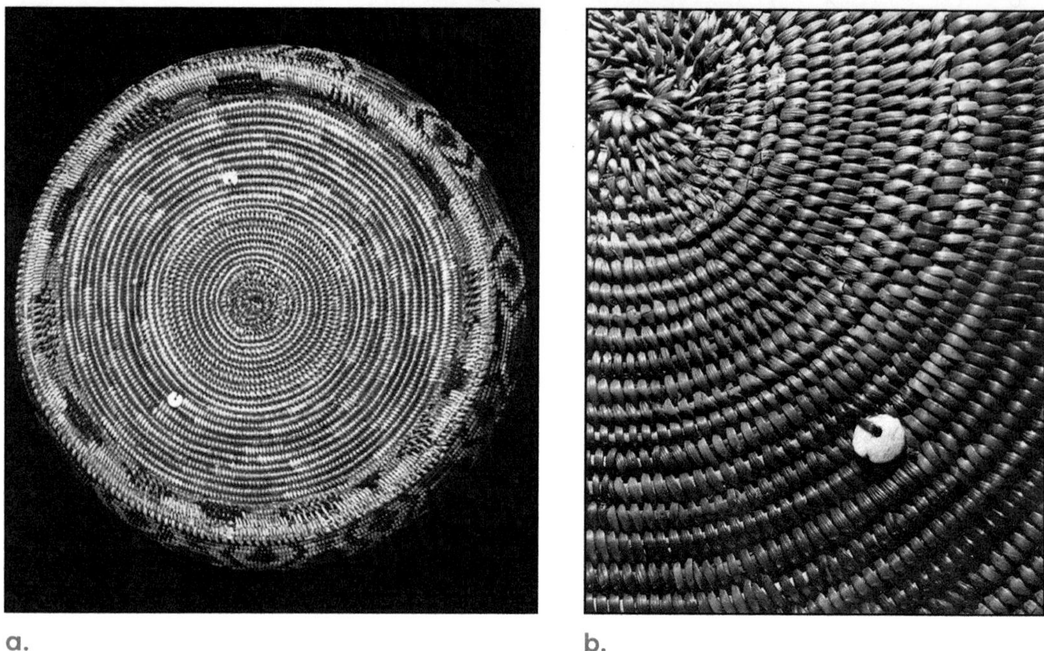

a. b.

Figure 6.15. (a) Bottom and (b) Olivella shell bead decoration on Chumash storage jar (570-113).

feature consists of an added decoration to the bottom of the jar in the form of two Olivella shell disk beads which were attached by passing the sewing strand through the bead perforation. Olivella shell-beaded baskets are not associated with the Chumash, and no other examples are known. However, one ethnographic reference does mention them: "They decorate baskets that they are going to burn at fiesta. They sew on shell ornaments or small beads on the basket so that they dangle" (Hudson and Blackburn 1986:235). We do not know if this description referred only to pendants or was also applicable to beads that were attached during construction, but it is conceivable that MAE 570-113 served some very special purpose. Because of its form and flaring skirt, it is likely that the basket was made in imitation of European forms and quite probably for European consumption. The Chumash were producing baskets specifically for Europeans at an early date, and in fact had adopted certain European conventions by the time of Vancouver's visit in1793. If this basket represents a style made expressly for and influenced by Europeans, it is the only such artifact observed in the Russian collections.

Chapter 7

Interacting with the Supernatural

Ritual Dress

Ceremonial dancing in central California was prayer in visible form.[1] Since it involved direct interaction with the spirit world, dancing was a supernaturally dangerous act. The performances—which were held during the winter months in large, semisubterranean earth-covered structures—have been characterized by anthropologists as comprising part of the "Kuksu Cult" complex of activities. The cult activities were carried out by a secret society consisting of both men and adolescent boys. A similar female society often assisted in the dances, which were designed to insure prosperity and health.

Kuksu cult dances were not only complex in their execution, the associated ritual costuming was also quite varied and elaborate. Most items of regalia were made from feathers, but regardless of the material used, every item was believed to be endowed with supernatural power which could cause sickness or death if not properly handled. Obviously, dancing was not something to be engaged in lightly. Participating in such performances was a serious undertaking—one which involved a lifetime commitment. The following description written by Vasilyev in 1821 provides a glimpse of the complex regalia and costuming that would have been observed on such occasions:

> They stain themselves in stripes of black and red, strew white bird down on their entire chest and face and in stripes on their arms, and around their head wear bands of small reeds, dyed red, with small black feathers on the ends. They also stick a feather in their hair and a crow's tail feathers in a stick, and they tie crow's feathers either to their back or to an entire waistband. They told us that in the mountains the women also dance naked and on their head wear a kind of helmet of black

Treasures from Native California: The Legacy of Russian Exploration, Travis Hudson and Craig D. Bates, Edited by Thomas Blackburn and John R. Johnson, 109–158.

feathers or a headband of down, and they mark time, swinging and flicking their arms. We saw another kind of dance: at a signal from a conductor, apparently, two come running, dressed alike except that on one's head there is a hat of black feathers and on his lips there is a long beak like a crane's made of feathers. In both of their mouths there is a whistle made of pelican feet, and both run back and forth, whistling, with sticks in their hands, and the others sing....

The savage Indians tie a reed band, dyed red, around their head and pass black feathers under it from above and below. In their hair they stick two or three sticks or bones, around which are tied red feathers from a sort of bird that has red feathers on its neck and part of its wings and black feathers elsewhere, and on the very ends they tie several condor feathers. Around their neck they wear several round bones, cut cleanly from fish, and pearl shells, and white fish bones and pieces of pearl shell are strung on a string. They pierce their ears with bones with designs and similar [illegible], and they have large waistbands of bones. (Gibson 2013:174–175)

The regalia used in these dances was constructed according to tribally accepted styles, and adherence to traditional aesthetic conventions was considered an important and necessary factor. Generally, the regalia was carefully made, and at least some individuals thought that taking the time to create objects of rare beauty—rather than simply costumes in which to dance—was all important. Their workmanship exhibited a commitment not only to dancing, but to display respect for the spirits that lived on the earth by giving them the very best one had to offer.

Because of the supernatural power inherent in the regalia, there were strict rules surrounding their handling, use, and ultimate disposal. Showing respect was essential. When an object began to show signs of wear, for example, it was often ritually destroyed; it was also carefully disposed of upon the death of its owner. Because of the respect that was given to central California items of regalia—such as headdresses, dance capes, aprons, and so forth—it is amazing that any examples should survive, particularly in the variety and quantity present in the Kunstkamera's holdings. It is also extremely fortunate that these materials to some extent document ritual behavior in pre-1841 California; after that date, nearly a half century passed before American ethnographers and collectors started to secure such objects, thus creating a chronological gap (bridged only by speculation) in our knowledge concerning the manufacture, use, and distribution of native California's most sacred objects.

There is still another way in which the Kunstkamera's collection of ceremonial regalia holds great significance to scholars: unknowingly, the Russians were collecting among peoples about whom today we know the least. The Ohlone and the Coast Miwok, for example, are presently known primarily from fragmentary information that was recorded either by early visitors or by anthropologists who interviewed native elders and inquired about their memories of objects that had been in use 50 years or more before. Few contemporary accounts exist that give us detailed information regarding the ritual objects that were used by these people, and the drawings of such artists as Tikhanov and Choris help only to establish the existence of basic object types—the renderings of such items were so indistinct that diagnostic details can not be ascertained. Data on the Plains and Bay (Saclan) Miwok are almost entirely lacking, and the bulk of the available information on the Valley Nisenan comes from one exceptional man's memory in the early years of this century.[2] Although many of the items of regalia in the Russian collections are similar to others that were used across a wide area of California—from the Sierra Miwok and Maiduan peoples to the Pomo—it is difficult, if not impossible, to ascribe a specific tribal origin to many of the pieces.

In this chapter, we shall describe the ritual regalia collected by the Russians in California. The objects range from elaborate headdresses, flicker bands, and feather capes to extremely beautiful and very rare feather belts. Many of the items found in St. Petersburg have no counterparts elsewhere.

Headwear

Flicker-Quill Headbands

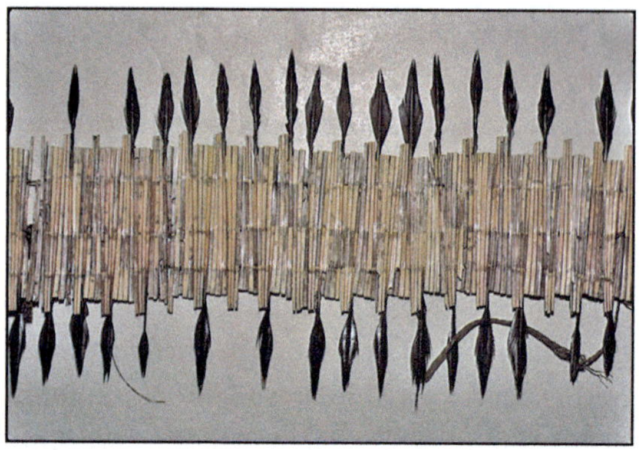

a.

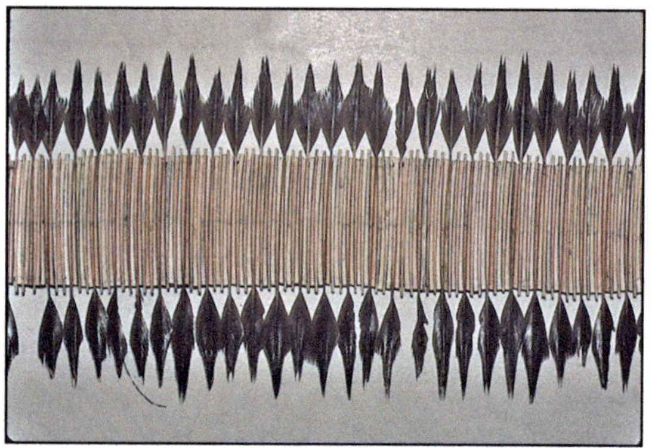

b.

c.

Figure 7.1. (a-c) Flicker quill headbands (570-16, -17, and -18). *Photos courtesy of Brian Bibby.*

The flicker-quill headband is perhaps the best known and most widespread article of ritual dress in central California, and one that is still used today by many native groups. The bands were composed of the stripped salmon-orange quills of the common flicker (*Colaptes cafer*), placed side by side like an elongated mat and held together by three or four parallel threads sewn through each quill. Specific styles of flicker bands were created using this manufacturing technique by varying the arrangement of wing and tail quills used and/or by trimming the band edges in different configurations. It is these distinctive traits which most non-Indian visitors to ceremonial functions have found to be of the greatest interest. Langsdorff, for example, described them as follows while visiting Mission San Francisco:

> Their most beautiful head-ornament is made of the two middle tail-feathers of the golden-winged woodpecker (*Picus auratus*), the shafts of which are naturally of a brilliant vermillion color. They are stripped to within an inch of the end, and then very cleverly strung and bound together so as to form a sort of bandeau for the head, the effect of which is very pleasing. (1814:II:59)

There is little doubt that Langsdorff did return to Europe with a flicker headband, for he later illustrated it in a book, and wrote:

> Among other curiosities that I procured from these people [at Mission San Francisco] in exchange for European glass beads, silk ribbon, knives, and other articles, was one of those bandeaus, which consisted of four-hundred and fifty feathers. (1814:II:60)

We can surmise that since one of the necklaces illustrated in his book appears to have ended up in the Kunstkamera, the flicker headband he illustrated may well have been deposited there as well. We do know that one band from his collection was deposited in Munich, but since it lacks the ornamental detail seen on the illustrated piece, we will focus first upon the bands in Russia.

The Kunstkamera's catalog lists five flicker headbands (MAE 570-15 to -19; see Figure 7.1). It was not possible to examine band MAE 570-15 very thoroughly since it was placed on a mannequin in an exhibit case; permission to remove it from the display could not be obtained. However, we can discern something about its style and make some inferences about its provenience from its general appearance in the display.

Since the purpose of the museum exhibit is to illustrate the manner in which this sort of head ornament was worn, we should begin our discussion of 570-15 by commenting on the display. What is most obvious is that the Russian museum staff was unfamiliar with the correct placement of the band on the wearer: such bands were not worn well above the eyes, nor were they tied so that they encircled the head with the exterior face of the feather quills in the band facing outward. Instead, a band was worn in such a way that the reverse (or inner) side of the feather quills faced outward. (The practice of wearing the inner side out began to change among the Patwin/Nomlaki and Pomo people in the 1930s. Today, some of these people wear either side of the band out.) The band was then attached to the head at points on the band which corresponded to the temples, thus allowing the end sections of the band to flap freely back and forth as the dancer moved. The dancer also invariably wore the band low on the forehead (Figure 7.2), in order to prevent spectators from looking directly into the dancer's eyes as the band ends flashed across his face.

Figure 7.2. Chris "Chief Lemee" Brown, Southern Sierra Miwok, in dance regalia from about 1936. Note position of the flicker quill headband covering the eyes. *Photo by Ralph Anderson, courtesy of Yosemite Research Library, National Park Service.*

Although we cannot tell from the exhibit, it is possible that 570-15 lacked the forehead ties, and thus was arranged on display as it is. Such tieless bands do occur, especially if they were made for sale or trade by skilled specialists; the ties, as well as any auxiliary ornaments, such as abalone pendants or beads, were usually provided by the ultimate owner.

The band features both wing and tail feathers in its construction. Apparently, only the center four (or possibly six) out of 10 tail feathers of the flicker were used in this band's construction. This indicates that at least 30 to 50 birds were required to make it. A similar phenomenon is seen in other early flicker-quill headbands collected by Ferdinand Deppe and Edward Belcher and now curated at the Museum für Völkerkunde in Berlin and the British Museum in London, and suggests that flicker populations were relatively large in early nineteenth century California.

Stylistically, a close look at MAE 570-15 reveals that it is made with three threads sewn through the quills. It has a serrated edge, which was accomplished by alternating the butt and tip ends of wing quills, and clipping the butt ends evenly a quarter of an inch or so below the trimmed edge of the tip ends. Four of these wing quills alternate with two tail quills, which retain the distinctive naturally-pointed tips of these feathers. The side points of the resultant "diamonds" of the feather tips left on the tail quills barely touch one another, which was a highly regarded feature of flicker-quill band manufacturing among native peoples in the early years of the twentieth century (Azbill, personal communication, 1969; Tadd, personal communication, 1984). The combination of these features identifies the band as falling within the style used by the Yuki, Coast Miwok, and Pomoan peoples (Azbill, personal communication, 1969; Barrett 1952:Pl. 42; Kelly n.d.:489; A. Kroeber 1925:267b). However, such information alone does not reliably limit the band's origin to any one of these people, and one must also be aware of the possibility of trade. A similar band with this distinctive serrated edge was collected from the Maidu high in the Sierra Nevada in 1911 (OPM 16-1449), and such bands were purchased from a Yuki band maker, John Maggentrick, by at least one Maidu gentleman in the 1920s (Azbill, personal communication, 1969). Moreover, no reliable information exists regarding the specific styles of bands used by the Ohlone, Bay and Plains Miwok, or Valley Nisenan peoples, the most obvious sources for MAE 570-15. Therefore, the Kunstkamera example could well have originated among any one of several tribes.

Band MAE 570-16 also has alternating quills, along with the three-thread construction characteristic of Miwok style. This band, which measures 64.0 cm in length and 9.8 cm in width, consists of all tail feathers, 100 of which are center tail feathers, while the rest are next to the center. Uniquely, this band has a pair of reversed quills at seven locations across the band. Spaced approximately 9.2 to 11.6 cm apart, they give a black stripe at each reversal. There are two tie strings on the band, unevenly spaced. Instead of leaving the natural, pointed tip of the tail feathers, the flicker band has been trimmed straight across each margin, approximately an inch from the quill edge (Figure 7.1a).

MAE 570-17 presents an entirely different design aesthetic (Figure 7.1b) that is suggestive of Yuki-style flicker bands. It is 57 cm in length and is constructed with only two center tail feathers, with wing and outside tail feathers predominating. These are arranged in groups consisting of three wing and one tail feather in an alternating orientation. The quills are dipped in a crenellated fashion, rather than having the more common straight margin to the quill band. Outside tail feathers are used more towards each end of the band. There are three lines of native hemp thread, and the tie strings are still present. One small quill of a white feather is attached at the end of the band.

The last flicker-quill band (Figure 7.1c) example in the Kunstkamera catalogue is MAE 570-18, and it is possibly of Pomo origin. It is 50.8 cm in length, with three thread lines, and is a comparatively narrow band, 10.8 cm in overall width, with only a 4.4 cm quill band width. The outer thread bands run very close to the edge of the quill band. Regular care has been used in arranging the quills, with two tail feathers and then four wing feathers alternating the length of the band. However, the black feather tips are not so evenly aligned, giving the band an uneven appearance. The margin is trimmed in a staggered fashion, and there are no ties remaining on the specimen.

A flicker headband is also present in Etholen's collection in Helsinki (FNM VK-1033). The salmon-orange quills on this piece are held together by the traditional three vegetable-fiber threads, apparently of native hemp cordage, which run parallel to one another. The band is 53 cm long and 12 cm wide.[3]

We mentioned earlier that one of the flicker quill bands in Munich that was collected by Langsdorff was probably obtained at Mission San Francisco in 1806 (Figure 7.3). This band (SMV 368), which has a length of 63 cm and a width of 10.5 cm, is made from the usual salmon-orange quills with black tips of flicker tails as a border. As is true of many such pieces, the band is held together by three parallel threads which extend beyond the ends. However, the unusual manner in which the quills have been arranged is noteworthy: groups of three quills with the basal ends together alternate basal and tip ends. In addition, the fact that the central quill in these groups is a tail

Figure 7.3. Chochenyo Ohlone dancers at Mission San José in 1806. The lithograph is based upon a sketch by W. G. T von Tilenau (Langsdorff 1814). *Courtesy of the Honold Library.*

feather flanked on either side by a wing feather quill is particularly important. This particular arrangement has not been recorded for any known California group, nor has it been found during an exhaustive study of flicker quill bands in major museums and private collections, among native people, or in photographs. The only example (BM 8182) that is somewhat similar is one of the three flicker quill bands in the British Museum,
lacking provenience, which were collected in California by Sir Edward Belcher. Unfortunately, no information exists as to where Belcher may have collected these items: Belcher visited San Francisco, Monterey, and San Jose as a member of Beechey's staff in the 1820s; a decade later, he returned to San Francisco and Monterey, explored the navigable limits of the Sacramento River, and visited Mission Santa Clara. He also stopped briefly at Santa Barbara, San Pedro, Ventura, Catalina Island, and San Diego (Beechey 1831; Belcher 1843). Since the British Museum collections also include a bow and five arrows (BM 8184-9) collected by Belcher—items which he specifically mentions as having seen being made during visits to villages along the Sacramento River (Belcher 1843:I:127)—it is possible that the flicker bands were collected in the same area. If that is the case, then the bands probably originated among the Valley Nisenan.

Nevertheless, the feather groups on the Belcher piece are composed of three tail quills, and no wing quills are used. Perhaps neither style was being made by 1900, and they either represent a tradition that was once popular but had lost favor by the beginning of the twentieth century, or they were styles characteristic of a group from whom no bands were collected—such as the Ohlone, Plains and Bay (Saclan) Miwok, or the Valley Nisenan peoples.

Feather Topknots

Feather topknots have long been an integral part of the regalia used in many dances, although extant examples in museum collections come primarily from the Pomo, Yuki, and Northwestern Valley Maidu peoples. A member of Drake's expedition, for example, described what was most likely just such a headpiece observed among the Coast Miwok as early as 1579:

> When he brought with him (as a present for the rest) a bunch of feathers, much like the feathers of a blacke crow, very neatly and artifically gathered vpon a string, and drawne together into a round bundle; being verie cleane and finely cut, and bearing in length an equal proportion with one another; a special cognizance (as wee afterwards observed) which they that guard their king's person, weare on their heads. (Fletcher 1947:283)

Similarly, Langsdorff described what was probably one style of this same type of headpiece at Mission San Francisco:

> Another head ornament, which is usually worn by these Indians at their dances, is made of the feathers of a vulture very common in these parts, *Vultus aura*. The tail and wing feathers are woven together in such a way that the ornament resembles a Turkish fez. (1814:II:60)

Louis Choris sketched a group of dancers at Mission San Francisco who appear to be wearing variations of these topknot style headpieces (Figure 7.4); his more detailed drawings of the headgear worn by native Californians likewise illustrate a variety of feathered headpieces (Figure 7.5). Tikhanov's 1818 sketch of a Bodega Bay (Coast Miwok) scene also shows such a headpiece being held

Figure 7.4. Dancers at Mission San Francisco in 1816 (Choris 1822). *Courtesy of the Honold Library.*

Figure 7.5. California Indian men in dance regalia (Choris 1822). *Courtesy of the Honold Library.*

Figure 7.6. Death of Coast Miwok chief at Bodega Bay, 1818. This remarkable watercolor by Mikhail Tikhanov apparently shows the death of the old chief (Farris 1998). Note the headdress held by one of the men in the foreground. *Courtesy of the Scientific Research Museum of the Russian Academy of Fine Arts, St. Petersburg.*

in the hands (Figures 7.6 and 7.7). Other Russian visitors described similar examples. Golovnin (1979:149) recorded that "their headdress, made of feathers, can be said to display great taste," while Khlebnikov, who shared a similar view, noted that "their head decorations of feathers are also beautifully done" (1940:333).

Virtually all of the central Californian peoples used such headpieces, but few details are available today that might help differentiate those made by one tribal group from those made by another. Excluding drawings, our earliest pictorial evidence for such pieces comes from the Sierra Miwok, where a group of dancers in the town of Sonora in the late 1870s

Figure 7.7. Two views of young Coast Miwok man named Valthazar as painted by Mikhail Tikhanov in 1818. He is wearing what appears to be a fur headpiece adorned with feathered bird wings attached with a cord, and is holding a reflex, sinew-backed bow. This is the same man that is shown in Figure 4.3. *Courtesy of the Scientific Research Museum of the Russian Academy of Fine Arts, St. Petersburg.*

Figure 7.8. Central Sierra Miwok dancers in Sonora, California, circa 1856–1860. Note the large feather topknots—especially those with white feather pendants tied to the tips of the topknots' feathers—as well as the topknots of upright groupings of magpie tail feathers worn by the men at left center and left rear. *Photo by Daniel Sewell Studio, Sonora, courtesy of Yosemite Research Library, National Park Service.*

posed for their photographic portrait wearing large topknots (Figure 7.8). All extant specimens—from the Pomo, Nomlaki/Patwin, Yuki, and Northwestern Maidu—appear to share the same basic method of manufacture, one in which feathers are attached to a cord, usually by means of a special single-string tie which utilizes half-hitches to secure the

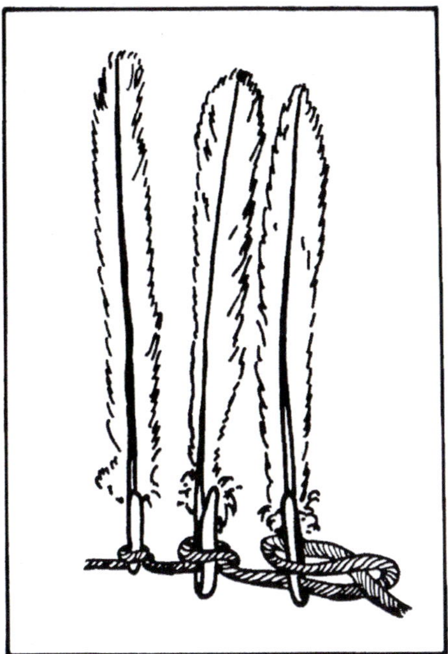

Figure 7.9. Sketch showing topknot construction. This method of feather attachment, using a series of half-hitches, was employed by the Pomo, Yuki, and Northwestern Maidu people.

feathers next to one another on the cord (Figure 7.9). The resultant feather strip is then wound spirally, and attached with cordage (using one of several methods) to a hoop, usually a willow or hazel shoot just slightly larger in diameter than the feather-strip bunch (see Wallace 1978a:458, Fig. 11).

Several types are represented among the examples in Russia; unfortunately, data regarding attachment to the base hoop are lacking for all but one of them: MAE 570-4 (Figure 7.10). This headpiece, for which we have the most data, is made from the long primary feathers of the brown pelican; the feathers are about 38 cm in length and average about 3.5 cm in width. White fluffs from the brown pelican have been tied to the tips of some of the feathers as a form of decoration. Each feather was attached to a single, two-ply native hemp string in the usual manner; that is, the quill end was bent over the cord, then the string was looped around it and secured to itself using a half-hitch. The supporting hoop is 13 cm in diameter; the feathered string was attached to this hoop using a chain-stitch in four lines radiating from the center of the piece, which was a common method of attachment found among a variety of groups. The feathers appear

a.

b.

Figure 7.10. Two views (a, b) of feather headpiece (570-4). *Photos courtesy of the MAE.*

upright in the photograph because of a wire wrapping which the Russian exhibitors placed about the feathers to form a bundle; this wrapping has inadvertently shaped the headpiece into the usual form used for storage among California people; in actual use, the feathers would drop into a more hemispherical position. It is interesting to note that the wire wrapping appears to have been in place in the 1873 photograph (Figure 2.2) that shows this piece. The wire may have been placed on the object for shipment from California to St. Petersburg and never removed!

The attachment of the white fluffs to the feathers on MAE 570-4 is unique. A similar, though slightly different, variant of this type can be seen in the circa 1870s photograph of Central Miwok people in Sonora (Figure 7.8). In this case, the feathers were tied so as to hang loosely from the large feather tips. This may have been an older style of headdress which eventually lost favor, or the style may have been peculiar to coastal peoples. Nevertheless, the feathers and fluffs used come from the pelican, a bird found close to the seashore and that ventures inland to California's central valley only on rare occasions (Grinnell and Miller 1944:51). Although these feathers could have been obtained in the central valley, we suspect that the headpiece originated among one of the coastal groups contacted by the Russians, such as the Ohlone, Coast Miwok, or Kashaya Pomo.

Two other topknots in the Kunstkamera collections fall into this same simple style, and were also made from complete, unmodified feathers. MAE 570-5, for example, is made from either raven or crow feathers, each about 16 cm long and 4.5 cm wide, with a wooden hoop foundation that is 6 cm in diameter. A few of the feather tips on this headpiece have been ornamented with short strings of white, blue, and white-centered red glass beads. The beads are of mixed sizes, and one clamshell disk bead is included in the assortment. Such a decoration of feather topknots has been recorded for

Figure 7.11. Feather headpiece (570-7).

Figure 7.12. Feather headpiece (570-8).

the Pomo, who occasionally also attached small pendant squares of flicker quill work to the feather tips along with the beads (FM 54418).

MAE 570-7 is constructed in a similar way with a hoop, but it lacks the bead decoration and is made from a variety of feathers, including barn owl and crow (Figure 7.11). The longest feathers are about 14 cm in length, while the hoop is 7.5 cm in diameter. Many of the feathers in this piece have been split down the rachis and scraped, or the vanes have been stripped from the quills; either operation would have produced their naturally twisting form.

Another headpiece in the Kunstkamera collections, MAE 570-8, is made entirely of stripped or split and scraped feathers. The presence of iridescent purple with black bands and white tips on these feathers suggests that they are from the wing patch of the mallard duck. Only the colored side of each wing feather was used. The feathers are about 9 cm in length, while the hoop is 9.5 cm in diameter (Figure 7.12). The cordage used to bind the feathers into a long rope, to half-hitch the rope into a coil, and to lash the coil on to the oak or ceanothus hoop, is all two-ply native hemp, S-spun and Z-plied.

Another feathered object at the Kunstkamera, MAE 570-9, could be an unfinished version of this same variety of headpiece, although unfortunately we can not be certain. The feathers are from the stripped vanes of an unidentified bird. The feathers appear to have originally been white, but have turned a light brown color, probably due to smoke or age. An examination of the feather vanes reveals that they most closely resemble the secondaries (or primaries) of certain large white waterfowl—perhaps the white pelican (*Pelecanus erythrorhynchos*) or the trumpeter swan (*Cygnus buccinator*). They are about 15 cm in length and are attached to a cord 115 cm long. The naturally downy basal ends of the feathers give the appearance of a fluff- or down-wrapped cord, which the unintentional twisting of the cord that commonly occurs on such unfinished headpieces accentuates. If the piece is an unfinished headdress, it would fit well within a category of stripped feather headdresses reported for the Northwest Valley Maidu, where it would constitute a variant of the *batsawi* (Azbill, personal communication, 1969) or *wai-et-ti* (Culin 1908:60) headpiece. A number of extant examples have been collected from these people (BKM 08.491.8807; AMNH 50/277, 50/3131; OPM 16-2322), and the style may have been present among other groups as well.

The remaining topknot headpieces collected by the Russians in California are in a different style, one that involves the use of a wreath of black feathers surrounding an upright cylindrical section of magpie tail feathers. Two examples of this style of headpiece are known: St. Petersburg's 570-6, and Frankfurt's E-0169.

MAE 570-6 is notable for its lack of a foundation hoop to which the bundle of feathers would have been secured. Perhaps it is incomplete. The top knot is made of large white tail feathers, possibly from pelicans or seagulls. The feathers are trimmed straight across at their tips. They are tied singly to the foundation cord. There are four spokes of chain stitching that bind the foundation cord into a coil. Two long cordage ties are present.

The Kunstkamera specimen (MAE 570-6) could not be removed for close inspection because it was placed on the mannequin in the exhibit case (Figure 2.1). However, it could be determined that the long, upright feathers were magpie tail feathers, and that only the two central ones from a magpie tail were used. It appears that there may be 100 or so such tail feathers in this headpiece, so that at least 50 birds were used in its manufacture. The feathers were apparently attached to extensions at their bases (thereby increasing their overall length) by either wrapping the bases on other feather quills or on stiff cordage. The wreath of surrounding feathers consisted of crow or raven feathers. These were split down the center of the quill; the pithy inner section was then cut into quarter-inch sections, and every other such section was removed. Crow feathers (like those of many other species) will not strip readily without breaking, so this particular method of preparing the quills was devised specifically for this type of headpiece.

The second of these headpieces is Frankfurt's EO-169, which was collected by Wrangell in the 1830s, possibly from among Pomo or Coast Miwok people. It has been described at some length by Vatter (1925:102–103). The headpiece is 36 cm in height, with a lower wreath that is some 37 cm in diameter (Figure 7.13). The wooden hoop foundation is oval and is 14 cm long and 11.5 cm wide. The specimen differs from the others in that the feathers in the wreath are simply split, and the magpie tail feathers are arranged in a more cylindrical manner. After being bound to quill extensions using deer sinew, the quill bases were attached to a cord in the usual fashion for feather topknots. The quill extensions were then held in their cylindrical form by two rows of plain twining with cordage. Like the MAE specimen, this example uses only the center tail feathers of the magpie, and 30 to 50 birds were required in its manufacture.

These two headpieces differ from the Patwin-Maidu variant of this form of headpiece, and more closely resemble the type made by the Yokuts (Wallace 1978a:458, Fig. 11) and Chumash (Hudson and Blackburn 1985:180–184). A number of examples exist in museum collections representing such groups as the Yokuts (FM 70594-1; USM 200090; HMA 1-9148, 1-10745, 1-10762), the Eastern Mono (Steward 1933:pls. 8, 9), and the Chumash (SBMNH NA-CA-XX-lH-1). The illustrative material mentioned earlier indicates that this form of headpiece was present among the Ohlone, Coast Miwok, and Central Sierra Miwok (see Figure 7.6). This style of headdress therefore seems to have been widespread over much of central California, and the Russian pieces were undoubtedly from the northern portion of this distribution.

Figure 7.13. Topknot headdress (WKM E-0169).

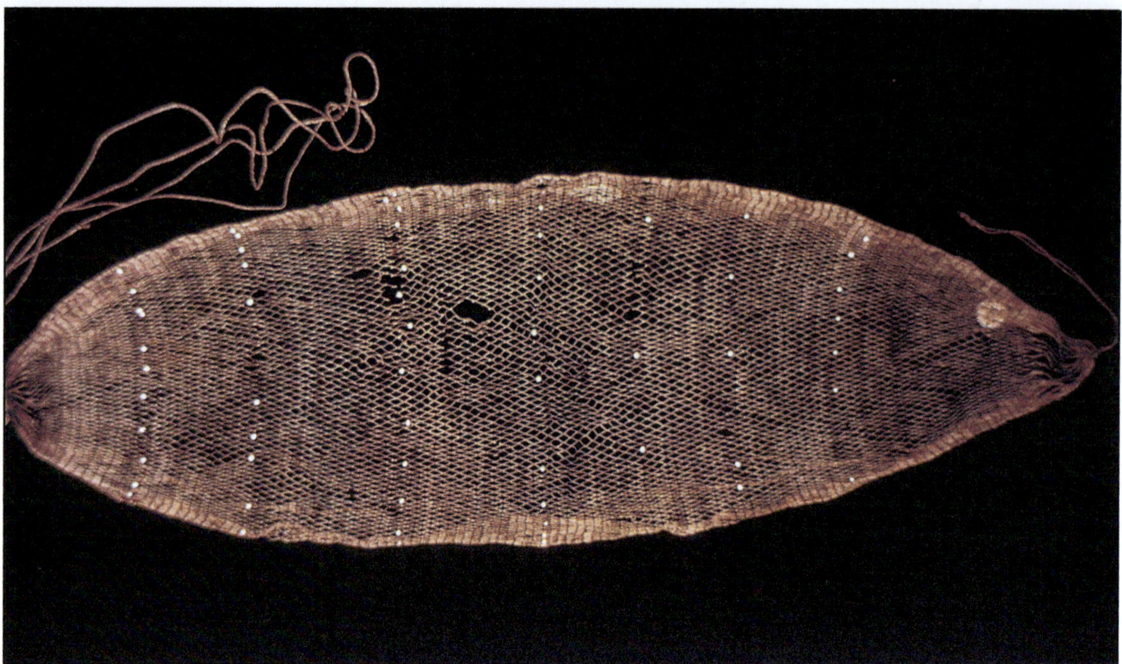

Figure 7.14.
Hairnet (570-67).

Hairnets

Hairnets were worn—primarily by men—on both a daily and a ceremonial basis, and served to keep the hair out of the eyes while various tasks were performed. In the context of rituals, the net was also used to shape the hair into a resilient mass into which various ornamental hairpins could be inserted.

A few early descriptions of hairnets were provided by European visitors. Fletcher, the chaplain during Drake's 1579 visit to the Coast Miwok area, briefly described what must have been a hairnet: "The crownes were made of knitworke, wroght vpon most curiously with feathers of diuers colours, very artifically placed." (1947:284). Similarly, Fr. Vicente Santa María, a Spanish priest who accompanied the first European entry into San Francisco Bay in 1775, wrote a short description of these items, stating that they were worn by the local native men, and that the Spanish found "pieces of the little nets with which we have seen the Indians cover their hair" as offerings at a sacred place (Galvan 1971:49, 61–63). A few Russian sources also provide information on hairnets; for example, Tikhanov's 1818 drawing of Coast Miwok people showing a man wearing a beaded hairnet while holding a headdress (Figure 7.6) and Voznesenskii's brief comment that "both men and women bind their hair on the crown of their heads... with a beaded band or a netting" (Lipshits 1950:417).

Although hairnets were apparently widespread in California, there is little documentation on hairnets decorated with beads, and extant examples in museum collections are rare. One Eastern Pomo consultant reported that when a boy reached eight or ten (puberty), his parents would prepare a feast, at which he would be presented with a hairnet. If this hairnet were elaborately decorated with beads, the boy was destined to become a member of the secret society, in which case the hairnet was set aside for use on ceremonial occasions (Loeb 1926:270; McLendon 1977:15). Sometimes, Sierra Miwok leaders wore beaded hairnets (Barrett and Gifford 1933:223), while those living near Sonora also required a girl undergoing a puberty ceremony to wear one as well (Dixon 1903). The Choo-hel-mem-sel Patwin also had beaded hairnets which were worn by the rich and were considered very valuable (Merriam 1967:272). The Valley Nisenan in the Sacramento region possessed them as well, and called the hairnet *ma'tap* or *ma'tcap* (A. Kroeber 1929:287).

The Kunstkamera catalog indicates that they have two beaded hairnets, both of which are on exhibit. One, MAE 570-67 (Figure 7.14), is 85 cm in length and 28 cm in width and is made of very fine native hemp cordage. It is decorated with seven rows of white glass beads in the netting. The second example, MAE 570-68, is much smaller, measuring 56 cm in length by 38 cm in width, excluding the tie strings; it is exceptionally well made (Figure 7.15), with a mesh size of 5 mm and a centrally-placed netted section decorated with white glass beads that measures 27 by 33 cm in size.

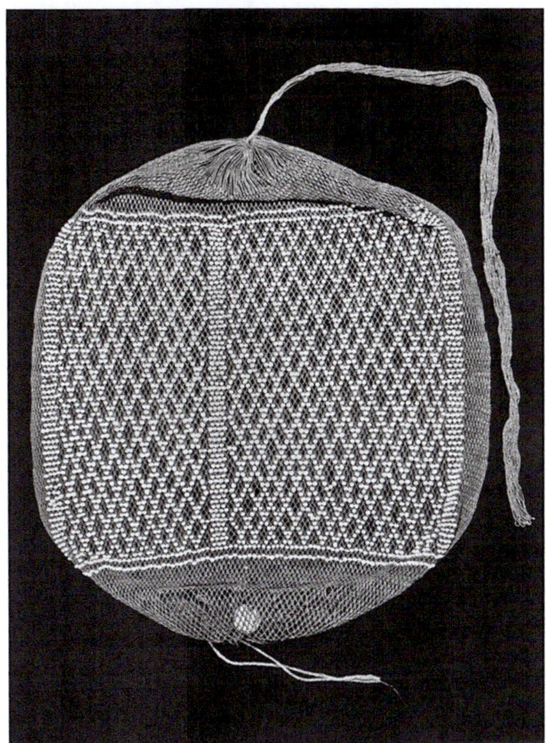

Figure 7.15. Hairnet (570-68).

One cannot help but marvel at the workmanship exhibited by 570-68, especially with regard to the way the beads (4 mm in diameter) were worked into the rows of knotting. We can infer how the latter was done: it appears that the beads were added individually by means of a technique in which the "loops" of the previous row of netting were pulled through each bead, with the next row of knots then being cast below the bead. Solid rows of beads form borders, with a pattern worked out in the central space. This piece, which is a remarkable example of the net maker's art, shows no knotting of the native hemp cordage anywhere which would mark the addition of the new strings that were needed as the work progressed. Since enough string could not be carried on a shuttle to finish the net—particularly with such a small mesh, and drawing several hundred feet of cord through each mesh hole would have been highly impractical—it is likely that the string was manufactured as the net was in production. If this was the case, it is possible that a few yards of cordage were made and wrapped around a fine, thin shuttle. After the bulk of this was used, the two loose ends of the two-ply cordage would be added to the new fiber, making several more yards of string that were then rewound onto the shuttle. This allowed the net maker to manufacture the piece without having to splice the cordage with bulky knots. The fact that many hairnets made in later times with commercial cotton cordage have additional string spliced in with coarse, overhand knots lends credence to this suggestion.

Although (as we mentioned previously) museum examples of beaded hairnets are rare, there are a few interesting exceptions. One of them (USM 2561), which is nearly identical to MAE 570-68, was collected in 1841 during the Wilkes expedition to California; unfortunately, no provenience exists for the item. As far as illustrations of the item being worn are concerned, several drawings from the mid-nineteenth century exist which possibly show a Nisenan and a Patwin or Nomlaki man wearing this type of beaded hairnet (Kroeber, Elsasser, and Heizer 1977:156, 170, 269). It is interesting to note that the men in this particular drawing are also wearing the stripped-feather type headpiece described earlier (see "Headdresses" earlier in this chapter), which is affixed to the back of the head and held in place with decorated hairpins. Another early drawing which shows this type of hairnet is Tikhanov's 1818 sketch of some Bodega Bay Miwok people, which we noted earlier (see Figure 7.6). We have been unable to locate any photographic records which might show this type of hairnet in use, which suggests to us that the style may have become very rare by the beginning of the twentieth century.

Hairpins

Hairpins in a variety of styles were commonly used in a number of ritual performances. An agent of the Russian-American Company at Fort Ross provided this early description of what must have been a simple hairpin of manzanita wood: "the men fasten the bunches of hair by means of little pieces of wood rather artfully carved from a red palm" (Kostromitinov 1974:7–8).

This description seems to apply to the plain, bipointed manzanita wood pins used by a variety of California peoples, including the Northeastern or Salt Pomo (OPM 16-2045, and part of 16-2034), the Pomo of Upper Lake (OPM 16-2851), and the Chico Maidu (BKM 08.491.8700). Among the Pomo, such pins were also a part of the paraphernalia of curing doctors (Barrett 1952:I:Pl. 12, Fig. 2). The pins were always highly polished and evenly carved, and were used to secure the feather topknots that were pinned to the hair using a hairnet. Such pins are not easily manufactured, for a large piece of manzanita, usually eight centimeters or more in diameter, must be secured in order to obtain the rich reddish brown wood. Because of the twisting grain of the wood, it must be carefully split, carved, and eventually scraped to obtain a fine pin from the innermost portion. The final highly polished finish is usually accomplished by drawing the finished pin rapidly back and forth through two sharp split sections of hardwood held like a vise. Although the Kunstkamera collections contain eight hairpins (570-25 to -29, -32 to -34) of uncertain style that could not be located, six hairpins of this particular style (MAE 570-36, -55 to -59) were found, the longest of which was 72 cm in length. One of these is decorated with a fine vegetable-fiber string that is attached to the end; it has glass beads strung on it, and it terminates with what appears to be a long, black grasshopper leg. Such a usage of insect parts has not been recorded for central California, and it may represent one individual's personal style or relationship with the supernatural, or it may have been a style that was once in vogue but had died out early on.

The Etholen collection in Helsinki also contains four hairpins (FNM VK-343); one of these is missing (no description is available), while another consists of paired bone rods and will be described later. The remaining two specimens are made of carved, highly polished manzanita. The longest of these is bipointed and is 58 cm in length and 1 cm in diameter. A sinew-wrapped band occurs near one end, with two long sinew strings strung with red and white glass beads tied to it; each string terminates in an abalone shell pendant. The other pin is pointed at one end and blunt at the other; the blunted end is also wrapped with sinew, to which is attached a string of clam disk beads that terminates in four complete flicker tail feathers. The pin is about 46 cm in length. Although the locations where these pins were collected is not given in the catalog, the majority of the Etholen material is described as coming from the Sacramento River area, specifically the Plains Miwok village of *Seuamne*.

Fancy, decorated hairpins of the long, single-rod variety were also widespread. Northern Miwok women wore one type in the *Wokile* Dance; these were about a foot in length and were covered with woodpecker scalps (Gifford 1917a), while other similarly decorated rods were used by the Maidu (Bates and Bibby 1983:49; Dixon 1905:150) and the Pomo (OPM 16-2854); other groups undoubtedly used them as well. Although no Miwok or Patwin examples appear to be extant, several single-rod hairpins have been collected from the Northwestern Maidu (BKM 08.491.8812; AMNH 50/274, 50/368; OPM 16-1542, 16-2322) and the Pomo. The

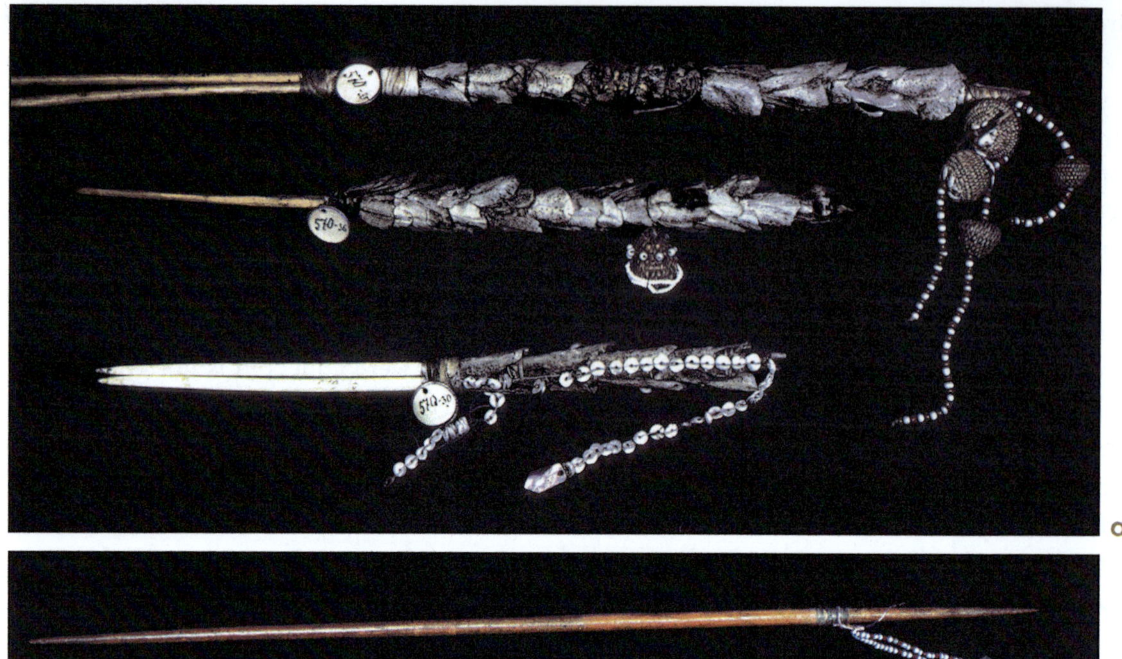

Figure 7.16. Hairpins: (a) MAE 570-35, -36, and -30; (b) FNM VK-343.

majority of the Pomoan examples consist of pins of spliced mammal bone that have been carefully incised, feather decorated, and finished, and all were made by one individual, William Benson, who created the pieces specifically to sell to non-Indian collectors (DAM FPO.6.Pd, FPO.7.Pd, FPO.8.Pd, FPO.9.Pd; MAI 11-2959, 11-9248, 16-3306). Some doubt exists as to whether these specimens are accurate reproductions of an old style or are more modern interpretations of a style described to the artist in his youth.

A second style of hairpin consists of two rods bound side by side; the only documented example was apparently collected from the Maidu people (FM 79944). However, there are three examples of this type of hairpin in St. Petersburg, and one in Helsinki (Figure 7.16). MAE 570-36, which is some 34 cm in length, is made of a single wooden shaft of a light-colored soft wood. It is covered with over 40 bird (apparently woodpecker) scalps, although the feathering is missing; sections of mallard duck scalps may have also been used. The base of the scalp decoration is wrapped with sinew. Olivella shell disk beads decorate the end of the hairpin, held on with native hemp string. This hairpin has one coiled basketry pear-shaped ball-like form, 2.5 cm in diameter, suspended from the hairpin shaft. This ball is ornamented with glass and Olivella shell disk beads. The white glass beads appear to be uneven Italian 12/0 seed beads, sewn in two rows near the bottom of the ball. The ball-like appendage is quite unusual, and although it does not appear in

California collections in the United States, it is present on a second hairpin in the Kunstkamera collections.

That second example, MAE 570-35, is made of two hardwood shafts that are bound together side by side. They appear to be made of chamise (*Adenostoma fasciculatum*) due to their alternate leaf scars, and have a hard, fine polish. They are mostly covered (as were those on the previous specimen) with bird scalps, although almost no trace of the original feathering remains. The few dark feathers that are still present might lead one to suspect that the black feathering which surrounds the red patch of the acorn woodpecker was included in the original feathering—this was a common practice among Maidu and Nomlaki peoples when making feather belts of entire bird scalps, and when the Konkow Maidu manufactured hairpins. The overall length of this particular specimen is 48 cm. The two shafts are bound together with a split piece of tule or cattail leaf. More than half of the hairpin is covered with 22 woodpecker scalps, bound in place by fine native cordage. At the base of the scalps is a strip of hide, wrapped at its base with sinew. Four solid, ball-shaped forms like those found on the previous hairpin, all made in coiled basketry, are suspended from strings of glass beads on the tip end and are decorated in a few places with Olivella disk beads attached with the coiling strand. These small basketry balls are made with sedge root sewing strands and may have been fully feathered. The largest such ball is 2.7 cm in diameter. Three of the balls are suspended with a string of beads made with extremely fine native cordage. The dark beads are green-centered with brick red exteriors. The fourth ball is more simply attached to the hairpin with an undecorated length of string and a small toggle stick.

The next example of the fancy hairpins, MAE 570-30, is 31 cm long and is made of two mammal bone pins bound together side by side. The bone pieces are extremely well formed and polished, with each one tapering to a short point. The bones are from a large mammal, but seem longer than typical deer leg bones. The bones appear to have been wrapped together with sinew. About half of the hairpin is covered with a series of overlapping bird scalps, which appear to be those of the acorn woodpecker, although most of the actual red feathering has been eaten away. The scalps are tied to the hairpin with a fine string that is "button-holed" from the base of one scalp to the next. At the bottom of the scalp wrapping, near the middle of the hairpin, the scalps are wrapped with some hide, which in turn is lashed with fine cord and a bit of sinew. The scalp decoration is further ornamented with a row of Olivella shell beads. These are chain-stitched together and laid along the length of the hairpin, covering the seam. At the apex of the hairpin, extending from the row of Olivella beads, is a pendant strand of Olivella shell beads, also chain-stitched. A second string attached near the mid-point of the hairpin is made of Olivella beads as well, but is incomplete and has lost any pendants.

MAE 570-31 is a feathered hairpin constructed of two mammal bone pins. Each of these is finely made, is 32.4 cm long and slightly more than 0.6 cm in diameter, and is tapered to a blunt point at the decorated end and to a sharp point at the functional end. The animal source must have been a large mammal. The two bones are bound together for just under half their length with fine native hemp cordage. The cord appears to be wrapped around both bones twice, then in a figure-eight twice, with these wrappings then repeated alternately for 16.5 cm. The feather decoration near the center of the hairpin consists of four overlapping woodpecker scalps. These scalps are secured in opposite pairs using fine hemp cordage. Each scalp has four or five Olivella shell disk beads sewn on concave-side down with chain-stitched sinew. At the bottom of the lower pair of scalps, a wrapping of fine, thin hide covers the binding cord. This piece of hide is secured by a 1 cm wrapping of sinew. A flicker quill pendant is suspended from the top of the hairpin. Each of the two pairs of projecting black tail quills contains a center and a next-to-center woodpecker tail feather. The flicker quill pendant is sewn with sinew in three vertical rows. On the suspending threads of the pendant are three 8/0 white pony beads and two chained Olivella disk beads. A remnant of a bird scalp or quail topknot is visible under the cordage wrapping where the pendant is attached to the hairpin.

Our last example of hairpins is the Etholen specimen in Helsinki (FNMVK-343). It is made from a pair of bone shafts held together with a vegetable twine wrapping; traces of bird skins indicate that the binding had once been completely incased by what probably were red woodpecker scalps. The butt end of the pin is ornamented by a twine string of white and red glass beads that terminates in an abalone pendant. The hairpin itself is 29 cm long.

Bodywear

Women's Skirts

Although MAE 1901-1 was attributed to the Iroquois by Siebert (1975:16, Fig. 15) and was exhibited as such in St. Petersburg, the piece was recently examined by Feest and others and correctly attributed to California. The characteristics that distinguish this item as being from California involve its general form and the particular type of ornamentation employed—Olivella cupped disk beads. The skin, which has had the hair removed and been tanned, is medium brown in color and is 110 cm in width and 158 cm in length. It has been trimmed, removing the hide from the lower limbs and leaving only a small segment from the upper limbs. The base is somewhat irregular, although the sides are straight and the upper or top edge is also somewhat straight.

The edges of the skin are decorated with a continuous fringe made by chain-stitching about six or so Olivella disk beads together, ending with a half-Olivella shell pendant. Along the edges of the hide are four rows of bead decoration. The two outer rows are formed by Olivella disk beads sewn in a chain-stitch directly to the skin, while the two adjacent and parallel rows are formed by long strings of light and dark blue glass trade beads that are attached in a "lazy stitch" fashion and occasionally separated by a single red or yellow glass bead.

Most of the decoration, however, occupies the entire lower half of the hide, from edge to edge (158 cm) and from about the center line down (about 55 cm); the upper half is undecorated. The decoration consists of densely clustered Olivella disk beads sown on to the skin in straight horizontal and vertical rows. There are three horizontal rows, each eight beads in width; the bottom row follows the bottom edge of the skin, while the upper row follows the center line. The middle row is equally spaced

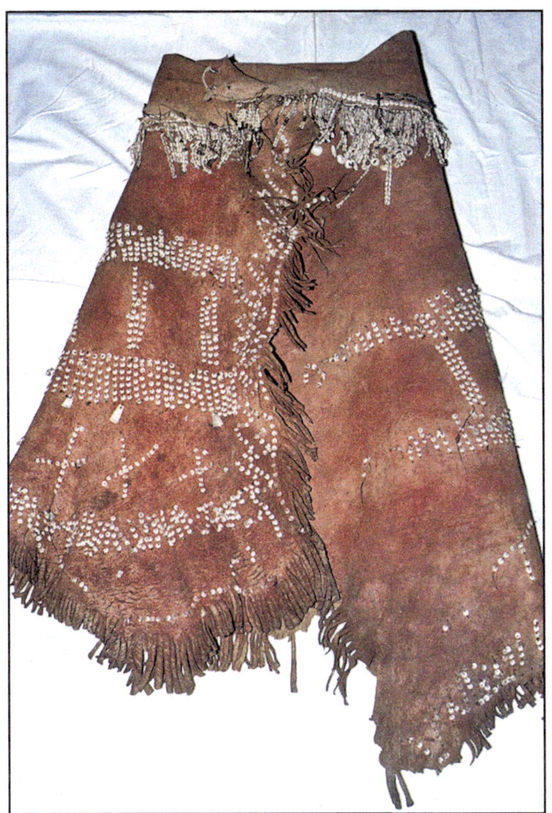

a.

b.

Figure 7.17. Two views (a, b) of woman's skirt (1-1061). *Photos courtesy of Brian Bibby.*

between the two. The 14 vertical rows run perpendicularly; each is about four beads wide, and each is equally spaced, thereby forming a negative pattern of "squares" which actually consist of the natural hide bounded on all sides by rows of beads. There are about 13 of these squares in each of the two horizontal rows, one above the other. The Olivella beads are occasionally interspersed with square abalone beads of about equal size, with a blue glass bead centered over the square; their common central perforation was used to sew them to the hide together.

The most obvious function of this item—as Feest (personal communication, 1985) has suggested—was that it served as the back part of the two-piece hide skirt worn by many California Indian women. The back part was always made from a larger hide than the front; when wrapped about the body, the upper portion (which would extend perhaps to the breasts) was folded down, thus creating a slight overlapping about the waist. In form, MAE 1901-1 certainly seems to be such a piece, and even the lack of decoration on the upper portion (where it would have been folded over and therefore covered) is highly suggestive. Most skirts were about 100 cm long (although MAE 1901-1 is longer than usual at 158 cm), while the width would be about the same (the item in question is 110 cm wide). Indeed, its size is not unlike that of a lower Klamath River woman's back apron, which "droops" in the front and is thus much wider than the wearer's hip measurements would suggest.

A second skirt, MAE 1-1061, was found in the Northwest Coast collection in 1998 (Figure 7.17). It consists of a brain-tanned hide that is stained with red ochre; the thickness

Figure 7.18. Photo showing details of ornamentation on skirt 1-1061. *Photo courtesy of Brian Bibby.*

of the hide suggests that it might have come from a tule elk rather than a mule deer. It is decorated (Figure 7.18) with Olivella beads, a surprising variety of glass beads, and abalone shell ornaments which are present primarily on the lower central Olivella band design. The abalone ornaments occur in the shape of round and square disks which are sewn on either shingle style or with a bead "washer," or as oblong shell pieces sewn on as pendants at the bottom of the central band. The shell beads were sewn on in the same manner as is seen on MAE 1901-1, and their shingling is identical to that found on the woven feather belts and fancy baskets described later in this chapter and in the following chapter. Olivella beads are sewn across the bottom third section of the skirt in a series of fourteen "X" designs. An Olivella bead fringe, 7.6 cm wide, hangs at the top fold and is attached to a narrow band of buckskin that is baseball-stitched to the skirt proper. Each strand apparently once terminated in a halved Olivella shell bead, but most strands now lack these. The most common of the glass trade beads is a transparent "trader blue" 7/0 bead, but also present are 7/0 pony trader blue, clear amber, and green-center/brick red exterior beads. There are also 4/0 clear beads, 8/0 greasy yellow beads, and a few 8/0 butterscotch beads. The back of the hide (the inside of the skirt), which is unstained, was once the epidermal side, while the decorated side of the skirt was the flesh side of the hide. The bottom of the skirt, when open flat, is 152 cm in length, and the length from the folded edge to the bottom is 129 cm. The decoration suggests that it may have been worn as a one-piece wrap-around skirt that overlapped in the front.

a.

b.

Figure 7.19. Two views (a, b) of feather cape (570-3). *Photos courtesy of the MAE, St. Petersburg.*

Feather Cape

Feather capes were made by attaching large wing and tail feathers to a net foundation. They were an ancient part of the regalia that was used by various California peoples; they are mentioned, for example, in Konkow Maidu legends, where two powerful doctors who came from the north wore cloaks made from black eagle feathers, which all later capes were to be patterned after (Azbill, personal communications, 1968, 1969; Powers 1877:297). Louis Choris illustrated their use in dances observed at Mission San Francisco as early as 1816 (Slaymaker 1977:99, 101; see Figure 7.4); here, members of the Coast Miwok, Bay Miwok (Saclan), and perhaps other groups are represented as wearing these capes. In 1821, Karl Gillsen mentioned their use in conjunction with feather blankets for clothing:

> They clothe themselves in blankets interlaced with black and white feathers; across their shoulders as far as their knees they wear a kind of cloak. Around the middle of their body they wind bast-like matting of their own making, and the rest is bare. (Gibson 2013:163)

The sole example of such a cape that was collected by the Russians is MAE 570-3, which is on exhibit in St. Petersburg (see Figure 2.1). It is about 70 cm in length and about 50 cm in width. The foundation that was used appears (on the basis of severed cords along each selvage) to have been cut from some sort of larger net, possibly one used in fishing. Four rows of feathers have been attached to the net; they are primarily from the California condor, with a few bald eagle feathers included in the top row (Figure 7.19). These feathers were attached by coarsely cutting off the back side of the quill end; the quill ends were then folded over a knot in one of the courses of netting and lashed to the feather quill with a piece of cordage. The tie string, at the top of the cape, terminates on one end with the entire tail of an immature golden eagle, with the upper and lower tail covert feathers still in place.

If the stylistic characteristics of such cloaks from the Maidu, Pomo, Yuki, and Miwok peoples are examined, we must conclude that it is not always possible to distinguish ethnic origins, since there are often no differences between them. The Kunstkamera specimen has no features that can help in attributing it to any particular group; even the use of condor feathers is of little assistance since capes made from their feathers have been reported for a number of California groups; for example, the Pomo (Barrett 1952:II:280, 305), the Northwestern Valley Maidu (Azbill, personal communication, 1970), and the Coast Miwok (Slaymaker 1977:98).

Kukshui Cloak

The Kukshui cloak in St. Petersburg (MAE: 570-1) is one of only two such objects known. As a supernatural, the Kukshui was considered very powerful, and was the most dangerous entity in any spiritual performance; it was feared and respected by native people, and only certain individuals would take this part or assist the performer in dressing for it, so great was Kukshui's power.

This specimen is one of the only two objects in the Kunstkamera which we can attribute to the collecting activities of Voznesenskii with some certainty. The sole reference to the item—along with the condor-skin cloak, or Molok, which is discussed later—occurs in this brief passage in Voznesenskii's notebook:

> When I brought the mo-lok and kukshui costumes to [handwriting difficult to read, the "to" might be "from"] the Sacramento River, the Indians who saw them were terrified and were astonished that I could keep such a thing in my room as a kukshui, in which Satan himself lived; whereupon they considered me a shaman. (Voznesenskii, quoted in Liapunova 1967:26)

Such a reaction is completely in keeping with the regard in which such objects were held. Even a member of the secret society, unless he had been properly trained to impersonate this particular spirit, would be hesitant at best to handle such a cloak.

The construction of the Kunstkamera specimen, which is on exhibit and could not be removed for study (see Figure 2.1), involved a net foundation of fine cordage with a mesh about 2 cm square. The cloak, which is sack-like in shape, covered the entire body and was affixed to a wooden hoop ring which rested on top of the head. The net was covered with pairs of crow wing feathers with their butt ends bent over a knot in the mesh; they were then lashed to themselves using hemp bark strips or short pieces of hemp cordage. At the top, a feather topknot was constructed of raven or crow feathers, with a very few turkey vulture pointers added to the mass. This topknot, and the net foundation of the cloak, is attached to a hoop made of a bent shoot. The diameter of the hoop is slightly smaller than that of the display mannequin's head. A few short, broad, white feathers, probably from some sort of water fowl, were mixed in as well.[4] The Kunstkamera's exhibit is in error in that the face of the wearer would not be exposed; in actual use, the wearer was completely hidden from head to toe.

As was mentioned above, only two examples of these cloaks have survived, although three cloaks of a similar style used by the Moki spirit impersonator among the Chico Maidu and Patwin/Nomlaki people do exist. Parenthetically, the other Kukshui cloak, which is housed in the Smithsonian (USM 3326), was also obtained in 1841, although it was collected by the American expedition under Captain Charles Wilkes. Unfortunately, there are no provenience data except for a general designation of "California." The two cloaks were constructed in a similar way, although the net mesh on the Wilkes piece is much larger (5.5 cm square), and it also has turkey vulture feathers and white feathers mixed into the crown section. On this specimen, the vulture wing pointers were added by being lashed onto short, unscraped shoots that were thrust into the foundation and then bent back onto themselves, where the wing feathers were then lashed. Unfortunately, the display status of the Kunstkamera specimen made an examination of such constructional techniques as these impossible.

Because of the close similarity between these two cloaks in nearly every detail of construction, we may surmise that they may have been made by one individual or were the product of a standardized, ritually controlled formula for the manufacture of such regalia. Such ritual formulae for the production of sacred regalia are known to have existed among the central Sierra Miwok (Gifford 1955:267). The term Kukshui is identical to that used by the Valley Nisenan, and it is most likely that this cloak originated among that group.

a.

b.

Figure 7.20. Two views (a, b) of *mollok* cloak (570-2). *Photos courtesy of the MAE, St. Peterburg.*

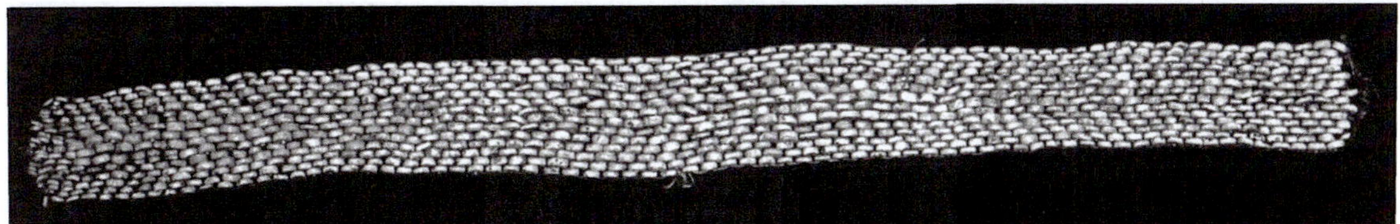

Figure 7.21. Clamshell disk bead belt (570-14).

Mollok Cloak

A condor-skin cloak (570-2), which was labeled *mollok* by Voznesenskii, is the second of the two objects which he is known to have acquired someplace in the Sacramento region. The cloak, which was made from the entire skin of a California condor, is the only such object known to exist. It measures about 2.74 m from wing tip to wing tip, and the pointers or wing spikes are approximately 60 cm in length. An unpeeled shoot was inserted into the base of the tail to keep the feathers somewhat spread (Figure 7.20). The presence of some slightly whitish feathering on the wings indicates that the bird was an immature adult (Hamber, personal communication, 1984).

The condor was venerated throughout much of central California, and the use of the skin of a condor in certain sacred dances was common among such people as the Patwin near Colusa (A. Kroeber 1932:387; Loeb 1933:213), the Valley Nisenan at the villages of Pusuni and Ol.ac near the present city of Sacramento (A. Kroeber 1929:269) which Voznesenskii visited, and among the Sierra Miwok (Gifford 1955:287). The Valley Nisenan term *mo'lo'ik* for the ceremony suggests that Voznesenskii may have collected the item from these people, not far from Sutter's Fort, or was given the condor pelt by Sutter himself.

Clamshell Disk-bead Belt

Clamshell disk-bead belts are uncommon in ethnographic collections, but at one time they were objects of wealth and prestige among such groups as the Pomo, and were presented as gifts of exchange at weddings (Allen 1972; Barrett 1952:312, Pl. 50; Bean and Theodoratus 1978:292; Merriam 1967:299; Purdy n.d.:12). They were also found among the Yuki (Miller 1978:252). Although little information exists on these belts, the Valley Nisenan were reported by Alfred Kroeber (1929:271) to have made a belt called *cu'dut'* of red or white glass trade beads; the *cu'dut'* may thus have been a replacement for an earlier belt made from clamshell disk-beads and produced using a netted stitch technique.

Museum examples are rare, but a few such belts have been collected and deposited in North American collections. Those in major collections have all come from the Pomo (MPM 15927) and the Yuki (USM 21375). A study of these examples reveals little, if anything, which can be used to distinguish ethnic styles.

The Kunstkamera example, MAE 570-14, is 71 cm in length and 6.5 cm in width (Figure 7.21). The belt was made using a fiber twine and the usual netted stitch technique, where the work progressed from one horizontal selvage to the other, adding one bead and then going through a previously fixed bead, until the opposite selvage end was reached. The progression was then repeated in the opposite direction. Thus, although the belt was 14 rows in width, only seven beads were added each time a selvage was reached.

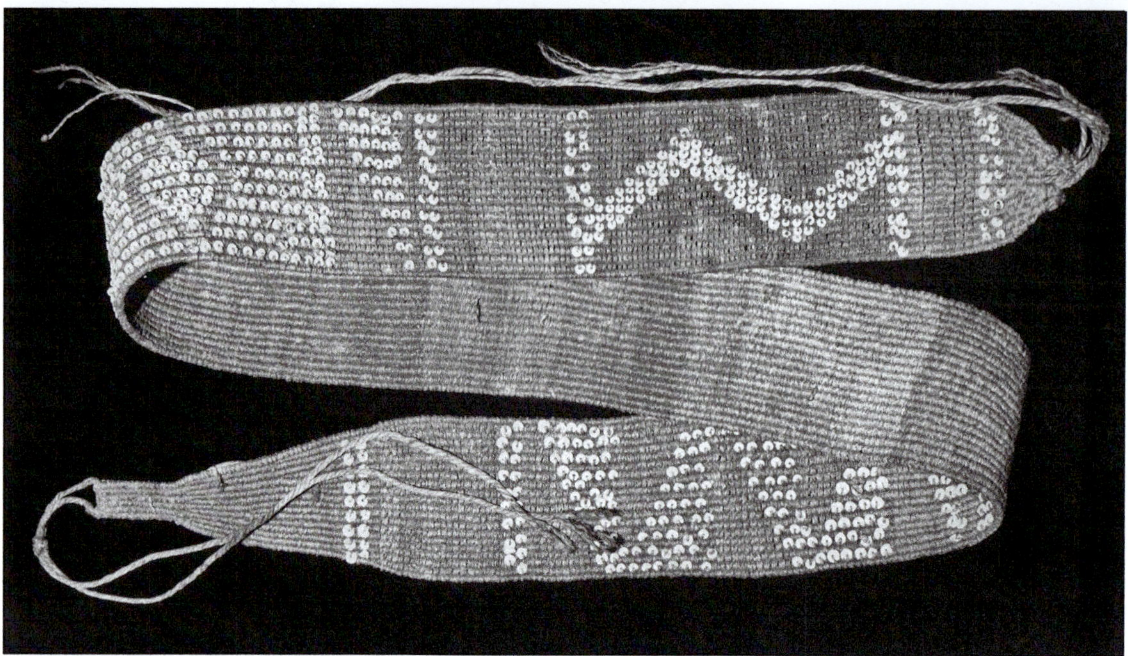

Figure 7.22. Feather belt (570-13).

Feather Belts

Feather belts played a prominent role in the material culture of California peoples, and were prized above all other material possessions. These objects, which were usually nearly a fathom in length and were woven with a weft-face technique using yards of cordage, were decorated with the scalp feathers of the mallard duck (iridescent green) and woodpecker (bright red), as well as with shell disk-beads (white) that were incorporated into the fabric as it was woven (Figures 7.22 and 7.23). Among the Wappo, these belts were worth more than three times the value of a first-class feathered basket or a bear-skin robe; that is, they had a value of some 15,000 clamshell disk-beads in the native economy (Driver 1936:194). Such a value made them the most expensive objects in aboriginal California.

Early European visitors to California were also impressed by the beauty of these objects. Choris, while describing the ceremonial clothing worn by the Indian people at Mission San Francisco during an 1816 visit, had this to say:

> When the service [Sunday mass] is ended, the Indians gather in the cemetery, which is in front of the mission house, and dance. Half of the men adorn themselves with feathers and with girdles ornamented with feathers and with bits of shell that pass for money among them. (Mahr 1932:97)

Choris also illustrated the scene, in which two men (one Coast Miwok and the other Bay Miwok) are wearing feather belts (Slaymaker 1977:101).

Captain Frederick Beechey may have also been describing feather belts when he wrote: "They also embroider belts very beautifully with feathers of different colors and they work with remarkable neatness" (Beechey 1831:II:62–63). Wrangell commented in a similar way on the regalia of the Coast Miwok and Pomoan peoples near Fort Ross: "Their headdresses, belts, earrings, etc., mostly made of feathers, betray not only their inventiveness, but also a certain penchant for beauty" (Heizer 1974:5).

Figure 7.23. Helsinki feather belt (FNM VK-1036).

Like feather headbands (which were made in the same woven style), feather belts are extremely rare in American collections. The complete inventory of objects in American museums from the post-1850 period consists of one Pomo feather belt (not illustrated) and four headbands, all of which were the work of one man who reinvented the technique for making the objects specifically for sale to non-Indians (and made them using a warp-face rather than weft-face weave); one headband collected from the Patwin/Nomlaki; and two belts made by the Chico Maidu. Only one belt in a private collection predates any of the above examples. However, there are 17 known examples in European collections: Oxford has two; St. Petersburg, four; Frankfurt, one; Oldenburg, one; Paris, three; Berlin, two; Copenhagen, one; La Rochelle, two; and Helsinki, one. The belt given to Wrangell by a "Tajon, i.e., Indian elder or chief, from New Albion" (Uhle 1886:15) is shown in Figure 2.3.

There may be still other belts in European collections in addition to these known examples. Uhle, for example, mentions one (1886:16) that was located in the Artillery Museum (presently the Musée de l'Armée), while Vatter (1925:96) states that he was informed by Stewart Culin that a feather belt was "said to be in Rome." Our efforts to locate both of these belts have failed.[5]

After a careful study of nearly all of these examples, we have found that the pre-1850 belts are similar in their manufacturing technique and in their use of feathers and Olivella shell beads for decoration. We have also found marked similarities in the type and placement of these feathers: large blocks of green mallard duck scalp feathers serve to separate blocks of red woodpecker scalp feathers upon which the shell bead designs are placed. The weaving was done using native hemp cordage, and there are also similarities in their dimensions. The dimensions of the belts[6] associated with Russian activities (Figure 7.23) in California are as follows:

Table 7.1 Dimensions of Feather Belts

BELT	LENGTH (in m)	WIDTH (in cm)
MAE 570-11	1.65	9.5
MAE 570-12	1.53	10.0
MAE 570-13	1.53	8.5
MAE n/n	1.83	11.0
WKM E 168	1.76	12.2
SNO 335	1.72	10.0
FNM VK 1036	1.71	9.5

The technique used to make these belts is unclear; the work involves a weft-face weave, although we do not understand the exact set-up that was used for the warp strands. Charlie Watham, who was perhaps the last person to produce this type of woven belt in the early twentieth century, is reported to have used a horizontal loom of sorts on which the warp strands were stretched. Perhaps the pre-1850 belts were similarly arranged. All of these belts share a common feature in that they have a square, loop-like "cinch" or tab on one end. This was the beginning of the belt, and the weaving technique involved the weft being woven over paired warps. Apparently, warp strands more than twice the length of the finished belt were stretched, but only half of those needed for the finished belt width. These were woven together in the middle using a weft cord; after several inches of weaving were accomplished, the piece was bent in half, thus creating warp strands that were only slightly longer than the total finished length of the belt, with a woven section equally placed at the end of the belt to form the loop. The warp strands were then integrated and woven with the weft strand, and slowly fanned out until the finished width of the belt was reached. At this point, the addition of the feathering began. From descriptions provided by native consultants, as well as from a study of the pieces, it appears clear that tufts of mallard feathers (those from the fore portion of the head were probably preferred) were carefully plucked from a dried scalp. The quill ends of the several feathers in the tuft were then twisted together; this was probably done by moistening them with saliva or water, as is done when such tufts are prepared for inclusion in a feather basket. As the weaving progressed, the pass of a weft strand over the top of the paired warp strands would cover one such group or tuft of feathers, with the quill ends then being carefully placed in the trough which resulted from the pairing of warp strands. Such a pairing of warp strands makes wide lanes in the weaving, and explains the erroneous information provided by some consultants who stated that such belts were produced by sewing, as in the production of a coiled feather basket. The weaving continued to the far end of the belt; then, when the feathering was completed, the end (or "tongue") was created by subtracting warp strands from the outer edges and covering the rough edges with the weaving of the weft strand, forming a neat, carefully finished selvage. When in use, the belts were wrapped about the waist and overlapped, with the tie string cinched through the "loop" in somewhat the same way that the cinch strap on a western saddle is fastened.

MAE 570-13 exemplifies this construction technique, with some exceptions. This feather belt (Figure 7.22) appears to be made of native cordage, with Olivella shell disk bead decoration. The Olivella beads were threaded on to the weft cordage and then placed to create the pattern as the weaving progressed. This belt was once fully feathered. The warp cords differ from those in the general method described above. In this specimen, only six pairs of warp cords form the starting loop. Additional warps to make the full width of the belt were gradually added in after the loop was complete. The ties are made of three-ply cordage that is knotted through the loop end.

Details concerning the exact use and ownership of such belts have been confused in the literature, and conflicting reports exist for the same ethnic group. What can be stated with certainty is that they were a valued prestige item. Zavalishin, a young Russian officer who was honored by being presented with such a belt, made the following statement: "By tradition [it] had been passed from generation to generation in one tribe from one chief to the

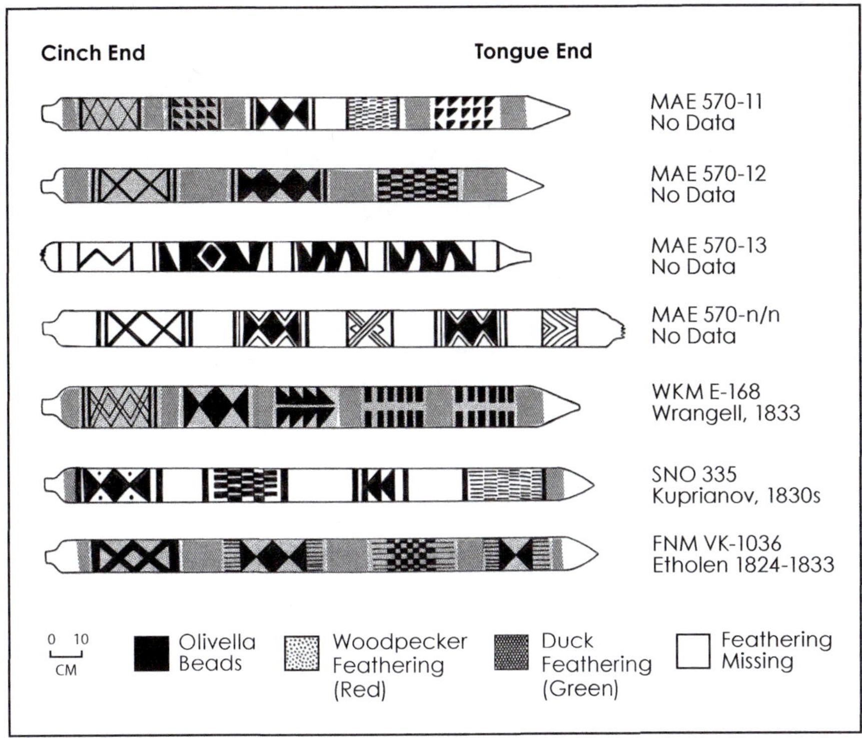

Figure 7.24. Sketch of feather belts collected by the Russians.

next as one of the symbols of their esteem, and it had not lost any of its freshness, despite long use" (Gibson 1973:382–383).

Mary Azbill, a Chico Maidu woman, stated at the turn of the twentieth century that some decades earlier "everyone of any wealth and importance had a belt" (Culin 1908:71).

Among Mary Azbill's people, and apparently among her Patwin neighbors to the west, such belts were reserved primarily for use in the Hesi ceremony, which twice a year marked the beginning and end of the dance cycle. They were used in dance performances during the Kenu and Toto, where their appearance bore testimony to the wealth of the wearer (Azbill, personal communication, 1973). Information is lacking, however, as to the particular dances in which the Valley Nisenan people used such belts, but it is known that belts were regarded by them as highly valuable objects (A. Kroeber 1929:271).

The ceremonial use of these belts suggests the possibility that the various designs on them may have had some symbolic meaning. If they did, however, such information is lost. Certain characteristics do stand out in a comparison (Figure 7.24) of the designs on all known complete examples, which suggests that a great deal of consideration was given to design style and placement. For example, the number of design fields was restricted to three, four, or five; 30 percent of the belts have five fields, or just slightly fewer than those with three (35 percent) or four (35 percent) fields. The figures also indicate a tendency for odd numbers to be preferred, with 65 percent of the sample having either three or five fields.

There are also marked similarities between the known belts in terms of the type and placement of designs that were used. The "cinch" or "tab" end of the belt has the same "winged diamond" motif 70 percent of the time. No

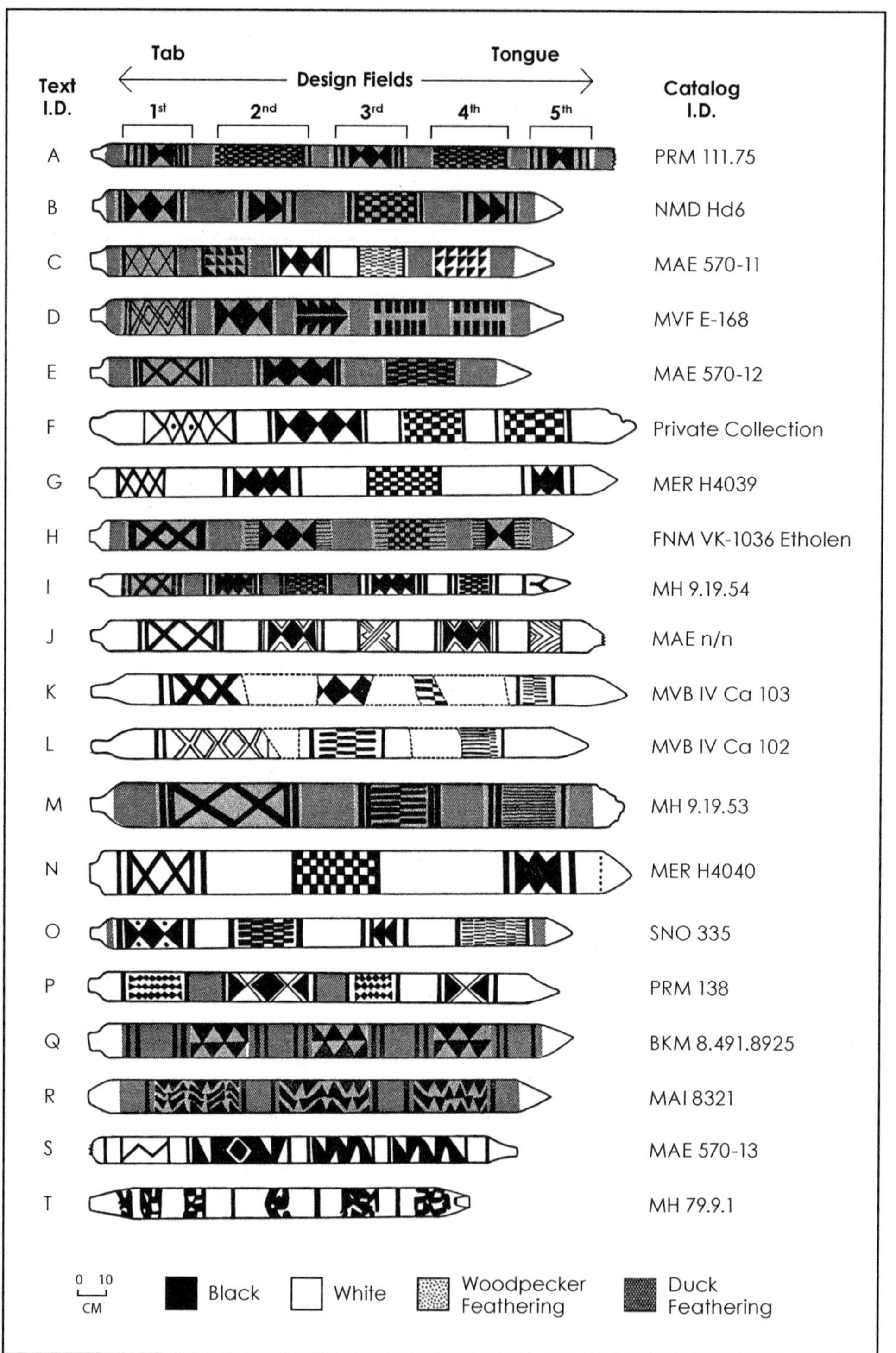

Figure 7.25. Sketch of extant feather belt patterns.

specific pattern appears to have been selected for the opposite, tongue end of the belt; none of the patterns reoccur on the six known five-field belts in existence. Photographic data suggest that some of the tongue-end patterns did duplicate; this can be seen in a photograph of two Chico Maidu dancers that was taken about 1910, whose feather belts exhibit a checkerboard pattern similar to that of Belt I in Figure 7.25. Still another photograph of a Chico Maidu dancer, this one taken in 1902, shows him wearing a belt that exhibits a terminal checkerboard motif next to the tongue, while the same design is repeated in the adjacent two field positions (Smithsonian Neg. 81-2121). Since we do not know if the photographed belt had three, four, or five (or more) fields, we can only surmise that it must have been somewhat similar to Belt F, which has this motif in its third and final fourth positions. A companion belt seen in the 1902 Chico Maidu photograph also exhibits a repetition of motif, although in this case the two similar designs are chains of diamond-like elements. Nevertheless, it is clear that even though existing museum specimens do not show a duplication of motifs in the fifth position, such duplication probably sometimes occurred. However, the placement of the checkerboard motif is even less obvious than the use of clustered, smaller elements (made up of geometric shapes) in the final position in the older belts, and (apparently) as favored designs in each position in the belts used by the Chico Maidu at the end of the nineteenth century. If we accept the idea that these people preferred to decorate belts with row-and-file-arranged geometric elements in the third, fourth, or fifth positions, then the frequency of pattern duplication in this wider and more general sense reaches nearly 55 percent.

The "winged diamond" motif was the overriding preference for decorating not only the first field position, but the second position as well (45 percent); in the third and fourth field positions, its frequency of use was 15 percent and 29.6 percent, respectively. The checkerboard and alternating rectangle motifs were the next most frequently found elements (occurring 13.8 percent and 11.3 percent of the time, respectively), and their locations on belts were very similar to those of the checkerboards.

With so few surviving examples to work with, it seems pointless at this time to consider pattern variations of other elements, such as zigzags, triangles, chevrons, and so on, although it can be observed that they also have geometric similarities as a group; significant variations may exist as well. It is interesting to note that the two post-1850 examples (Belts Q and R) seem to have little in common with their older siblings.

However, some interesting comparisons can be pointed out. For example, the checkerboard motifs that are present in Belts E to I, which have counterparts among the Chico Maidu examples that are known from photographs, raise some interesting questions about sources and trends. Was there a trend after 1850 to make belt panels more symmetrical in pattern layout, and to make only three, rather than four or five, decorated panels? In other words, were the designs and design layouts undergoing change? Are such attributes as symmetry or non-symmetry in pattern layout characteristic of the particular regions in which the belts were made? Were certain patterns perhaps linked to specific ethnic groups, communities, or families, as the statement that among the Patwin, at least, the right to make such belts was inherited (McKern 1922:250) seems to imply? If so, it would stand to reason that the more southerly regions, which were visited by Russian, English, and other travelers, may have produced the extant older belts, while the more symmetrical belts, apparently characteristic of the Chico Maidu at the end of the nineteenth century, represent a more northerly style that favored the three-panel decorative scheme. If this premise is true, would we be correct in attributing the early belts (A–P) to the Patwin, Nisenan, Pomo, Ohlone, and Coast Miwok, and in suggesting that the Patwin and Nisenan probably made the pieces in Figure 7.25?

In addition, what can we say about belts S and T, which lack the longitudinal symmetry that is so typical of Belts A to R? They definitely pre-date 1850, yet they exhibit a marked preference for different design layouts. Could that preference reflect their ethnic origin, or is it in some way related to function? Since we have no data on either of these belts, our ignorance only allows us to note these variations and reemphasize the need for more detailed studies. It is possible that we may never know the answers to these questions. The religious leaders and regalia manufacturers from the coastal and inland regions of California are largely gone, and those still alive were too young at the turn of the twentieth century to have learned much about the woven feather belts they saw in their youth. Of course, the hope always exists that someday, somewhere, new information may surface and open new vistas for research.

Something might also be learned from a study of post-1900 belts, although few of these exist or are represented even in photographs. Judging by a series of images that date up to the 1920s, and conversations with elderly native consultants in the 1960s and 1970s, it is evident that woven belts underwent some changes; most lacked bead decoration, and others were replaced by canvas belts with bird scalps attached by sewing, or simply by cloth appliques that were used to create new patterns for belts that were then employed much as the feathered belts had been. Such cloth belts can be seen on some of the dancers who took part in the Hesi ceremony at Grindstone Creek Rancheria in 1923 (Merriam 1955:Pls. 2c, 3a, 4a), while two other performers at this function can be seen wearing woven feather belts that lack bead decoration (Merriam 1955:Pls. 6a and 6b, left, and possibly also 6c). While this dance was held at a settlement consisting primarily of Nomlaki and Patwin people, the primary manufacturer of the regalia in use had been trained at the Chico Maidu village; thus one would expect some of the regalia to be like types used there. It seems clear that the cloth belt had begun to replace the woven one by the 1920s. By World War II, woven feather belts were but a memory.

Feather Band

There is a feathered band in the small California collection at Moscow State University, but it was impossible to obtain permission to study or photograph any of the pieces curated there. It is an unusual piece, which seems matched only by a specimen in the British Museum (BM Van-199) that was purportedly collected in California during one of Vancouver's voyages. The Moscow example is about 30 cm long, and is made of feathers (each about 20 cm in length and 2 cm in width) that were placed side by side and then attached to cords. The edge of each feather has been trimmed to form a zigzag pattern. Although Curator Nina Smirnova believed that the medium-length white tail feathers were from a condor, they appear to more closely resemble those of a sea bird of some sort.

The method of attaching the feathers was also unique. The quill ends of each feather were cut and tucked over a cord, and the quill tip was then worked back inside the quill. Three rows of simple twining on the quill ends were used to hold the feathers in place. The twine that was used appeared to consist of some sort of vegetable fiber.

There are few objects from California that resemble these bands, and (with the exception of the Vancouver specimen) only Shasta feather bands are ethnographically described as being somewhat similar (Dixon 1907:403–406). The Shasta pieces resemble the Moscow specimen in that both have quill-attached feathers that were placed side by side, and some of the feathers were edge-trimmed into a zigzag form. However, there are also marked differences, especially in construction. The Shasta pieces do not have cut quill ends; instead, the uncut end was bent over the cord. This difference may be indicative of a different ethnic origin for the Moscow example; it should be noted that the feather waist and neck bands of the Northwestern Valley Maidu, Patwin, and Pomoan peoples that were used in the Hesi ceremony seem so different in outward appearance from the Moscow piece as to be completely unrelated. Depictions of what seem to be feather waist bands appear in several early illustrations of dancers at missions San Francisco and San Jose (Kroeber, Elsasser, and Heizer 1977:88, 95, 96). The Moscow piece may be one of these objects, but the lack of detail in the renderings does not allow us to make such an attribution with certainty. It appears that the band must remain an enigmatic object for the moment.

Ornaments

Ear Rods

Ear rods of various kinds—usually consisting of incised bird-bone tubes—were worn through a hole in the lobe of the ear. Judging by illustrations, descriptions, and abundant archaeological examples, these objects were a popular form of adornment. José Cardero, an artist with the Malaspina expedition, drew a Monterey Bay Indian woman in 1791 whose ear ornaments appear to have been made of incised bird bones, with the ends of the long tubes tipped with feathered tufts or feathered basketry disks and decorated chains of beads (Heizer 1974:90, Fig. 2; Iglesias 1980:Fig. 81; see Figure 6.11). Captain Frederick Beechey, who visited California in 1826 with stops at San Francisco and Monterey, also noted that "to their ears they [the women] attach long wooden cylinders, variously carved, which serve the double purpose of ear-rings and needle-cases" (1831:II:77). Tikhanov's drawing of a young woman at Bodega Bay in 1818 also shows her wearing a long, elaborate bone ear rod in her right ear (Farris 1998:4–5).

Although these objects were apparently very popular in late prehistoric and early historic times, few were being produced by 1900, and even those were often indifferently made, with simple "x" design elements replacing the more elaborate patterns of an earlier age (for example, the Chico Maidu ear rod BM 08.491.8826). Indeed, the few surviving examples of later historic bone ear rods collected from such groups as the Pomo, Sierra Miwok, Northwestern Maidu, and a few others consisted simply of an incised bone tube with a simple design and no additional decoration, although a few did incorporate such items as quail topknots, woodpecker scalps, and bead and abalone pendants into their composition. Rarely were any finished off with the forward

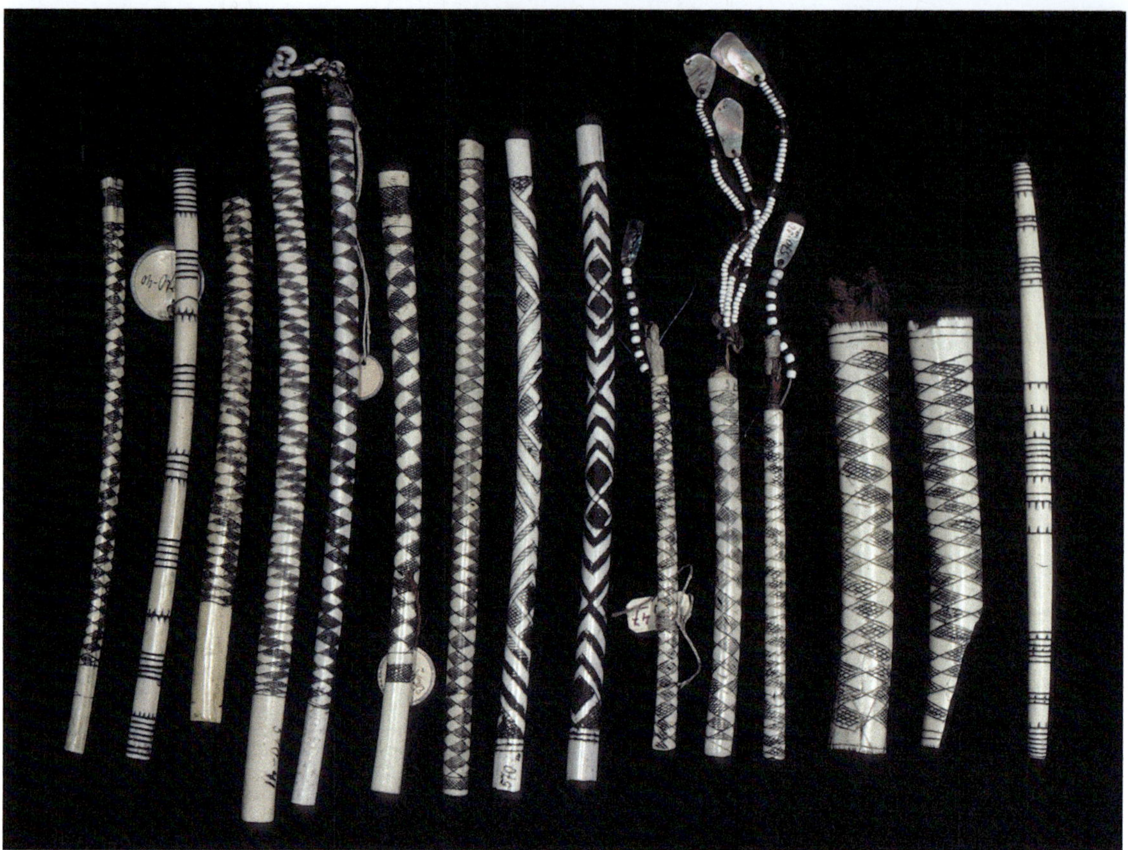

Figure 7.26. Ear rods made from incised bird-bone tubes: (*left to right*) 570-39, -40 (pair), -41 to -48, -50 to -52, and -119.

end of the tube terminating in a basketry disk covered with feather work and festooned with bead and abalone pendants.

Because of the relative rarity of such objects in ethnographic contexts, the 16 (out of 18 cataloged) examples of these objects in the Kunstkamera collections are of particular interest. Three more incised bird-bone tubes were found in the collections at Moscow State University, but permission to study them could not be obtained. The extant specimens in St. Petersburg are illustrated in Figure 7.26, while Table 7.2 provides information on their dimensions.

Many of the ear rods illustrated in Figure 7.26 closely resemble those reported in the archaeological record; MAE 570-52, for example, has nearly identical counterparts from archaeological sites in Pinole (Davis 1960:Fig. 6a) and Napa Valley (Heizer 1953: Fig. 11a, b, k), while MAE 570-45 and -46 resemble an example from a site in the San Francisco Bay region (Heizer 1951:55, Fig. 15). Obviously, design styles were widespread, and it is very difficult to ascribe a specific location to any one piece on the basis of similarities to archaeological examples. The same might also be said for ethnographic examples; MAE 570-47, -48, and -50, for instance, closely resemble three incised bird-bone tubes collected among the Pomo people in Lake County (OPM 16-2599) shortly after the turn of the last century.

MAE 570-48 (-49?) is an incised bird-bone ear decoration. The bead pendants are threaded on a fine cord of uncertain type, then tied with native hemp cordage to a

Table 7.2 Ear Rods in the St. Petersburg Collection

Cat. No.	Length Cm	Diameter Cm	Material	Decoration
570-39	16.5	0.6	Bird bone	Incised
-40	16.5	0.7	Bird bone	Incised
-40[a]	15.0	0.9	Bird bone	Incised
-41	21.0	0.9	Bird bone	Incised
-42	20.0	0.6	Bird bone	Incised[b]
-43	17.5	0.9	Bird bone	Incised
-44	18.5	0.7	Bird bone	Incised
-45	18.5	0.9	Bird bone	Incised
-46	18.5	0.8	Bird bone	Incised
-47	10.5	0.6	Bird bone	Incised[c]
-48	11.0	0.8	Bird bone	Incised[d]
-49 (missing—perhaps one of two catalogued as 570-40)				
-50	10.0	0.6	Bird bone	Incised[e] Object matches 570-47
-51	12.0	1.2	Bird bone	Incised[f]
-52	12.0	1.2	Bird bone	Incised Object matches 570-51
-119	—	—	Bird bone	Incised

a Cataloguing error resulted in duplicate numbers.
b Ends may have once been plugged with wood. There are sinew strands extending out at one end, connecting white and red beads 2 mm in diameter together, as well as a strand of clam disk beads sewn with a chain stitch.
c Has woodpecker scalp on one end, with a string of glass beads and an abalone pendant held in place with fiber twine.
d One end is plugged with vegetable fiber string from which extend three strands of white beads separated by red beads, ending in an abalone pendant.
e Has a woodpecker scalp and one string of glass beads on end.
f One end is plugged with a rag.

small stick wedged into the end of the bone. What remains of woodpecker scalp pieces are wrapped around the stick, which consists of a scraped shoot. The beads on the three drop pendants are 12/0 uneven white seed beads and oval, long clear red glass beads. The abalone pendants are very fine and small.

MAE 570-51 is another incised bird-bone ear decoration, but it is shorter in length than MAE 570-48. The bone is very large in diameter, and may be the upper wing bone of a pelican, crane, or swan. In one end there is a square tuft of red, plain wool cloth, which has simply been folded up and jammed in the end of the tube. The opposite end of the bone has a large crack in it.

The Kunstkamera collections, in addition to having a number of ear rods fashioned from bird bone, also contain two pieces (MAE 570-53 and -54) made from wood which are especially elaborate in form (Figure 7.27). These ear ornaments consist of a wooden tube made from either elderberry or possibly mock orange; the center of the wood is pithy. MAE 570-53 is 12.5 cm in length and 0.8 cm in diameter. The rear or back end of the tube has no decoration, while the front-facing end (next to the basketry disk) was once covered with woodpecker scalps secured with a cotton-string wrapping over another wrapping of narrow strips; there is also evidence of bits of green thread. The basketry disk was coarsely coiled using a three-rod technique, apparently using sedge root as the sewing strands; it is 4.2 cm in diameter and has two circles of white glass beads decorating it, a decoration that was created by stringing the beads on the sewing strands while the disk was being made. These beads are 3.5 mm in diameter. Two strings of red and white glass beads that end in abalone shell pendants, as well as another string of white and black glass beads with a similar decoration, hang from the tube itself. A 0.7 cm-thick clamshell disk bead 1.6 cm in diameter is centered in the middle of the basketry disk and secured by a wooden peg through its central hole, thereby connecting the basketry disk to the tube as well.

Figure 7.27. Ear ornaments (570-53 and -54).

MAE 570-54 is very similar to 570-53, although it lacks the large clamshell disk bead. The tube itself is 10 cm in length and 0.9 cm in diameter, and the attached basketry disk is 3.7 cm in diameter. The strips of cotton cloth wrapping under the woodpecker scalps are of a pink floral pattern, and there are two remaining woodpecker scalp coverings. Two strings of beads terminating in abalone shell pendants hang from the rod, and the center of the basketry disk has a group of six short strings of red and white glass beads, each terminating in an abalone shell pendant. Several types of glass beads were used in the pendants on both MAE 570-53 and -54, including red with white hearts, green-centered/red brick exterior, both small and large black and milky white, and a few porcelain off-white beads. The workmanship of the basket disk on MAE 570-53 is finer than on MAE 570-54; in addition, each basket disk may have once been covered with feathers, although evidence for that is now gone.

Earrings such as MAE 570-53 and -54 have been reported for the Pomo (DAM FPo-10-DP) and Chico Maidu (BKM 08.491.8856), as well as for the Southern Miwok (YPM 737); there is also the Cardero sketch mentioned at the beginning of this section (Figure 6.11). It is very probable that the use of such ornaments was widespread.

Ear Pendants

Two ear pendants (WKM EO-170), which were collected by Admiral Wrangell in 1833 and—according to the catalog—apparently associated with topknot headdress WKM EO-169 (described in the "Feather Topknot" section of this chapter), should also be mentioned. Judging from a sketch of one of these items (Figure 7.28), the ear pendant originally consisted of woodpecker scalps from which a plant fiber cord, decorated with five Olivella shell beads and ending in an abalone shell pendant, was suspended. The overall length of the item is 12.5 cm at present.

According to the Frankfurt catalog, this item was worn affixed to the crown over the ear, rather than being suspended in some manner from the earlobe itself.

Figure 7.28. Sketch of ear pendant collected by Wrangell (WKM E-0170).

Necklaces

Necklaces of either shell or glass beads have long been an important part of the trade economy among California Indian people, and as such are widespread in their distribution. In precontact times, clam disk beads were commonly used by various Central California peoples, with the primary suppliers being the Coast Miwok and the Pomo. After contact, there was a reduction in population among the Coast Miwok, and (having also gained access to the rich clamshell resources at Bodega Bay) the Pomo became the major suppliers.

Clam disk bead-making was an art unto itself, and it required great skill. A bead maker started production by first breaking the shells of the Washington clam into small pieces, and then chipping these into roughly circular disks. Next, a single, centrally-located hole was drilled in each disk; the disks were then strung and rolled on an abrading surface until they became perfectly round and had a smooth, polished surface. Such beads were used not only as constituent parts of necklaces and other decorative objects but, more importantly, were used as a form of currency by various Indian peoples.

The glass beads introduced by European traders also became an important element in decorating or fashioning objects, and in many cases became a substitute for shell beads. The Russians, however, may have also introduced an imitation clam shell disk bead made from a dull-lustered glass.[7] At the turn of the century, Pomo people told J. W. Hudson (1975:108) that in 1816 Kuskov had ordered such beads to be used in the California trade at Fort Ross, and that the Pomo people considered these *charlil kol* (or devil's beads) to be a counterfeit currency designed to cheat them; according to these aged Pomo consultants, three Russian traders were taken unawares and "their heads burnt with the beads" as a punishment (Hudson 1975:18; Farris 2001).

We can not say whether or not the story is true, but we do know that clam disk bead money was certainly very important to California Indian people. Francis Fletcher, Drake's chaplain during his 1579 visit to the Coast Miwok, wrote our earliest description of these objects: "The chaines seemed of a bony substance; every linke or part thereof being very little, thinne, most finely burnished, with a hole pierced through the middest" (Fletcher 1947:287).

Over two centuries later, Langsdorff also described these beads—and necklaces made from them—during his visit to Mission San Francisco in 1806:

> Their ornaments are of many kinds, and are generally fashioned of shells and feathers. Among the shells chiefly used is a sort of sea-ear, probably the Haliotis gigantea, which abounds on these coasts.... Small rings are made of another sort of shell.... These rings are all of the same size, and are of perfectly accurate make, and bored through the middle without the aid of any kind of instrument. In appearance they are much like glass beads, and are strung together to make necklaces. (Langsdorff 1814:II:59)

We noted in Chapter 2 that two of the California necklaces illustrated in Langsdorff's work were deposited in European museums, one (Figure 2.4) in Munich (SMV 213), and the other in St. Petersburg (MAE 570-23). Louis Choris, during his 1816 visit to California, depicted similar necklaces (Figure 7.5) being worn by men in ceremonial regalia. Kostromitinov, who wrote a short description of the Indian people in and about Fort Ross, stated only that "both sexes decorate themselves with pearls from mussels" (1974:8).

Figure 7.29. Shell necklaces (top to bottom: 570-20 to -23).

The five necklaces in St. Petersburg are most interesting. Only one of them, MAE 570-24, is a simple string of clam disk beads; it is 1.35 m in length and is identical to the more common form of clamshell disk bead necklaces that were used in the latter part of the nineteenth century. The remaining four examples are more ostentatious, and have abalone shell pendants with glass or shell beads that provided a means by which the pendants were displayed (Figure 7.29).

MAE 570-23, the Langsdorff piece mentioned above, is some 36 cm in length and 1.5 cm in width, and is composed of four rows of clam disk beads woven in a "gourd stitch." In this technique, the necklace maker works from one horizontal margin to the other, back and forth across the band, connecting the beads together with two-ply native hemp. The exceptionally fine beads used in this example were 5 mm in diameter. Below the band (and attached to it) are a series of rare clamshell disk tube beads which were positioned in pairs to receive the eighteen abalone pendants, which are pentagonal in shape and range in length from 2.2 to 4.7 cm and have an average width of 2.5 cm. The pendants were worn so that the convex side faced outward; they are thin and well formed, which indicates that they were worked from very large shells. The necklace appears to have been broken in several places; one pendant and two tube beads are missing. The end ties are knotted and bound together to keep the necklace from unraveling.

This necklace, with its pentagonal pendants of abalone shell, is similar to specimens in some American collections: historic Sierra

Miwok examples (HMA 1-71822) are similar, as is an example from the Nisenan of the Sierra foothills that is known photographically (USM photo 2854a); archaeologically, the form is found in such widely scattered locales as the Napa Valley (Heizer 1953:343, Fig. 12t), Marin County (Meighan 1953:Pl.2g; Slaymaker 1977:190), in Sierra Miwok territory near Mokelumne Hill, in the Sacramento Valley, in the San Francisco Bay and intervening Delta region, and north to Marysville (Gifford 1947:23). Because of this widely scattered archaeological distribution, and because such multiple abalone pendants have been reported for the Miwok, Maidu, Patwin, Nisenan, and Pomo peoples, it is impossible to ascribe a specific tribal origin to the piece. The only helpful clue may lie in the clamshell tube beads, which are found archaeologically in Coast Miwok territory along the coast, but do not occur along the shores of San Francisco or San Pablo bays (Slaymaker 1977:188). In historical times, the beads were produced and used by the Pomo (J. Hudson 1975:15).

The remaining three necklaces in the Kunstkamera present us with similar problems of identification. MAE 570-20 is similar to -23 in its gourd-stitch beaded band, although in this example the clam disk beads were replaced by opaque white (both milky white and bright white) beads and green-centered/brick-red exterior beads that average about 4 mm in diameter. The sewing material, as was the case with MAE 570-23, was a fine two-ply native hemp cordage string, with a finished band 29 cm in length and 3 cm (eight beads) in width forming a white zigzag design against a red background. The pendants, which are suspended along the bottom edge of the band by short strings of glass beads, are again of abalone, although they are rectangular in form and are 3.5 cm long and 2.5 cm wide. The abalone shell work is very fine; two of the pendants are drilled along the slightly curved bottom edge with seven small pits. Three small holes in the top of each pendant permit the attachment of the bead strings. This necklace shows signs of having been broken in two places and sewn back together with native hemp string. The ends of the necklace are furnished with ties, a double strand from the top band and a double strand from the band bottom, which were each knotted together and then joined by a knot and twisted into a long cord with an end knot.

Attributing this necklace to a particular ethnic group presents problems. The Pomo, for example, made wide bands of clamshell disk beads, but none made of glass beads are known. As far as other groups are concerned, narrow bands of glass beads—two or four beads wide—are occasionally found among the Miwok and Maiduan peoples. The white and red beads, which are termed "Hudson Bay" and "Spanish" beads, were used by the Valley

Nisenan of the Sacramento area in making belts (A. Kroeber 1929:271), quite possibly in conjunction with the netted gourd-stitch technique. The use of such beads, which were perhaps secured in quantity by those people living near Sutter's Fort, may have extended to the manufacturing of necklace bands. If such was the case, MAE 570-20 may have been collected by Voznesenskii, although we can only suggest that as a possibility.

The last two necklaces in the St. Petersburg collection, MAE 570-21 and -22, are similar to the one just described in that the abalone squares are suspended from a band of woven cordage, apparently produced by using a cord to create a figure eight-like binding between two parallel cords. This produced a weft-faced band similar in appearance to the feather ropes described in the next section. Tribes such as the Northwestern Maidu used this technique in producing a specific style of choker (BKM 08.491.8855; OPM 16-2345) that indicated an individual's intention to participate in a future mourning ceremony. MAE 570-21 is 46 cm long; the band supports 11 abalone shell pendants (although it appears that two are missing), each of which is suspended on strings strung with large (4 mm in diameter) glass beads. The beads are green-centered/brick red exterior glass beads and opaque white paste beads, some of which have a porcelain-like appearance. The pendants average 2.1 cm in length and 1.3 cm in width, and have two holes (one near each corner) on the top edge for suspension.

MAE 570-22 is 40 cm in length, and has a fastener consisting of a small loop in the cord that is decorated with three glass beads and two clamshell tube beads. Seven rectangular abalone pendants, which average 2.8 cm in height and 2.6 cm in width, are suspended below, with suspension strings that are strung with large white 4 mm glass beads. Each pendant has two holes drilled on the top side for suspension, while a series of small, partially drilled "pits" are lineally placed along the basal or outside face.

The decoration of abalone shells by the drilling of small pits is restricted in time to the prehistoric and early historic periods, for it is known only from the archaeological record and from certain early nineteenth-century pieces in European collections. Archaeological excavations have produced examples of pit decoration from a variety of sites, including ones in the Napa Valley, the Delta region, and near Red Bluff (Gifford 1947:22; Heizer 1953:344; Treganza 1954:Fig. 5h). In addition, necklaces consisting of large square or rectangular pieces of abalone shell were also widespread historically; they appear to have been most frequently used by the Miwok (HMA 1-71828, 1-71829, 1-71831, 1 71832, 1-71834; FM 70214; OPM 16-549) and Maiduan peoples, including the Nisenan (Azbill, personal communication, 1973); also in photograph USM 2854a). This style of necklace has also been noted among the Pomo (Barrett 1952:II:Pl. 40) and the Patwin or Nomlaki (Kroeber, Elsasser, and Heizer 1977:269). Archaeologically, they are found in the central part of the state, in sites throughout Miwok and Maidu territories and near Red Bluff (Treganza 1954:Fig. 5f, j), as well as in the Delta region, on the southern California coast, in Mendocino County, and in Round Valley (Gifford 1947:22). Because of such a diverse distribution, it is impossible to attribute MAE 570-22 to any particular ethnic group.

The first of the two shell bead necklaces collected by Langsdorff and now curated in Munich (SMV 213) is similar to MAE 570-23 (see Figure 2.4). SMV 213, which is about 35 cm in length, consists of pairs of clam shell beads (each about 5 mm in diameter) that have been strung together, and from which a series of six (originally seven) pentagonally shaped abalone shell pendants are suspended. The pendants are 5.5 cm long and 4.5 cm wide, and they have two suspension holes along their upper edges. The position of the missing seventh pendant (see Figure 2.4) is marked by a break in the clam bead chain; one row of beads is apparently missing, and the broken ends of the sewing twine have been tied together.

The other Munich necklace (SMV 204) simply consists of a long string of Olivella shell disk beads that average about 6 mm in diameter. The strung beads may or may not have served as a necklace, but it is worth mentioning that because of the early replacement of Olivella disk beads by glass trade beads, this piece is exceptionally rare—in fact, it is the only known specimen to have been collected ethnographically (Hudson 1984:36). Since the beads from which it was made were once widely distributed over much of central California, we are unable to assign it to a particular ethnic group, although Langsdorff probably acquired it from Mission San Francisco Ohlone or Coast Miwok peoples.

Figure 7.30. Feather rope (570-10).

Feather Ropes

Feather ropes were used in a number of dances. They were made from either small body feathers or from the vanes of larger, stripped wing feathers; the quills were bound together by two parallel cords, usually employing a figure-eight technique. The use of these ropes was indeed ancient, for the Northwestern Valley Maidu told stories of how—when the world was made—these feather ropes were used to tie the new land down upon the water so that it would not float away. In addition, when the world was about to be made, the creator came from the sky on a feather rope. In possible recognition of this event, the people later held the Aki dance, in which a spirit performer entered the dancehouse by sliding down through the smokehole on a feather rope (Azbill, personal communication 1969, 1973).

Nearly all central Californian groups used these ropes in dances. The Central Sierra Miwok often tied a rope around a woman's head, with the ends hanging down the back, to form a type of headdress that was worn in certain dances (Gifford 1955:305). The Coast Miwok called the rope *sukuti* (Slaymaker 1977:61–68), while the Patwin called it *p'okal* (Kroeber 1932:342); the Chico Maidu employed the term *pokelma* for this ritual item (Azbill, personal communication, 1970), and women often held the ropes in their hands when dancing. Among the Chico Maidu, the *mesti* or leader held a black feather rope while dancing with the Earth Mother or Du spirit, and the latter also held a white rope while dancing in the Hesi. Among the more affluent families in this settlement, the dead were tied into a fetal position prior to burial using lengthy ropes of this sort (Azbill, personal communication 1970).

The one example (MAE 570-10) of these ropes that was collected by the Russians, and which is now on exhibit in St. Petersburg, is approximately 5 m in length (Figure 7.30). It was made with alternating bands of color; the white sections average about 4.5 cm in length, while the black sections are only 3 cm in length. Similar ropes with alternating black and white color bands have been collected from the Northwestern Maidu (AMNH 50/4181; HMA 1-2323, 1-2634, 1-2635), but there are no examples from the other groups that apparently made and used them.

Chapter 8

Objects for Festive Occasions

Music, Gifts, and Games

The collections compiled by the Russian explorers—indeed, those assembled by most European visitors to California—notably lack many of the objects, such as charms and charmstones, doctor's kits, shamanic sucking tubes, pipes, medicines, cocoon rattles, and so on, that were used in ceremonial contexts . While the Russians may have ignored such objects in favor of more ostentatious items of ritual costuming, it is probable that most of these items were considered to be so endowed with supernatural power that they would never have been available for sale, let alone for viewing by outsiders. By the turn of the twentieth century, however, a few American ethnographers were able to secure examples of such objects as charms, cocoon rattles, and so on, probably as a result of changing attitudes, better relations between Anglos and native people, and the need for money in a new, cash economy. Attitudes about supernatural power were also changing; as various diseases increasingly decimated native peoples, growing doubts in the efficaciousness of the old curing methods allowed such exchanges to take place. However, whatever the reason may have been, only a few musical instruments and a number of non-utilitarian fancy baskets that were intended for ritual use were acquired by the Russians. We will begin our survey of these items with a discussion of musical instruments.

Musical Instruments

Although several visitors had the opportunity to observe native dances, there are surprisingly few descriptions of the kinds of instruments employed. The following brief comment by Vasilyev (1821) is one such exception:

Treasures from Native California: The Legacy of Russian Exploration, Travis Hudson and Craig D. Bates, Edited by Thomas Blackburn and John R. Johnson, 159–184.

We saw their dances at Mission San Francisco. They sing and clap; some beat time with a split stick and some dance and pose, marking time by striking the ground hard with their /right/ foot, and in their mouth they have a whistle made from a bird's foot, with which they keep time.... We saw another kind of dance: at a signal from a conductor, apparently, two come running, dressed alike except that on one's head there is a hat of black feathers and on his lips there is a long beak like a crane's made of feathers. In both of their mouths there is a whistle made of pelican feet, and both run back and forth, whistling, with sticks in their hands, and the others sing. (Gibson 2013:174)

Gourd Rattle

According to the Munich catalog, Krusenstern[1] and Langsdorff collected a gourd rattle in California. The item (SMV 183; Figure 8.1) consists of a gourd with a painted wooden stick handle extending through it; the top of the gourd is decorated with bright green feathers, probably from a parrot. The overall length is 25 cm.

Figure 8.1. Gourd rattle attributed to Langsdorff (SMV 183).

Gourd rattles were unknown in northern and central California in precontact or early historic times; they were only used in the southern region of the state, among such groups as the Chumash and Gabrielino (Hudson and Blackburn 1986:336), after the missions were established—although even then turtle shells or tin cans were preferred. Although SMV 183 could have been collected at one of the California missions, we suspect that it was not; because of the rattle's general form and parrot feather decoration, we suspect that it may have originated instead in tropical South America—another location where Langsdorff is known to have collected (Müller 1980). Our guess is that the rattle came from Surinam.

Bird-bone Whistles

Bird-bone whistles, bound in pairs, were a very commonly used item in dances among most central California peoples. Two examples (570-62, -63) are on exhibit in St. Petersburg; the catalog states that two others (570-60 and -61) were considered to be South American and were transferred. Since there is a great deal of similarity between California and South American bone whistles, an effort was made in March, 1983, to locate the latter to verify their origin; unfortunately, they could not be found.

The two extant specimens (Figure 8.2) both show evidence of having once been decorated with bird skins; these were probably acorn woodpecker scalps, which would have encased the instruments in a shimmering coat of red. Today, as a result of insect damage, only the dried brown skin remains. Whistle 570-62 is 11 cm in length, and has an Olivella disk bead decoration that was affixed by means of two bands of pitch which encircle the whistle on either side of the note holes. The other example, 570-63, is 9.5 cm in length; it also has an Olivella shell disk bead decoration affixed with pitch, which in this case forms the plugs at the end of the whistle. Both examples are bound with native cordage; 570-63 appears to be wrapped with a bark-like twine, consisting perhaps simply of prepared hemp bark which had not yet been twisted into cordage.

Figure 8.2. Bird-bone whistles (570-63, *left*, and -62, *right*).

Bird-bone whistles differ little, if at all, from one group to the next in central California. The holes in the center of these examples are rounded in shape, and compare nicely with those on archaeological specimens from across the state from contexts prior to 1850; the availability of steel files after that date often tended to produce rectangular holes. Examples resembling the Kunstkamera specimens come from widely scattered regions and peoples; whistles made by the Nomlaki (OPM 16-2087 thru 2089, 16-2831), the Northwestern Maidu (OPM 16-1569; FM 79894; HMA 1-16,694), the Pomo (OPM 16-506, 16-508), the Northeastern (Salt) Pomo (OPM 16-2011, 16-2043), the Patwin (OPM 16-1159, 16-1997), and the northern Sierra Miwok (HMA 1-10037, 1-10038) are so similar that they discourage any attempt to discern meaningful ethnic differences. However, few such whistles are decorated with bird feathers. Among the Yokaya Pomo, whistles were sometimes decorated with red-shafted flicker tail feathers as a sign of graceful dancing, or with mallard duck scalps as a symbol of astuteness and watchfulness (J. Hudson n.d.a:184). A few extant whistles that were collected among the Pomo were decorated with mallard duck and woodpecker scalps (MAI 12-2927, 14-7365, 5-6469; DAM MPO-2-P), although the technique that was used was markedly different from that employed on the Kunstkamera specimens.

It is possible that other groups, such as the Coast Miwok, decorated whistles in a similar fashion. The technique of smearing the whistle's bindings with pitch appears to have been largely abandoned by the turn of the century, although a few archaeological examples of such coated wrappings exist that came from sites such as the Patterson Mound in Alvarado on the east shore of San Francisco Bay (Davis and Treganza 1959: Pl. 2A, r–s). Thus, the whistles, like many of the objects in the Russian collections, provide us with few clues that can be used to ascertain their specific tribal origin.

Ceremonial Basketry and Presentational Items

Many of the "fancy" baskets in the Russian collections also leave us perplexed when we try to identify possible places of origin. With the partial exception of that produced by the Pomo, the basketry made by many of the groups who lived in the area visited by the Russians is little known. Only six extant coiled baskets from the Ohlone region, for example, have believable documentation that links them to these people (Larry Dawson, personal communication, 1981). Although charred fragments of twined ware have been recovered archaeologically from Coast Miwok sites, almost no similar remains of coiled basketry have ever been found. Our sole knowledge of the art of basketry among these people is based upon the memories of aged consultants (Kelly n.d.), and upon one photograph of a Coast Miwok woman holding a basket which she or her relatives may—or may not—have made (Kroeber and Heizer 1968:105). Although other groups, such as the Wappo, the Lake Miwok, and the Patwin, are better represented in museum collections, there are many gaps in the record, especially for more southerly groups such as the Patwin and Pomo. In addition, some southern groups, such as the Northern Valley Yokuts and the Plains and Bay Miwok, are either not represented at all or are represented by a mere handful of specimens. Such a dearth of information makes the task of attributing any of the Russian fancy baskets to a particular group difficult at best.

Fancy or ornate baskets—resplendent in their shell, feather, and bead trim—are usually called "ritual" or "ceremonial" pieces in the literature; that is the reason we are discussing them here, rather than in conjunction with household activities (see Chapter 6). Such fancy baskets served as symbols of wealth and affluence during their owner's lifetime, and also had the potential to be used as valuable trade items; they were surpassed only by woven feather belts in the esteem in which they were held and their purchasing power. Baskets of this kind were most commonly fated for eventual destruction upon the death of an individual or at an annual Mourning Celebration. Among the Chico Maidu, their burial with the owner insured that the basket's spirit, along with that of the owner, would travel to the spirit world as an offering, thus giving thanks to the spirits for the good life that the owner had had on earth (Azbill, personal communication, 1968). Fancy baskets, with their crimson woodpecker scalp feathers, beads, and abalone pendants, were widely used in this way throughout central California, and their importance to native peoples was remarked upon again and again by European visitors to the state's heartland.

The earliest description of such very ornate baskets was written by a member of Drake's party, and probably applies to the Coast Miwok:

> Their baskets were made in fashion like a deepe boale, and though the matter were rushes, or such other kind of stuffe, yet was it so cunningly handled, that the most part of them would hold water; about the brimmes they were hanged with peeces of the shels of pearles, and in some places with two or three linkes at a place, of the chaines aforenamed: thereby signifying, that they were vessels wholly dedicated to the onely vse of the gods they worshipped; and besides this, they were wrought vpon with the matted downe of red feathers, distinguished into diuers workes and forms. (Fletcher 1947:287–288)

Another English visitor, Captain Frederick Beechey, also wrote a description of the baskets of this region:

> Their closely wove baskets are not only capable of containing water, but are used for cooking their meals. A number of small scarlet feathers of Oriolus phoeniceus are wove in with the wood, and completely screen it from view on the outside and to the rim are affixed small black crests of the Californian partridges, of which birds a hundred braces are required to decorate one basket; they are otherwise ornamented with beads and pieces of mother of pearl. (Beechey 1831:II:75–76)

Russian accounts of basketry are quite extensive, beginning with that of Langsdorff at Mission San Francisco:

> I saw baskets made of the bark of trees. These were so ingeniously woven, compact, and impervious to water, that they are used as drinking vessels, food-dishes, and even as roasting pans.... Many of these baskets, or vessels, are ornamented with the scarlet feathers of Oriolus phoeniceous, or with the black crest-feathers of the California partridge (Tetraonis cristati) or with shells and corals. (1814:II:58)

Descriptions were also provided by Chamisso and Choris. Chamisso mentioned only that the women made neat and waterproof baskets of "coloured blades of grass" (Mahr 1932:85); Choris, however, went into more detail:

> The Indians at the missions to the south of San Francisco—particularly that of Santa Barbara—make charming vessels and vase-shaped baskets, capable of holding water, from withes of various running plants. They know how to give them graceful forms, and also how to introduce pleasing designs into

> the fabric. They ornament them with bits of shell and with feathers. (Mahr 1932:99, 101)

The sketch made by Choris of native people traveling in a balsa on San Francisco Bay (Figure 5.3) is also of interest, for the drawing contains a depiction of a basket in the shape of a truncated cone; the details in the sketch allow us to ascertain something about its decoration. The vertically-arranged design elements, as well as the conical form, are attributes shared with a documented Ohlone basket (USM 313,234), and are features that provide a basis for sorting out ethnic affiliations for these baskets.

Golovnin was another Russian visitor who wrote about California Indian basketry:

> [They make] baskets woven so closely and firmly from roots and grass that they hold water and in which they boil their food by means of heated rocks; or their hats, woven from the same material and frequently decorated with seashells; both these items are not only well made but are very attractive. (1979:149)

Khlebnikov (1940:333) noted only that very neat and firmly woven baskets were made from roots and "decorated with red and azure feathers and blue shells."

Other visitors were equally impressed with the fancy baskets they encountered, and some secured examples for themselves. Bryant's visit to Earl Livermore's ranch in the first half of the nineteenth century resulted in his acquisition of a small feathered basket (Bryant 1849:307; Heizer 1968). Livermore's ranch was located on the eastern edge of Ohlone territory, only a few miles south of Bay Miwok lands. It is unfortunate that Bryant's basket cannot be located today, because the extant documented baskets from the Ohlone area all came from south of Santa Clara, and we have no examples from the tribelets in the northern half of Ohlone territory, nor any from their Bay Miwok neighbors. If the surviving examples are truly representative, the types of feathered baskets that were made by the Ohlone at Santa Clara, San Juan Bautista, Monterey, and Santa Cruz were markedly different, and one would probably be correct in assuming that such differences existed in the basketry of the more northerly Ohlone peoples as well.

Judging from surviving specimens and from incomplete ethnographic data, it appears that feather and bead decorated basketry was produced in a variety of forms by the bulk of central California peoples, including the Ohlone, the Coast Miwok, the Patwin, the Pomo, the Nisenan (Valley Maidu), the Northwestern Maidu, the Sierra Miwok, the Esselen, the Salinan, and probably the Plains and Bay Miwok (Saclan). The Russians, at one time or another, were in contact with most of these peoples. Therefore, it is not surprising that 35 of the 46 known baskets presently found in collections fall within the category of "fancy ware"; that is, ware intended for ritual or ceremonial use and elaborately decorated with feathering and/or beads. All but eight of the Kunstkamera's 27 such baskets were located for study in 1983. Moscow State University's two examples were seen briefly, but it was impossible to get permission to study them. Frankfurt and Munich each has three such baskets in its collection, and they were examined by Hudson. Similar baskets present in collections in France, England, and elsewhere in Germany were not amassed by the Russians, which suggests that such elaborately decorated objects were considered excellent souvenirs that reflected the workmanship of California Indian peoples. One can speculate as to the effect such an interest may have had on the production of these baskets, but the question is certainly moot at present since little is known about precontact examples. However, we do know that one change certainly took place: glass trade beads replaced beads made of shell.

Because of our limited knowledge of these baskets, and because the examples found in St. Petersburg, Moscow, Munich, and Frankfurt are rather diverse, we have found it convenient for descriptive purposes to subdivide them into three general categories on the basis of their shape and size: ceremonial baskets, feast baskets, and gift baskets. While any one of the functions ascribed to one category might well have applied to another—since we have no evidence that highly decorated cone-shaped baskets were used in serving food, nor can we say that a ceremonial basket could not have been an exchange item, nor that a gift basket could not have served as a funerary offering—our designations are used simply to divide the collection into smaller and more easily handled descriptive units. The items that we have categorized as being "ceremonial" and "feast" baskets are baskets that are relatively large; the former are somewhat globular or hemispherical in form, while the latter have the shape of a truncated cone with flaring sides. We consider gift baskets to be smaller in size, with either a hemispherical or truncated cone shape; a few have string handles, and some even have bead decoration on the interior surface.

Examples of each type of basket will be presented next. Unless otherwise noted, all three categories of fancy baskets share certain basic constructional features. All were made by three-rod coiling with an outside work face and a leftward coiling direction, and all had fag ends that were concealed in the bundle foundation, while the moving ends were either trimmed on the back face or were bound under successive stitches. Sewing strands consisted of split sedge (*Carex* sp.) roots.

Figure 8.3. Ceremonial basket (570-78).

Figure 8.4. Ceremonial basket (570-79).

Figure 8.5. Ceremonial basket (570-90).

Ceremonial Baskets

Examples of these large, globular, elaborately decorated baskets can be found in St. Petersburg (where three out of the six cataloged specimens were available for study, and a fourth was located in 1998) and in Helsinki (which has one specimen).

MAE 570-78 (Figure 8.3) is 44 cm in its maximum diameter and is 24 cm high; the orifice is 37.5 cm in diameter. Traces of red feathering appear on the outside surfaces, with clam disk beads sewn onto the rim with cordage in three locations; glass beads have also been occasionally sewn to the exterior.

MAE 570-79 (Figure 8.4) is 14.5 cm high, with a maximum diameter of 26 cm; the orifice is 22.5 cm in diameter. Clamshell disk beads, in groups of three, are equidistantly spaced in thirds about the rim, sewn on with milkweed string or possibly linen fiber. Both large white pony beads and small irregular porcelain glass beads have been attached by means of the coiling strands to the dark design areas; a few smaller white glass beads have been attached to the uppermost three rows of coiling by what appears to be cotton string. The thread was carried along under the coiling strands with the rod foundation; a bead was then strung on it and left on the outside of the basket, with the thread returning to its previous location next to the rods. In this specimen, and possibly in the preceding piece (570-78; see Figure 8.3), the black design material consists of dyed and split bulrush root. Red feathering was once scattered on the buff-colored background area of the upper one-fourth of the basket and on the rim. The start is an overhand knot with one row of down to the right twining; then the warps were bent to the left and stitched over. It is possible that a row of twining is under the first row of coiling. The design on the base consists of tooth-like triangles, and it appears that the materials of bulrush and sedge floated under one another rather than being clipped with each new material being used. There are an average of 20 stitches per inch and 5.9 rows per inch, with the bottom being of a coarser weave.

MAE 570-90 (Figure 8.5) is globular in shape, and is some 18 cm high and 40 cm in diameter. The walls of the basket have an elaborate black patterning, while the base has a six-pointed star pattern which has been expanded outward by the addition of "petals" to the basic star figure to form a much larger, six-pointed star where the base begins to turn upward to form the vertical walls of the basket. This basket, which was also originally decorated with red woodpecker feathers on the buff field, is elaborately ornamented with both clam disk and glass beads. The clam shell beads are attached in groups of four at three equally distant locations about the rim. The glass beads, which measure 4 mm in diameter and are an opaque white in color (although a few red beads with white centers and brick red beads with green centers also occur), are strung on the sewing strands and thus attached to the basket. The materials are bulrush and sedge; the start consists of a large knot, followed by tight twining for two rows, which in turn converts to three-rod coiling. The sedge roots are very rounded, which indicates that they were split and culled without much further trimming. The rim is bound off with a three-strand-like braid for four stitches, then finished with two plain stitches.

MAE 570-80 and -81 are probably ceremonial baskets as well, but they were missing in March, 1983, and therefore could not be studied. Our only source of information on them comes from Kojean (1979:8, Table II, 7), who stated that MAE 570-80 was a globular feather-decorated basket from the Sacramento River area that was collected by Voznesenskii. We do not know the basis for this attribution (for it is not given as such in the catalog), but it was followed by the statement that the basket was of Pomo origin, which was an obvious contradiction since these people did not reside in the Sacramento River area. Kojean also attributed MAE 570-81 to the Pomo, and stated that it was globular in shape, although he did not mention whether or not the basket was feathered or beaded. MAE 570-82 is a three-rod Maidu-style basket made of sedge and redbud, with some bulrush root in the last row of coiling. The design consists of black rectangles worked in a spiral layout, with red woodpecker feathers scattered about. There is an oval start, and the sedge roots are very wide or hefty in appearance, allowing the interior root to be split. The fag end is concealed, and the moving end is bound under or clipped (with a great deal of floating along the single line design area).

One basket which is documented as coming from the "Rio Sacramento" is a fine Etholen piece (FNM VK-341) that is housed in Helsinki. It is globular in shape, and measures 29 cm in maximum diameter by 17 cm in height; the orifice is 23 cm in diameter. In addition to the elaborate body designs (done in redbud), there are traces of red feathering that once covered the buff-colored background areas. A mixture of clam disk and white glass beads, attached with thread, are scattered about the design areas.

The baskets in the Kunstkamera collections, as well as this example in Helsinki, appear to be most like the baskets produced during the historic period by both Pomoan and Patwin peoples. The globular form, the grouping of clamshell disk beads at the rim, the decoration of negative areas with a scattering of red woodpecker scalp feathers, and the ornamentation of the black design areas with white glass beads are all features that are common to the basketry of these people—and probably at one time to that of their neighbors, the Wappo.

Feasting Baskets

As previously mentioned, feasting baskets are relatively large baskets in the shape of a truncated cone with flaring sides. They are very beautiful pieces; unfortunately, only four are known to exist: two in Leningrad, a third (collected by Wrangell) in Frankfurt, and one in the Etholen collection in Helsinki.

Figure 8.6. Feasting basket (570-91).

MAE 570-91 (Figure 8.6) is some 18 cm in height and 35 cm in diameter. Traces of red feathering appear on the body of the basket, along with small white glass beads strung on a fine, light thread in the manner described in the previous section in conjunction with MAE 570-79; one bead is sewn on using the coiling material. One hanging thread about 2.5 cm in length suggests that there was a pendant at one time. The material is sedge and bulrush root, with very fine stitches in a diagonal winged pattern. The start is a large knot that protrudes on the outside bottom surface; the sedge is next twined before the coiling begins. The knot nearly disappears on the interior side, showing mostly the twined start. The fag end is concealed, and the moving end is bound under or clipped. Clamshell disk beads, in groups of three, are spaced equidistantly in thirds along the rim. The coil ending is plain.

MAE 570-96 (Figure 8.7) is exceptionally beautiful, with nicely arranged vertical patterns in sedge and bulrush. Scattered red woodpecker scalp feathers once decorated the buff ground, and Olivella shell disk beads were attached by stringing them on the sewing strands. A few pendants of the same shell beads, tipped with abalone shell, further decorate the sides. Equidistant groups of seven clamshell disk beads can be seen just below the rim, attached with native cordage. The rim was overstitched by passing around twice and grouping the previous stitches into pairs.

WKM EO-171, the Wrangell piece, is some 46 cm in diameter and 24 cm in height. Its

Figure 8.7. Feasting basket (570-96).

decoration consists of a series of triangles worked on a spiral, with the addition of red feathering. Clamshell disk beads were placed in three equidistant groups of four about the rim, and white glass beads were sewn on a fine thread that carried along the foundation rods. The white beads appear only on the last four rows prior to the final row at the rim, while the clamshell beads are strung on the last row. Unfortunately, the basket was unavailable for detailed study and photography because it was on exhibit at the Deutsches Leder-und Schuh Museum in Offenbach.

Figure 8.8. Feasting basket (FNM VK-342).

FNM VK-342, the Etholen piece in Helsinki, differs markedly from the others in form; it is hemispherical, rather than conical (Figure 8.8), and is 36.5 cm in diameter and 19 cm in height. The basket, which is documented as having come from the "Rio Sacramento," has a decoration involving a cascade pattern; no traces of feathering exist, and only a single glass bead, attached with the coiling strand, is present.

The catalog notation for this basket states that it was one of six given to the Torku Academy; all were given the number 63, with each individual specimen receiving a separate letter designation. An old Russian tag on the basket identifies it as No. 63 B. Four of the original six baskets in this series are presently missing, while one other cannot be distinguished from other baskets in the collection.

All of these examples—particularly MAE 570-91 and WKM E-171—are similar to Pomoan and Patwin pieces from the recent past. The remaining example (MAE 570-96), however, defies attribution to a particular group. This basket, which is exceptionally beautiful, has vertical design patterns that resemble other central California coastal motifs; that correspondence does not apply, however, to the use of Olivella shell beads on both dark and negative design areas, the overstitching of the rim, or the unique designs worked in Olivella beads on the negative areas. The authors know of no other comparable piece in any collection of California materials in the world. It is possible that this object represents a basketry tradition that is relatively little known—such as that of a tribelet of the Coast Miwok or the Ohlone, or even of the Bay Miwok. Of course, such a suggestion is simply a guess, and we must be content with the overwhelming beauty and artistry of the piece itself, which was created long ago by an unknown California Indian woman.

Gift Baskets

The last category consists of baskets which are smaller in size and have globular, truncated cone, or bowl-shaped forms. Some have feather decorations, and most have bead attachments; a few also have string handles with bead ornamentation. There are 27 examples in collections of Russian origin: 19 of these are in St. Petersburg (four are missing); two each are in Moscow and Frankfurt; three are in Munich; and one is in Helsinki.

MAE 570-92 (Figure 8.9) is an unusual coiled basket 8.2 cm in height and 32.5 cm in diameter. This particular specimen is the only known example out of all of the gift baskets described in this section that was made with the work face on the interior in a leftward coil direction; it is also one of only two baskets produced using a one-rod, rather than a three-rod, foundation. There is an unusual wrapped start or knot, and the rim finish is plain (it is not overstitched in any way). Large (3.5 mm) opaque white glass beads which have been attached with the coiling strands decorate the interior of the basket; in

Figure 8.9. Gift basket (570-92).

Figure 8.10. Gift basket (570-93).

Figure 8.11. Gift basket (WKM E-0173).

addition, this particular basket (unlike other baskets, which have such bead decoration on the inside) lacks any bead attachment to the exterior face. There are many split stitches on the exterior, with a great deal of abrasion to both the exterior and interior bottom. The zigzag pattern, which was done with bulrush root, is unlike any other in the collections. It is reminiscent in some respects of the pattern present on a Pomo basket illustrated by J. W. Hudson (1893:570).

So far as attribution is concerned, 570-92 is as enigmatic as many of the others collected by the Russians. The combination of one-rod coiling and an interior work face is suggestive of any of a number of Patwin groups who are known to have used slightly basin-shaped trays with these constructional features for use in sifting acorn flour. However, the application of decorative glass beads certainly eliminates the possibility that this piece had a utilitarian function, which leads us to surmise that 570-92 may have been a gift version of this type of basket.

MAE 570-93 (Figure 8.10) is 11 cm in diameter and 5 cm in height. Its sole decoration consists of large (3 mm in diameter) white glass beads located just below the rim, and a few white-centered red glass beads (3.5 mm in diameter) that were attached to the basket in the last three rows of coiling by being strung on the sewing strands. Unlike most of the other gift baskets in the collection, 570-93 was produced (as was 570-92) using a one-rod technique. We cannot say whether or not the piece was also originally feathered, but we can state that the features present on this basket make it unique among central California examples.

WKM E-0173 (Figure 8.11), which was collected by Wrangell, is rather cylindrical in form, and is 18 cm in height and 21.2 cm in diameter. The upper half of the basket is decorated with white glass beads which were sewn on, with the beads located on both the linear black design elements and on the buff background. There is a scattering of red woodpecker scalp feathers on the negative design areas, as well as one abalone shell ornament suspended with cordage. The overall appearance of the basket and the large knot-type start lead us to attribute this piece to one of the Pomoan groups.

Figure 8.12. Gift basket (570-95).

MAE 570-95 (Figure 8.12) is a unique basket. It is 15.5 cm in height and 20.5 cm in diameter, and shows no signs of wear. It is somewhat bucket-shaped, and has a black design made from bulrush root; tufts of red woodpecker feathers, Olivella disk beads, and one white glass bead contribute to the decoration. It is interesting to note that the feathering and the vertically arranged Olivella shell bead patterns appear to be separate from the black design motif. There is an oval start that is reminiscent of the Chico Maidu, and the stitches are slightly spaced with sedge used for the background material. The fag ends are concealed; the moving ends are bound under. There is a string handle.

An Etholen basket (FNM VK-203) in Helsinki, 22 cm in diameter and 16.5 cm in height, is similar in form (Figure 8.13). It also has diamond-like shapes, made with Olivella disk beads that were attached with the sewing strand in five equidistant positions about the body. Traces of mallard and woodpecker feathers are present. The bottom of the basket is decorated with two parallel ticked lines, with each of the three groupings equally spaced. We do not know where Etholen collected the piece, but it may well have come from the "Rio Sacramento" area.

MAE 570-95 and FNM VK-203 are similar to each other in form, and were probably collected from the same people. Still another basket of this general form is housed in Oxford (PRM 824); it was collected by Captain Beechey during his 1826 visit to California. However, the Oxford basket is distinct in terms of its design.

Although larger cylindrical baskets are known to have been used in California for such utilitarian purposes as cooking acorn mush by stone boiling, smaller feather and bead decorated baskets of this shape unfortunately are not represented in museum collections.

The next five baskets share certain features which today we would tend to associate with the basketry that the Patwin and Pomoan peoples produced about the turn of the twentieth century. Two of the baskets (SMV 142, 143) were collected by the English rather than by the Russians, and later assembled by Sir Joseph Banks—Banks's California materials stemmed from Vancouver's 1791–1794 voyage and from visits to San Francisco and Monterey (King 1981), and were subsequently obtained from the Banks estate by a Nuremberg zoologist, J. Wagler. These items were later mixed with others, such as those collected by Krusenstern and Langsdorff, during the time of King Ludwig I, when the basis for Munich's collection was established (Müller 1980:21). Since there is thus good reason to believe that both of these baskets came from Ohlone territory (either from San Francisco or from Monterey), we cannot rule out a northern Ohlone origin for the five baskets under discussion. Moreover, some of the motifs on these baskets—for example, the diamond patterns made from Olivella shell beads on a basket shaped like a truncated cone—are also suggestive of Ohlone affinities. Many of these elements, in solid rather than in outlined or reticular forms, will be described later in this section in relationship to Ohlone basketry.

MAE 570-101 (Figure 8.14) is decorated with a reticular arrangement of diamond shapes that were created by attaching Olivella shell disk beads to the basket with the coiling strand. The background field was once covered with red woodpecker scalp feathers. Clam shell disk beads were attached to the rim with cordage, and just below the rim vestiges of quail plumes can still be seen. There is an unusual design in black sewing strands just below the rim consisting of short horizontal lines, and pendant strings composed of glass beads in several colors and ending with abalone shell pendants adorn the exterior. Overall, the basket is 32 cm in diameter and 15 cm in height.

Figure 8.13. Gift basket (FNM VK-203).

Figure 8.14. Gift basket (570-101).

Figure 8.15. Gift basket (SMV 142).

a.

b.

Figure 8.16. Two views (a, b) of gift basket (SMV 143).

SMV 142 (Figure 8.15) is very similar to 570-101. The Munich basket also has a reticular arrangement of diamond shapes done in Olivella shell beads, and has clam disk beads attached to the rim. Traces of red woodpecker scalps can be seen on the body of the basket. Pendants made of strings of Olivella disk beads, terminating with abalone shell pendants, are also present. The basket is 31 cm in diameter and 12.5 cm in height.

SMV 143 (Figure 8.16) is also similar to the baskets just described. It is 31.5 cm in diameter and 13 cm in height. The rim is decorated with clam disk beads, while the body of the basket has a reticular arrangement of Olivella shell disk beads that form a series of diamonds, most of which are partially bisected by a single vertical row of Olivella beads. When viewed from below (Figure 8.16b), the diamonds form the petals of a six-pointed star. Traces of red woodpecker scalps are also present.

MAE 570-102 (Figure 8.17) appears to be a simplified version of these baskets, in that it lacks the elaborate reticular design on the body. The traces of feathering present suggest that the entire basket may have been covered with red woodpecker feathers. The base has one ring of 16 black bulrush and sedge bands. The rim is decorated with clamshell disk beads, and pendant strings are again present; in this case, some of the pendants are composed of strings of Olivella shell disk beads that terminate in nicely-shaped rectangular abalone shell pendants with two perforations. A string knot at the rim indicates that there may have been a cordage handle that is now missing. The basket is 27.5 cm in diameter and 9.5 cm in height.

MAE 570-105 (Figure 8.18) is the last of the five baskets in this series. It is 8.5 cm in height and 19 cm in diameter, and is of exceptional workmanship. A "handle" of cordage,

Figure 8.17. Gift basket (570-102).

Figure 8.18. Gift basket (570-105).

Figure 8.19. Gift basket (570-104).

decorated with a series of knots that anchor glass beads (4 mm in diameter) about 2 cm apart, is present. Two sizes of glass beads also decorate the body of the basket: black and red beads 4 mm in diameter are attached to the body of the basket; smaller white glass beads 2 mm in diameter are strung to form dangles which also terminate in abalone shell pendants. The rim is decorated with clamshell disk beads which are sewn on side by side with native cordage. A black "tick-like" pattern made with bulrush is present on the base of the basket.

MAE 570-104 (Figure 8.19) is 9.5 cm in height and 23 cm in diameter. It is one of two baskets in the collections that are decorated in a heavy spiral pattern using large (4 mm in diameter) white glass beads strung onto the sewing strands, instead of being ornamented with Olivella shell disk beads. In addition, smaller white and white-centered red glass beads (3 mm in diameter) and an abalone

Figure 8.20. Gift basket (SMV 9-48).

Figure 8.21. Gift basket (570-94).

Figure 8.22. Gift basket (570-106).

shell pendant have been strung on cordage to decorate the exterior. The negative design areas on this piece were once covered with red woodpecker scalp feathers.

SMV 91-48 (Figure 8.20), an undocumented basket in the Munich collections that resembles MAE 570-104 (Figure 8.19), is 17 cm in diameter and 7 cm in height. It also has heavy spirally arranged patterns made from large white glass beads, and glass bead pendants. Traces of red woodpecker scalp feathers appear in the negative design areas of the basket. However, this basket differs from MAE 570-104 in that very large white glass beads were used to imitate clamshell beads and form a continuous row just below the rim. This specimen clearly shows that designs previously created with shell beads were later copied with glass ones. The attachment of clamshell disk beads, arranged either singly or in a continuous manner to the rim of a basket with cordage, is a feature that is found on some of the fully feathered baskets that were made by Pomo and Patwin peoples. MAE 570-102, were it not for the Olivella shell beads, would be identical to a plethora of later baskets made by the Pomo in which the early twentieth century use of Olivella beads was supplanted by the use of beads made of clamshell or glass. Baskets MAE 570-101 and -105 are somewhat less similar to most such pieces, although the areas decorated with beads cause them to bear a certain resemblance to some of the Pomo examples collected at Stewart's Point (SC Sheedy Coll. 6242) or in the Sonoma Valley (SC Sheedy Coll. 5947), or to some of the specimens collected from the Patwin at Rumsey (OPM 16-2774). Because the features found on baskets of this kind have a very wide distribution, and because of the possible northern Ohlone connection that we suggested earlier in this section in relationship to baskets SMV 142 and

143, it certainly appears that this is a very old type of basket, and one perhaps associated with the San Francisco Bay region—as is the use of heavy, bold designs formed by glass beads on a red feather background, like those present on MAE 570-104 and SMV 91-48.

Two other baskets, MAE 570-94 and -106, are interesting in that they are characterized by an all-encompassing reticular pattern. MAE 570-94 (Figure 8.21) is a small globular basket 8 cm in height and 15 cm in maximum diameter, with an opening some 9 cm across. It was once fully covered with woodpecker scalp feathers that would have formed a striking contrast to the reticular pattern made from white Olivella disk beads that covered the surface in a series of diamonds. The base of the basket shows some sign of wear. The rim was finished with simple stitching, which was accomplished by stitching over the top rod in the last coil. A few stitches appear to have been "doubled" at the coil ending on the rim, a feature not uncommon in rim finishes of this type.

MAE 570-106 (Figure 8.22) is 11 cm in height and 23 cm in diameter, and has the shape of a truncated cone. Triangular patterns made of Olivella disk beads are arranged in a connecting, reticular design, with a few pendant strands of strung Olivella shell beads arranged like chains and terminating in thin abalone shell bangles. The cordage used for the pendants appears to consist of finely twisted hemp and commercial thread; in one place near the bottom some beads were sewn on with commercial thread using a needle, possibly representing a later repair. Another indication of repair is a small hole in the base of the basket, with four rows missing; several stitches of sedge were added from the coils below to coils above and then stitched horizontally, perhaps to simulate the regular coiled rows. Another possible repair involved one of the pendants; the shell disks were not chained, but were separated by knots. The basket was once fully feathered with acorn woodpecker feathers inserted two stitches apart, and with quail plumes set in every stitch one row below the final row. There are ticks of bulrush on the base, and rather than the sewing strand being cut to add new material, it was "floated" under the bulrush, and the bulrush was run under the sedge.

Both MAE 570-106 and MAE 570-94 appear to represent a "connecting, reticular design" style that was once common in central California's heartland. A basket similar to MAE 570-94, for example, was collected from the Miwok (USM 313,260), although it may have originated among the Plains Miwok or their foothill neighbors.[2] In addition, such reticular patterns, worked out in triangles, appear commonly in Maiduan basketry; they are even present on a documented Plains Miwok basket (UMP 8011), although the triangles on that specimen were done with feathering, rather than with shell beads. It is possible, therefore, that MAE 570-106 and -94 originated among the Plains Miwok, or one of their neighbors.

We now turn our attention to a large number of baskets which we have begun to call "classical forms," in that they share a number of features. They are all heavily decorated with Olivella disk beads, and the vertically arranged patterns consist of solid diamonds and triangles, or simply of triangles appended to a real or imaginary vertical line. These "classical" baskets have the shape of a truncated cone, and most have a continuous series of shell beads—usually made of Olivella shell, although a few are made of clamshell—along the rim. Their striking beauty and fine workmanship certainly set them apart from the rest of the corpus of Ohlone basketry to which they belong.

Figure 8.23. Gift basket (570-97).

MAE 570-97 (Figure 8.23) is an excellent example of the classical form. The beads on this basket, which is 36.5 cm in diameter and 16.5 cm in height, were attached by means of the sewing strands. Native cordage was used to suspend pendant beads and abalone shell pendants, which were probably added during the construction of the basket in order to conceal the string-ends within the foundation bundle. Three kinds of bird feathers were used in covering the background on the exterior surface of the basket: red woodpecker scalp feathers; a dark-colored feathering; and a row of quail topknots that were used around the rim. The attachment of Olivella beads to the rim was done singly with cordage, with the pattern conforming beautifully to the curvature of the basket edge. The vertically placed designs, which consist of triangles attached to vertical lines, are noteworthy.

MAE 570-98 (Figure 8.24), which is another classical basket, is 32 cm in diameter and 14.5 cm in height. The base of this piece is ornamented with black "ticking" that was done with the sewing material. Olivella shell beads, worked into a vertical design layout, decorate the exterior, while the interior has similar beads worked into six chevron-like patterns. The basket appears to have once been feathered, since traces of fine black feathering can be found in the exterior stitching.

MAE 570-99 (Figure 8.25) is a magnificent classical basket, 14.5 cm in height and 30.5 cm in diameter. Although the rim is not beaded, the basket maker devoted a great deal of attention to the Olivella bead design, which begins close to the starting knot on the base of the basket (Figures 8.26a, b). When viewed from below, the pattern appears to consist of a four-pointed star, but when viewed from the side, the pattern is transformed into vertically placed lines with pendant triangles, not unlike the design seen on MAE 570-98. The placement of Olivella shell beads on the interior

Figure 8.24. Gift basket (570-98).

Figure 8.25. Gift basket (570-99).

a.

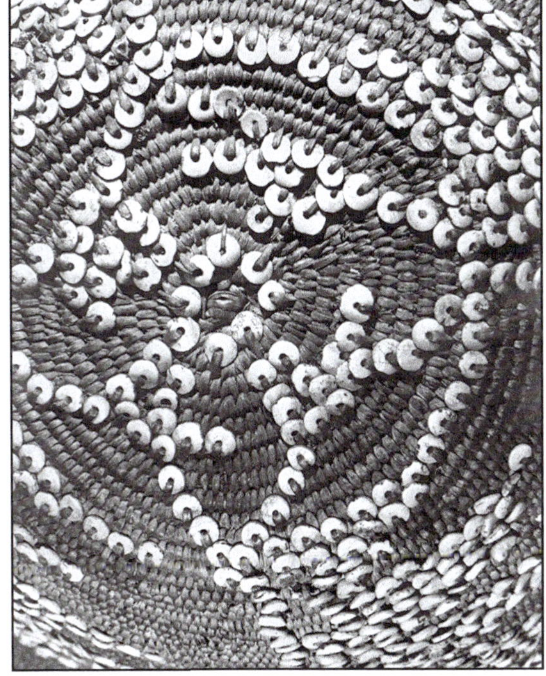

b.

Figure 8.26. Detailed views (a, b) of gift basket (570-99).

of the basket also resembles that present on 570-98, although in this case their placement seems random. There are a few pendant strings with shell beads that appear to have been retied without abalone shell terminations.

MAE 570-100 (Figure 8.27) is 14 cm in height and 28 cm in diameter. The designs on this example consist of vertically arranged columns of rectangles and stacked diamonds and triangles, with a rim finish that is similar to that on the previous two baskets. Curiously, the pendant strands sometimes end in entire Olivella shells, as well as in the more usual abalone shell pendants noted on others. A few Olivella disk beads randomly ornament the interior of this basket. One feature that is unique to this basket is the presence of quail topknot feathers, which protrude from the center holes of the disk beads about the rim. Like the other baskets discussed here, this specimen was once fully feathered.

Figure 8.27. Gift basket (570-100).

Figure 8.28. Gift basket (570-103).

Figure 8.29. Gift basket (4291-13).

MAE 570-103 (Figure 8.28) is 27 cm in diameter and 11 cm in height. Although it is larger than MAE 570-100, it is nearly identical in appearance. The major difference between the two baskets involves the way in which the abalone pendants are suspended; MAE 570-103 employs strings on which the beads are separated by knots, as well as beads that are tied together in a "chained" method, while the clamshell disk beads around the rim are attached singly, as they are on MAE 570-101 and -102. The rim on this piece lacks the overstitching that is found on MAE 570-100; instead, a few small clamshell disk beads with large perforations were attached to the interior surfaces of the basket.

MAE 4291-13 (Figure 8.29) is not included with the Voznesenskii materials; the catalog entry states only that the basket came out of an old collection from another museum and was accessioned into the Kunstkamera in 1931. The basket is 12.5 cm in height and 29 cm in

Figure 8.30. Gift basket (WKM E-0172).

diameter. It has the usual vertically placed decoration consisting of Olivella disk beads strung on the sewing strands. A few strings of Olivella disk beads, separated by knots, suspend abalone shell pendants, while clamshell disk beads are arranged in three groups of four about the rim, with a quail plume projecting from the perforation in the center of each. The interior of the basket is further ornamented with four Olivella disk beads attached by means of the coiling strand. It is uncertain whether or not this piece was once feathered.

WKM EO-172, one of the baskets in Frankfurt that was collected by Wrangell, is 31.4 cm in diameter and about 14.2 cm in height (Figure 8.30). It is decorated with Olivella disk beads, with additional clam shell beads attached singly at even intervals around the rim with cordage. Strings of glass beads suspend pendants made of abalone shell. The piece was once feathered.

Two baskets at Moscow State University are also of classical form; unfortunately, the curator would not permit them to be studied or photographed. Both baskets appeared to be made of sedge, with the direction of coiling to the left. The beaded patterns were created with Olivella disk beads that were affixed to the exterior, with the coiling strands used for attachment. No clamshell disk beads or glass beads were present on either specimen, although they were decorated with abalone shell pendants. Traces of red and black feathering indicate that they were once fully feathered. One basket was about 32 cm in diameter, while the other was slightly smaller.

Four baskets (MAE 570-83, 570-108, 4193-54, and 4291-12) which could not be located in 1983 would probably also fall into the classical category. They were all described by Kojean (1979:8–9) as having the shape of a truncated cone, and he stated that 570-108, 4193-54, and 4291-12 had shell designs. The Kunstkamera records provide no additional information on these baskets in terms of either description or documentation. Kojean's (1979) attribution of three of these baskets to the Pomo was not based upon any solid ethnographic or documentary information; indeed, he seems to have made guesses on the basis of very limited data.

Judging from a single documented specimen (USM 313,234) that was obtained from an old Spanish family in Santa Clara, it appears that a vertical placement of Olivella disk bead design patterns was favored by at least some of the Ohlone peoples. We do not know how widespread this design style was, but it may have extended to the Coast Miwok as well. Although it lacks good documentation, one classical basket (BM 6222) in the British Museum was thought by E. F. Hubby (an ardent basket collector at the turn of the twentieth century) to have been collected by Francis Drake (according to a statement contained in catalog record USM 313,234). While this specimen is otherwise undocumented, there might be a thread of truth behind Hubby's attribution. It is possible that the baskets that we refer to as classical in form represent both Ohlone and Coast Miwok styles—if that is the case, it would explain our inability to recognize Coast Miwok basketry in the Russian collections, since it certainly must be present as a result of all the interaction that took place between the Coast Miwok and the Russians at Bodega Bay.

Figure 8.31. Men gambling with stick dice at Mission San Francisco in 1816 (Choris 1822). *Courtesy of the Honold Library.*

Gaming Bones

A number of different kinds of games were played in native California. Games of chance were particularly popular, although to Indian people the concept of "chance" or "luck" did not exist; in their view, such games involved the opposition of supernatural powers, and the outcome was determined by the interaction of such forces. These games continued to be played in mission times, and a number of historical accounts mention such activities. Choris, for example, witnessed a gambling game during his 1816 visit to Mission San Francisco, and made it the subject of a sketch and a watercolor (Figure 8.31).

One of the most popular games was the "grass" or "hand bone" game, which was widely played throughout California. In the south, it was referred to by the Spanish term *peón*, and (as was true everywhere) it was played during most festivities or large gatherings. Teams of two or more people faced each other a few feet apart; accompanied by a song, one team hid two pairs of bones, with each pair being held by two players. One bone was unmarked and was white in color, while the other was marked with black bands of various sorts. Once hidden, it became the task of the opposing team to guess the hand in which the unmarked bone was being held. If the guessing team missed, then the team hiding the bone scored a point; if the guessing team was correct, it was its turn to hide the bones. Score was kept with counters, which were usually 10, 12, or 16 in number, and one team was declared the winner when it had acquired all of the counters. The counters frequently went back and forth as each team scored; the game could take as

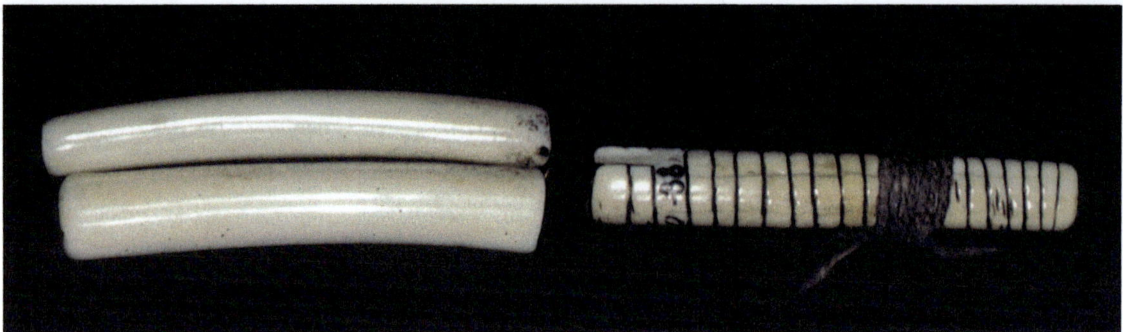

Figure 8.32. Gaming pieces (570-37 and -38).

little as an hour or as many as a dozen hours before it ended.

The Kunstkamera collections contain what seem to be examples (Figure 8.32) of the gaming bones used in the grass game. MAE 570-37 apparently represents only the white, unmarked bones from two pairs of gaming bones. The bones are each 6.2 cm in length, with slightly different diameters (8 mm to 10 mm). They are highly polished, the marrow has been removed, and the ends are nicely rounded. It is difficult to determine the kind of mammal the bones may originally have come from, since the bones of a wide variety of animals, such as deer, bear, mountain lion, and so on, were used by central California peoples. Another difficulty stems from the fact that gambling bones collected from the Maidu, Nomlaki, Patwin, and Miwok peoples are often so similar that identifying pieces made by different groups is impossible.

MAE 570-38 represents one of the marked gaming bones used in the grass game. It is 6.2 cm in length and 1.0 cm in diameter, and has darkened incised lines that circumscribe the shaft. A vegetable fiber wrapping is also present. The original Kunstkamera collection may once have included two such marked bones, in which case MAE 570-37 and -38 could well have comprised a single, complete set of gaming bones.

Chapter 9

Some Comments on Significance

During the first half of the nineteenth century, Russian ships plied California waters in conjunction with greater voyages of discovery, and Fort Ross and Port Rumiantsev became part of a Russian American outpost for sea-mammal hunting, trading, and agricultural activities. At the time, visitors such as Georg von Langsdorff, Dmitrii Zavalishin, Otto von Kotzebue, Vasilii Golovnin, Kiril Khlebnikov, Ferdinand von Wrangell, Ivan Kuprianov, and perhaps a host of others were scarcely aware of the importance of their collecting activities. Il'ia Voznesenskii seems to have been the sole exception to the rule; he deserves the honor of being recognized today as having been California's first systematic ethnographic collector. The efforts of these men—which ranged from sporadic and haphazard to deliberately comprehensive—resulted in the assemblage of not just a rich and varied assortment of tools, utensils, costumes, ornaments, and baskets, but in fact the accumulation of the largest such collection of nineteenth-century California materials in the world, and one which documents a segment of the life of the state's native peoples before American intrusion induced rapid and catastrophic changes.

Some of the objects that the Russians collected are the only examples of their kind still extant. The Kukshui and Mollok cloaks that were collected by Voznesenskii, for example, are unique items that reflect admittedly esoteric religious activities that would be unlikely to be represented in any collection today; however, even once commonplace items (such as the fire-making kit in St. Petersburg) have no known counterparts in American museum holdings. The many varied fancy baskets, feather belts, blankets, hairpins, necklaces, and other treasures in the Russian collections comprise a unique and priceless ethnographic statement about Native California peoples. These objects certainly greatly enrich the limited and incomplete

Treasures from Native California: The Legacy of Russian Exploration, Travis Hudson and Craig D. Bates, Edited by Thomas Blackburn and John R. Johnson, 185–186.

depictions of native life obtained from historical descriptions; they also provide the archaeologist with a glimpse of the many perishable materials which the agencies of time and decay have served to eliminate from the archaeological record. The integrity and complete state of many objects is of further benefit to the archaeologist; for example, the Kunstkamera arrow collection can provide detailed information on types of wood used, feathering techniques and materials, methods of hafting, and so on that greatly amplify and enrich reconstructions that otherwise would depend upon arrow points alone. It is tremendously exciting to have the opportunity to examine objects that are not only complete, but that appear to have been made only yesterday. The brilliantly shining, polished bird-bone ear rods are examples of objects which convey something of the grandeur and beauty of ceremonial regalia in central California; they are a far cry from their archaeological counterparts, which are brown and brittle as a result of their long entombment.

There is also a certain honesty in these collections as well. The face of California changed rapidly after Voznesenskii's departure, particularly after the Gold Rush, and by the time such American ethnographers as Stewart Culin, S. A. Barrett, or J. W. Hudson became active, much of the traditional way of life had passed. Native consultants were commissioned to reproduce the sorts of objects that had been used by their forefathers in "the old days," and some of the results can be considered little more than approximations at best. The attempts of collectors to obtain particular objects had similar results, since native people—in their desire to please as well as profit—often attempted to fabricate objects from intuition or memory.

In light of the various points raised above, the scientific value of the Russian collections seems obvious. However, there is another dimension to these objects that must be emphasized: they are of incalculable humanitarian significance, because they are inextricably linked to the artisans who once made and used them. That realization could be particularly meaningful to the living descendants of the Native Californians who originally traded and exchanged these objects with the Russians. The craftsmanship inherent in a feather belt or in the luxuriant beauty of a feathered and beaded basket is clear and striking evidence of a rich cultural and artistic heritage worthy of respect. Rescuing such objects from relative obscurity will hopefully promote a better appreciation and a deeper understanding of Native California arts; it should also foster a greater sense of pride and self-respect in the Native American community.

Afterword

The Bicentenary and Beyond

Glenn Farris

Fort Ross, the Russian-American Company settlement on the Sonoma coast, has been preserved as a California State Historic Park since its acquisition from the local ranching family of George Washington Call in 1903 by the California Landmarks League, and its subsequent donation to the State of California in 1906 (Sakovich 1998:27). Using this historic location as a focal point, the link to the Russian presence in early nineteenth-century California was maintained, thanks especially to the outreach of former ranger-curator John C. McKenzie, who corresponded widely with scholars in Russia and Alaska, maintaining ties even during the restricted years of the Cold War. Scholarship on this portion of the history of Russian America resulted in international conferences in 1979, 1987, and 2010 (Kidd 2013; Pierce 1990b; Starr 1987), each held in Sitka, Alaska, as well as the Irkutsk Conference on Russian America in 2007 (Afanasieva-Medvedeva et al. 2007); these allowed face-to-face meetings among scholars from several nations, principally Russia, the United States, and Canada. The change in government in the early 1990s that converted the old Soviet Union to the Russian Federation has marked an ever greater period of interest and cooperation between the United States and Russia in the study of this piece of Russian colonial history. In addition to the conferences mentioned above, there have been two notable traveling exhibits, organized by Barbara Sweetland Smith of Anchorage (1990, 2000), that made available some of the remarkable artifacts, drawings, and paintings that Russian visitors used to document the exotic land of California. However, we have not been as fortunate in having artifacts from the Voznesenskii collection brought to California for exhibit.

In conjunction with the celebration of the bicentenary of the founding of Fort Ross

Treasures from Native California: The Legacy of Russian Exploration, Travis Hudson and Craig D. Bates, Edited by Thomas Blackburn and John R. Johnson, 187–189.

(1812–2012), this renewed fascination with the history of the Russians and Alaskans in California reached even greater heights. A conference held in San Francisco in 2011, called "Hidden Stories" and sponsored by the California State Parks Foundation, increased interest in the broader story of Russians in early nineteenth-century California. This renewed focus, in turn, led to the publication of an anthology of various published and unpublished documents (Farris 2012). Most of these documents relate to observations by various Russian and foreign visitors on California life at that time. However, beyond bringing back descriptive stories of the era, there were a number of naturalists who also returned home with material objects of natural and cultural history. In 2012, another international conference on Fort Ross was held in Santa Rosa in April, followed by a roundtable in July featuring Russian and American scholars. At the meeting in April, Sergei Korsun of the Kunstkamera in St. Petersburg highlighted the Voznesenskii materials in his talk (Korsun 2012). This presentation was supplemented by Professor Yuri Chistov, director of the Peter the Great Museum of Anthropology and Ethnography RAS (the Kunstkamera), at the July roundtable (Chistov 2012). Another event in 2012 was particularly poignant when a group of seven Kashaya Pomo made a trip to the Kunstkamera to view the collections. One of the participants, Billyrene Marrufo Pinola (2012), wrote about the event and spoke of how it made the traditional stories passed down by her ancestors more meaningful.

* * *

Several books of documents which have been produced over the years have been of great benefit to people interested in the story of the Russians in California; these have provided wonderful grist for the further study of this piece of California history (Dmytryshyn, Crownhart-Vaughn, and Vaughn 1989; Farris 2012; Gibson et al. n.d.; Istomin, Gibson, and Tishkov 2005, 2012; Khlebnikov 1990; and Mathes 2008). These will soon be supplemented by two additional publications by Professor James Gibson which are due out in 2013 and 2014. These documents add a great deal to our image of not just Fort Ross, but other parts of early California as well, since while many of the visitors spent most of their time in San Francisco Bay or Monterey, they did make occasional trips down to Santa Barbara and even San Diego. Several of the observers were particularly interested in the bows and arrows and the basketry of the California Indians.

Archaeological studies that have added to our knowledge of material culture have been undertaken both at Fort Ross and in Sitka, Alaska. The excavation of the Native Alaskan village at Fort Ross under the direction of Professor Kent Lightfoot of U.C. Berkeley resulted in the discovery of numerous artifacts associated with both the Alaskan native peoples, who were brought down to California to hunt sea mammals, and their native Californian spouses (Lightfoot et al. 1997). Concurrently, Professor Lynne Goldstein, then of the University of Wisconsin-Milwaukee (and now at the University of Michigan), excavated the Fort Ross cemetery (Osborn 1997; Goldstein 2012). In Alaska, David McMahan of Alaska State Parks was in charge of a notable excavation at the site of Castle Hill (McMahan 2002) that turned up many intact artifacts, including some arrow points that could be sourced to California (McMahan 2012). Research was conducted by Francis Riddell (1955) and later by Thomas Wake (2013) on the Farallon Islands, where there was an *artel* or resident group of hunters maintained by the

Russian-American Company to hunt seals and sea lions to provision Fort Ross. Included there were artifacts used by the Native Alaskans who worked for the Russian-American Company on these islands. Most recently, there was an exciting find of a redwood box filled with artifacts discovered on San Nicolas Island off Santa Barbara (Erlandson et al. 2013).

Given the crescendo of research that has developed in recent years on the story of the Russians in California, and on what the documents they produced can tell us to augment the ethnohistory of the California Indians, the time is right to make available the present book on the truly remarkable collections of California Indian artifacts that were taken to Russian and other foreign museums. Among these, the Voznesenskii collection will remain pre-eminent as providing the most extensive sample of the material culture of pre-Gold Rush California Indians, since the bulk of the Voznesenskii collection was obtained directly from Indians who were still living their traditional lifestyle, many of them in the Central Valley of California.

June, 2013

Appendix

Catalog of California Indian Materials in European Museums Collected by the Russians

Museum of Anthropology and Ethnography, St. Petersburg (MAE)

570-	1	Kukshui Cloak
	2	Mollok Cloak
	3	Feather Cape
	4	Topknot Headdress
	5	Headdress
	6	Headdress
	7	Headdress
	8	Headdress
	9	Unfinished Headdress?
	10	Feather Rope
	11	Feather Belt
	12	Feather Belt
	13	Feather Belt
	14	Disk Bead Belt
	15	Flicker Band
	16	Flicker Band[1]
	17	Flicker Band[1]
	18	Flicker Band[1]
	19	Flicker Band[1]
570-	20	Necklace
	21	Necklace
	22	Necklace
	23	Necklace
	24	Necklace
	25	Hairpin[1]
	26	Hairpin[1]
	27	Hairpin[1]
	28	Hairpin[1]
	29	Hairpin[1]
	30	Hairpin
	31	Hairpin[1]
	32	Hairpin[1]
	33	Hairpin[1]
	34	Hairpin[1]
	35	Hairpin
	36	Hairpin
	37	Gaming Bones
	38	Game Bone

Treasures from Native California: The Legacy of Russian Exploration, Travis Hudson and Craig D. Bates, Edited by Thomas Blackburn and John R. Johnson, 191–196.

39	Ear Rod
40	Ear Rod
41	Ear Rod
42	Ear Rod
43	Ear Rod
44	Ear Rod
45	Ear Rod
46	Ear Rod
47	Ear Rod
48	Ear Rod
49	Ear Rod[1]
50	Ear Rod
51	Ear Rod
52	Ear Rod
53	Ear Rod
54	Ear Rod
55	Hairpin
56	Hairpin
57	Hairpin
58	Hairpin
59	Hairpin
60	Whistle[2]
61	Whistle[2]
62	Whistle
63	Whistle
64	Woven Mat[1]
65	Woven Mat[1]
66	Woven Mat[1]
67	Hairnet
68	Hairnet
69	Net Bag
70	Net Bag[1]
71	Unknown[1]
72	Carrying net
73	Carrying net
74	Hair Rope
75	Twined Basket
76	Twined Basket
77	Twined Basket
78	Coiled Basket
79	Coiled Basket
80	Coiled Basket[1]
81	Coiled Basket[1]
82	Coiled Basket[1]
83	Coiled Basket[1]
84	Twined Basket
85	Coiled Basket
86	Sifting Tray
87	Twined Basket
88	Winnowing Tray
89	Winnowing Tray
90	Coiled Basket
91	Coiled Basket
92	Coiled Basket
93	Coiled Basket
94	Coiled Basket
95	Coiled Basket
96	Coiled Basket
97	Coiled Basket
98	Coiled Basket
99	Coiled Basket
100	Coiled Basket
101	Coiled Basket
102	Coiled Basket
103	Coiled Basket
104	Coiled Basket
105	Coiled Basket
106	Coiled Basket
107	Basket[4]
108	Coiled Basket[1]
109	Seedbeater
110	Lidded Basket[3]
111	Lidded Basket[3]
112	Lidded Basket[3]
113	Coiled Basket
114	Model Balsa
115	Firedrill
116	Seed Cake
117	Pestle
118	Ear Rod[1]
119	Ear Rod
120	Gambling Sticks[1]
121	Spanish Spurs[1]
122	Decoy Headdress
123	Decoy Headdress
124	Self Bow

125 Bow[1]
126 Bow[1]
127 Sinew-backed Bow
128 Sinew-backed Bow
129 Sinew-backed Bow
130 Sinew-backed Bow
131 Sinew-backed Bow[1]
132 Sinew-backed Bow
133 Quiver
134 Arrow
135 Arrow
136 Arrow
137 Arrow
138 Arrow
139 Arrow
140 Arrow
141 Arrow
142 Arrow
143 Arrow
144 Arrow
145 Arrow
146 Arrow
147 Arrow
148 Arrow
149 Arrow
150 Arrow
151 Arrow
152 Arrow
153 Arrow
154 Arrow
155 Arrow
156 Arrow
157 Arrow
158 Arrow
159 Arrow
160 Arrow
161 Arrow
162 Arrow
163 Arrow
164 Arrow
165 Arrow
166 Arrow
167 Arrow
168 Arrow
169 Arrow
170 Arrow
171 Arrow[1]
172 Arrow[1]
173 Arrow[1]
174 Arrow[1]
175 Arrow[1]
176 Arrow[1]
177 Arrow[1]
178 Arrow[1]
179 Arrow[1]
180 Arrow[1]
181 Arrow[1]
182 Arrow
183 Arrow
184 Arrow
185 Arrow
186 Arrow
187 Arrow
188 Arrow
189 Arrow
190 Arrow
191 Arrow
192 Arrow
193 Arrow
194 Arrow
195 Arrow
196 Arrow
197 Arrow
198 Arrow
199 Arrow[1]
200 Arrow
201 Arrow
202 Arrow
203 Arrow
204 Arrow
205 Arrow
206 Arrow
207 Arrow
208 Arrow
209 Arrow
210 Arrow

211	Arrow [1]
212	Arrow [1]
213	Arrow [1]
214	Arrow [1]
215	Arrow [1]
216	Arrow [1]
217	Arrow [1]
218	Arrow [1]
219	Arrow [1]
220	Arrow [1]
221	Arrow [1]
222	Arrow [1]
223	Arrow [1]
224	Arrow
225	Arrow [1]
226	Arrow [1]
227	Arrow [1]
228	Arrow [1]
229	Arrow [1]
230	Arrow
231	Arrow
232	Arrow
233	Arrow
234	Arrow
235	Arrow
236	Arrow
237	Arrow
238	Arrow
239	Arrow
240	Arrow
241	Arrow
242	Arrow
243	Arrow
244	Arrow
245	Arrow
246	Arrow
247	Arrow
248	Arrow
249	Arrow
250	Arrow
251	Arrow
252	Arrow
253	Arrow
254	Arrow
255	Arrow
256	Arrow
257	Arrow
258	Arrow
259	Arrow
260	Arrow
261	Arrow
262	Arrow
263	Arrow
264	Arrow
265	Arrow
266	Arrow
267	Arrow
268	Arrow
269	Arrow
270	Arrow
271	Arrow
272	Arrow
273	Arrow
274	Arrow
275	Arrow
276	Arrow
277	Arrow
278	Arrow
279	Arrow
280	Arrow
281	Arrow
282	Arrow
283	Arrow
284	Arrow
285	Arrow
286	Arrow
287	Arrow
288	Arrow
289	Arrow
290	Arrow [1]
291	Arrow
292	Arrow
293	Arrow
294	Arrow [1]
295	Arrow [1]
296	Arrow [1]

2520-8	Feather Blanket [5]
4291-13	Coiled Basket
2520-9	Feather Blanket [5]
4296-6	Coiled Basket
4193-54	Coiled Basket [1]
N/N	Twined Basket
4208-5	Twined Basket [4]
N/N	Feather Belt
4291-12	Coiled Basket [1]
N/N	Mortar [6]
1901-1	Buckskin Skirt
1-1061	Buckskin Skirt

Notes

1. Object missing
2. Object sent to South American collections and missing
3. Object sent to Northwest collections and missing
4. Object probably Asian
5. Object misidentified as Polynesian
6. Object may be part of 570-117

Two objects on exhibit with California materials and not noted above are a Cree Indian necklace, 3266-2, which is worn by a female figure, and her grass skirt, which is a museum replica.

Anthropology Museum, Moscow State University (MSU)

n/n Coiled Basket
n/n Coiled Basket
n/n Ear Rod
n/n Ear Rod
n/n Ear Rod
n/n Feather Band
n/n Arrow
n/n Arrow
n/n Arrow
n/n Arrow
n/n Arrow

Note

No provenience; not permitted to study objects

Weltkulturen Museum, Frankfurt

(Wrangell Collection) (WKM)

E-0168	Feather Belt
E-0169	Topknot Headdress
E-0170	Ear Pendants-2 [1]
E-0171	Coiled Basket [1]
E-0172	Coiled Basket
E-0173	Coiled Basket
E-0174	(open number)
E-0175	Feather Blanket

Note

1. Objects on loan for exhibit, Deutsches Leder-und Schuh Museum, Offenbach

Staatliches Museum Für Völkerkunde, Munich

(Langsdorff-Krusenstern Collection) (SMV)

142	Coiled Basket [1]	213	Abalone Shell Necklace
143	Coiled Basket [1]	368	Flicker Band
183	Rattle [2]	91.48	Coiled Basket [3]
204	Olivella Bead Necklace		

Notes

1. Objects purchased by the museum as part of the "Cook Collection" and were not collected by Langsdorff-Krusenstern
2. Probably from South America, though attributed to California
3. Given to the museum by a private collector; origin of object unknown

Staatliches Museum Für Naturkunde Und Vorgeschichte, Oldenburg (SNO)

335	Feather Belt

National Museum of Finland, Helsinki

(Etholen-Cygnaeus Collections) (FNM) (Etholen)

VK-203	Coiled Basket	VK-341	Coiled Basket
VK-336	Sinew-backed Bow	VK-342	Coiled Basket
VK-337	Sinew-backed Bow	VK-343	Hairpins, 4 [2]
VK-338	Quiver (1)	VK-1033	Flicker Band
VK-339	Arrows, 20 [2]	VK-1036	Feather Belt
VK-340	Arrows, 18 [2] (Cygnaeus)	VK-4911:23	Sinew-backed Bow
VK-4911:38-47	Arrows,10		
VK-4911:77-78	Arrow Foreshafts, 2.		

Notes

1. Wooden-tube quiver probably from Asia
2. One item in group, missing

Estonian History Museum, Tallinn

AM 4168/61 K 1359	Coiled Basket
AM 4330/713 K 2136	Coiled Basket

Notes

Foreword

1. This denotes the sugar pine, not the redwood.

Chapter 1. Introduction

1. The term "New Albion," which originated with Drake, is replaced here with "Russian California," a designation suggested by Shur and Gibson (1973:38) for the settlements at Port Rumiantsev and Fort Ross.
2. During visits to 32 museums in 14 European countries, Hudson located over 7,000 objects from California. Particularly large collections were found in London, Paris, Berlin, Stockholm, Gothenburg, and Copenhagen (Blackburn and Hudson 1990). Although Spain's interest in California would suggest that large collections should be present in that country as well, the Malaspina collection at the Museo Naval in Madrid contains a mere 19 examples, and represents the only presently known California material in Spain.

Chapter 2. Documenting a Collection

1. Our classification (Table 2.1) gives the following figures for St. Petersburg: 186 hunting and gathering items, 64 ritual dress items, 33 religious items, and 17 tools and utensils related to household activities.
2. A pair of Spanish spurs (570-121) has been excluded from this study, although they are also attributed to Voznesenskii's California collecting activities.
3. There seems to be a problem with the 1901 catalog series as well. Christian Feest (personal communication, 1985) noticed that a piece exhibited as an Iroquois man's robe is actually a California woman's buckskin skirt (MAE 1901-1), complete with shell bead and abalone shell decoration, and another skirt was identified in 1998. This brings the actual total of California objects in St. Petersburg to 300, with the likelihood that more will be found in the future.
4. According to a curator at the British Museum (J. C. H. King, personal communication 1983), some of the Kotzebue collection was acquired by their museum in the following way. In 1929, a private collector, H. G. Beasley, sent an agent to Estonia in conjunction with the British Museum. The resulting collection acquired by the two parties was divided, with Beasley taking the larger share. Upon his death in the 1940s,

additional Kotzebue material was given to the museum. But some of the objects listed in Beasley's catalog of the collection are missing, and it is not known whether any of the items had originated in California. Christian Feest (1984), a curator at the Museum für Völkerkunde, Vienna, has located portions of the Beasley collection in many European museums, including those in Cambridge, Edinburgh, Oxford, and Liverpool; it is not known, however, whether most of the objects are from the Pacific or from America.

5. Possibly some of Wrangell's collection went to other museums as well. Wrangell was a member of the Imperial Academy of Sciences while he was a resident in St. Petersburg (Gibson 1969:205); he died in 1870 in Dorpat (=Tartu), the location of a Russian American collection seen by Pinart three years later. His original notes on California Indians were found in Reval (=Tallinn).
6. During World War II, the Nazis placed a very low priority on protecting the ethnographic collections in Frankfurt from Allied bombing. According to Münzel (personal communication, 1983), the collections were saved from certain destruction by a curator who defied regulations and moved the objects to a farm in the countryside. As a result, all of the Wrangell materials survived.
7. The curator of the ethnographic collections from America that are housed in the Finnish National Museum in Helsinki, Pirjo Varjola, contacted Estonian museums for us in 1985 to find out if any California Indian material was known to be in their collections. The response was negative. However, in 1995 Blackburn found two California baskets in the Estonian National Museum in Tallinn, one of which was apparently collected by Moller during Kotzebue's visit to California in the 1820s.

Chapter 3. A Superb Collector Visits California

1. Although in transliteration from Spanish to Russian and then into English the name comes out "Tijos," the individual involved was Fray Lorenzo Quijas of that mission, a priest who had an extensive knowledge of California Indian languages, and who was no stranger to such Russians as Peter Kostromitinov (Geiger 1969:200–203) or Russian Orthodox priest Father Ioann Veniaminov, who visited Mission San Rafael in 1836 (Gibson 1971). It is worth noting that Fr. Quijas also provided a number of native artifacts to the Wilkes Expedition in 1841.
2. In German, Strauch.

Chapter 4. Describing a People

1. According to an account obtained by Fr. Mariano Payeras from two Bodega Bay Indians living at Mission San Rafael, a Russian named Talacani (Timofei Tarakanov) presented gifts to the chiefs of the areas of Bodega Bay and Fort Ross (Farris 1993b).
2. Heizer (1978b:701) noted, however, that the Kashaya were forced into the concession as a result of the fact that the Russians had taken local people hostage as a guarantee of good behavior, and therefore the document did not represent a formal treaty between both peoples. Spencer-Hancock and Pritchard (1981) take exception to this, noting that the Russians made a special effort to avoid mistreating or adversely exploiting the Kashaya.
3. There may have been at least one occasion for disagreement between the Russians and the Pomo people, if a note written by J. W. Hudson (1975:17–18) has any truth to it; he remarked that for a time

the Russians had introduced counterfeit "bead money" into the Pomo economy (Farris 2001).

4. As Vancouver (1984:714, 721) phrased it, "their [the California Indians'] faces [were] ugly, presenting a dull, heavy, and stupid countenance, devoid of sensibility or the least expression; ... [they] appeared to be a compound of stupidity and innocence."
5. A. Kroeber (1925:884–886) noted that while California represents about 5 percent of the land area of the United States, its native population represented between 16 percent and 19 percent of the total for the country! Obviously, a hunting-gathering economy was able to support a high population density in California; a higher density, in fact, than it would have been able to support had the Indians abandoned their lifestyle in favor of horticulture based upon seasonal rainfall or primitive irrigation systems (see Blackburn and Anderson 1993).
6. Pinart (1955:135) thought that these Russian descriptions were erroneously applied to Hawaiian people whom the Russians had also brought to California.
7. Spelling variations are typical, even within a text by one author. The names and spellings given here are the ones most consistently used. Most California Indians, rather than being organized in tribes (a cluster of social groups forming a single entity characterized by a common language, territory, cultural heritage, and sociopolitical structure), were associated with far smaller, more fragmented entities, which anthropologists usually refer to as "tribelets." For additional information on the various indigenous groups in this area, see Millikan 1995 and 2008.
8. The Olamentko were the Coast Miwok, while the term "marginal" could also be translated as "distant" or "remote" (Stephen Watrous, personal communication, 1984).
9. Shur and Gibson (1973) have reviewed a number of Russian manuscripts—most of which are difficult if not impossible for American scholars to acquire—which contain ethnographic data on California Indians; unfortunately, most of these are equally unknown to Soviet scholars. Some examples would include the manuscripts of F. F. Matiushkin and F. P. Lütke, who were with Golovnin during his 1818 visit to California; the manuscripts of M. N. Vasiliev and G. S. Shishmarev, whose ships *Discovery* and *Loyal* wintered in San Francisco, 1820–1821—Vasiliev's notes in particular are of great importance, for Shur and Gibson (1973:44) noted that "perhaps in no other published source for the ethnography of this region are there such detailed descriptions of the life of the Indians of California at the Spanish missions;" and the manuscripts of M. K. Kiukhelbeker [Kukelbaker], whose notes contain information on Mission Indian life (Shur and Gibson 1973:40–44). We might also point out that any of these California visitors might also have contributed to the Kunstkamera collections, as well as to small museums tucked away inside the former USSR which await future "discovery." [Editors' note: Many of these accounts can now be found in James Gibson's *California Through Russian Eyes, 1806–1848* (2013), which was published just as the present book was about to go to press. Some excerpts from it have been incorporated here.]

Chapter 5. Objects of the Quest

1. It is worth noting that two sinew-backed bows (1884.15.21 and 1884.14.22) attributed to "Captain" Belcher with the date 1826 are found in the Pitt-Rivers Museum in Oxford, England (Blackburn and Hudson 1990:129). Although Belcher returned to California in 1837 as the captain of the *H.M.S. Sulphur*, at the time of his 1826 visit he was a lieutenant on the Beechey Expedition aboard the *H.M.S. Blossom* (Farris, Hodgson, and David 2004:45–46).
2. Judging by the large number that were seen by Hudson in old European collections, this type of bow must have been very popular in pre-1850 central California.
3. However, X-ray fluorescence analysis of the obsidian arrow points could be useful in sourcing the materials, although it would not be helpful in identifying ethnic origins. The method is nondestructive, and Russian scholars will hopefully soon begin to use it.
4. For example, Hudson's study (1987) of the 71 arrows collected by George Hewett along the California coast during the Vancouver visits turned up 15 arrows with wooden self points, or about 21 percent.
5. There is a wooden tube container (FNM VK-338) in the Etholen collection in Helsinki that is listed as a "California quiver." It is misidentified and is probably from Southeast Asia.

Chapter 6. Objects of Home and Hearth

1. For a detailed description and extensive discussion of these and all other extant blankets, see McLendon 2001a.

Chapter 7. Interacting with the Supernatural

1. Much of the following discussion of dance is based on conversations with tribal elders from central California over a period of many years: Elsie Allen (Pomo), Henry Azbill (Maidu/Wailaki/Hawaiian), Wallace Burrows (Nomlaki), Ernest Burrows (Nomlaki), Edith Burrows (Patwin), William Franklin (Northern Miwok), Oscar McDaniel (Pomo/Patwin), John Porter (Northern Miwok), Dorothy Stanley (Miwok), Mabel McKay (Patwin/Pomo), Nelson Hopper (Pomo), John Kelly (Central Miwok), Rosalie Bethel (Western Mono), Gene Day (Central Miwok), Mary Cox (Northern Miwok), and Viola Wessel (Northern/Central Miwok).
2. This was Tom Cleanso, who served as a major consultant on the Valley Nisenan for both Kroeber and Merriam.
3. A very old label attributes the piece to the "South Seas," but it is certainly from central California.
4. The constructional details drawn by Okladnikova (1981:55, Fig. 2) are incomplete and inaccurate, with some of the feathers shown going in a completely opposite direction.
5. In Rome, the Borgian, Latteran, Vatican, and Pigorini museums were searched. In Paris, Hudson found an 1880s photograph showing the belt in an exhibit at the Musée de l'Armée, but was unable to locate the object; it was suggested that this belt may have been sent to the Trocadero, which later became the Musée de l'Homme. The three belts at the latter museum, however, seem to have come from other sources: 09.19.54 and -55 were obtained in 1909 from the Musée St. Germain en Laye, which had in turn received them from the Musée de Marine (Louvre)—where Uhle

(1886:15–16) had reported seeing them on exhibit in 1884. Belt 79.9.1 was purchased in 1879 from A.M. Laglaize, and does not match the one shown in the Musée de l'Armée photograph.

6. Many of these belts belonged to governors of Russian America, such as Kuprianov, Wrangell, and Etholen. They may have been given to important Russian officials as special presentation gifts by chiefs or elders. Etholen appears to have had two other belts, which he donated to the Turku Academy in 1825; they were destroyed there in a fire in 1827.
7. Farris (2001) believes that it may have been magnesite beads rather than clamshell beads that the Russians were "counterfeiting."

Chapter 8. Objects for Festive Occasions

1. Since Krusenstern was never in California, the Munich records should note that the object was collected by Langsdorff.
2. This bead-decorated basket (USM 313,260) was acquired as part of the large basket collection assembled by E. F. Hubby. The catalog card for the object has a handwritten notation stating that the basket is very old and rare, and that it is "Mewuk," made in a canyon 25 miles from "Jollon, California." It might be surmised that "Jollon" referred to Jolon, a small town in Monterey County, in Salinan Indian territory. If the canyon mentioned was 25 miles north of Jolon, it would be in southern Ohlone territory, and the reticular patterning would not be too dissimilar to that on the baskets (MAE 570-101, SMV 142, 143) mentioned earlier in this section. However, the "Mewuk" reference and the form of the basket in relationship to others suggest to us that "Jollon" may be an early misreading of a longhand transcription of "Ione," a modern town in Northern Miwok territory, where a number of Plains Miwok people were living at the turn of the twentieth century when Hubby's basket collection was assembled. Therefore, we suggest that the Hubby basket should be attributed to the Plains Miwok, or be considered a trade item between them and their Northern Miwok neighbors.

Bibliography

Note: a number of significant references published since 1985 have been added.

Afanasieva-Medvedeva, G. V., T. A. Kriuchkov, Yu. P. Lykhin, A. K. Nefedieva and V. V. Tikhonov (Compilers)

2007 *Russian America: Materials of Third International Scientific Conference "Russian America"* (Irkutsk, 8–12 August, 2007). Irkutsk, Russia: AEM Talci.

Alekseev, Aleksandr Ivanovic

1977 *Il'ia Gavrilovich Voznesenskii (1816–1871)*. Moscow: Academy of Sciences.

1987 *The Odyssey of a Russian Scientist: I. G. Voznesenskii in Alaska, California and Siberia, 1839–1849*. Translated by Wilma Follette and edited by Richard Pierce. Alaska History Series, No. 30. Kingston, Ontario: Limestone Press.

1990 *The Destiny of Russian America, 1741-1867*. Translated by Marina Ramsay. Alaska History Series, No. 34. Kingston, Ontario: Limestone Press.

Allen, Elsie

1972 *Pomo Basketmaking, A Supreme Art for the Weaver*. Happy Camp, Calif.: Naturegraph.

Anonymous

1970 *The Museum of Anthropology and Ethnography Named After Peter the Great*. Pamphlet (in English). Leningrad.

Bancroft, Hubert H.

1885 *The Works of Hubert Howe Bancroft: California, Vol. II, 1801–1824*. San Francisco: A. L. Bancroft.

Barratt, Glynn

1981 *Russia in Pacific Waters, 1715–1825*. Vancouver: University of British Columbia Press.

Barrett, Samuel A.

1952 Material Aspects of Pomo Culture. *Bulletins of the Public Museum of the City of Milwaukee* 20(1–2). Milwaukee.

Barrett, Samuel A. and Edward W. Gifford

1933 Miwok Material Culture. *Bulletins of the Public Museum of the City of Milwaukee* 2(4):117–376. Milwaukee.

Bates, Craig D.

1978 The Reflexed Sinew-backed Bow of the Sierra Miwok. *San Diego Museum of Man Ethnic Technology Notes* 16. San Diego, Calif.

1983 The California Collection of I. G. Voznesenski. *American Indian Art Magazine* 8(3):36–41, 79.

Bates, Craig D. and Brian Bibby

1983 Collecting Among the Chico Maidu: The Stewart Culin Collection at the Brooklyn Museum. *American Indian Art Magazine* 8(4):46–53.

Bean, Lowell J. and Dorothea Theodoratus

1978 Western Pomo and Northeastern Pomo. In *Handbook of the Indians of North America, Vol. 8: California*, Robert F. Heizer, ed., pp. 289–305. Washington, D.C.: Smithsonian Institution.

Beechey, Frederick W.

1831 *Narrative of a Voyage to the Pacific and Beering's Strait....* 2 Vols. London: Henry Colburn and Richard Bentley.

Belcher, Edward

1843 *Narrative of a Voyage Round the World, 1836–1842....* 2 Vols. London: Henry Colburn.

Bennyhoff, James A.

1977 Ethnogeography of the Plains Miwok. *Center for Archaeological Research Publications* 5. Davis: Center for Archaeological Research at the University of California, Davis.

Blackburn, Thomas

1999 A 'New' Choris Watercolor. *Journal of California and Great Basin Anthropology*, 21 (2):154–157.

Blackburn, Thomas and Kat Anderson

1993 *Before the Wilderness: Environmental Management by Native Californians*. Menlo Park, Calif.: Ballena Press.

Blackburn, Thomas and Travis Hudson

1990 *Time's Flotsam: Overseas Collections of California Indian Material Culture*. Menlo Park, Calif.: Ballena Press.

Blomkvist, E. E.

1972 A Russian Scientific Expedition to California and Alaska, 1839–1849: The Drawings of I. G. Voznesenskii. *Oregon Historical Quarterly* 73 (June):101–170.

Bolkhovitinov, Nikolai N.

1986 *Russia and the United States: An Analytical Survey of Archival Documents and Historical Studies.* Translated and edited by J. Dane Hartgrove. *Soviet Studies in History:* Fall 1986.

Broadbent, Sylvia M.

1972 The Rumsen of Monterey: An Ethnography from Historical Sources. *Contributions of the University of California Archaeological Research Facility* 14:45–93.

Bryant, Edwin

1849 *What I Saw in California: Being the Journal of a Tour....* New York: D. Appleton.

Chamisso, Adelbert von

1986 *A Voyage Around the World with the Romanzov Exploring Expedition in the Years 1815–1818 in the Brig Rurik, Captain Otto von Kotzbue.* Translated and edited by Henry Kratz. Honolulu: University of Hawaii Press.

Chernykh, E. L.

1967 Agriculture of Upper California. *Pacific Historian* 11(1):10–28.

Chever, Edward F.

1870 The Indians of California. *American Naturalist* 4(3):129–148.

Chistov, Yuri

2012 Collections from "Russian America" at the Museum of Anthropology and Ethnography RAS (the Kunstkamera). Paper presented at The American-Russian Roundtable, "Fort Ross as Living History," July 27, 2012, Santa Rosa, Calif.

Choris, Louis

1822 *Voyage pittoresque autour du Monde....* Paris: Firmin Didot.

1913 *San Francisco One Hundred Years Ago.* San Francisco: A. M. Robertson.

Clark, Galen

1904 *Indians of the Yosemite Valley and Vicinity: Their History, Customs and Traditions.* San Francisco: H. S. Crocker.

Clewett, S. E. and Elaine Sundahl

1981 *The Archaeological Investigation of Eagle Court, a Partial Mitigation of Ca-Sha-266, Redding, California.* Ms. on file, Shasta College Archaelogical Laboratory, Redding, Calif.

Coe, Ralph

1976 *Sacred Circles: Two Thousand Years of North American Indian Art.* London: Arts Council of Great Britain.

Cook, Sherburne F.

1976 *The Conflict between the California Indian and White Civilization.* Berkeley: University of California Press.

Culin, Stewart

1908 Report of the Museum Expedition. Unpublished Manuscript, Brooklyn Museum, New York.

Cutter, Donald

1977 Malaspina's Grand Expedition. In *The Malaspina Expedition: "In the Pursuit of Knowledge....,"* Richard Polese, ed., pp. 28–41. Santa Fe: Museum of New Mexico Press.

Davis, James

1960 The Archaeology of the Fernandez Site, A San Francisco Bay Region Shellmound. Papers on California Archaeology 74 and 75. *Reports of the University of California Archaeological Survey 49:11–52.* Berkeley, Calif.

Davis, James,and Adan E. Treganza

1959 The Patterson Mound: A Comparative Analysis of the Archaeology of Site Ala-328. *Reports of the University of California Archaeological Survey* 47.

Davydov, Yu. V.

1956 *V moryakh i stranstviyakh.* Moscow: Nauka.

Dixon, Roland B.

1903 Sierra Miwok Field Notes. Unpublished ms. on file at the Bancroft Library, University of California, Berkeley.

1905 The Northern Maidu. *American Museum of Natural History Bulletins* 17(3):119–346.

1907 The Shasta. *American Museum of Natural History Bulletins* 17(5):381–498.

Dmytryshyn, Basil and E. A. P. Crownhart-Vaughan

1976 *Colonial Russian America: Kyrill T. Khlebnikov's Reports, 1817–1832.* Portland: Oregon Historical Society.

Dmytryshyn, Basil, E. A. P. Crownhart-Vaughn, and Thomas Vaughn

1989 *The Russian American Colonies, 1789–1867: A Documentary Record.* Portland: Oregon Historical Society.

Dridzo, A. D., and R. V. Kinzhalov

1994 *Russkaia Amerika: po lichnym vpechtleniam missionerov, zemleprokhodzev, moriakov, issledovatelei i drugikh ochevidzev.* [*Russian Amerika: Based on personal impressions of missionaries, pioneers, sailors, explorers, and other observers.*] Moscow: Mysl'.

Driver, Harold E.

1936 Wappo Ethnography. *University of California Publications in American Archaeology and Ethnology* 36(3):179–220.

DuFour, Clarence

1933 The Russian Withdrawal from California. *California Historical Society Quarterly* 12(3):240–276.

DuHaut-Cilly, Auguste Bernard

1946 *A Visit to the Russians in 1828.* Bohemian Grove, Calif.: Silverado.

1997 *A Voyage to California, the Sandwich Islands and Around the World in the Years 1826–1829.* Translated and edited by August Frugé and Neal Harlow. Berkeley: University of California Press.

Dzeniskevich, G. I., and L. P. Pavlinskaia

1988 Treasures by the Neva: The Russian Collections. In W. W. Fitzhugh and Alan Crowell, *Crossroads of Continents, Cultures of Siberia and Alaska*, pp. 83–88. Washington, D.C.: Smithsonian Institution.

Efimov, A.V. and S.A. Tokarev (eds.)

1959 Plemena Kalifornii i Bol'shogo Basseina [Tribes of California and the Great Basin]. In *Narodi Ameriki*, pp. 266–283. Moscow: Institute of the Academy of Sciences of the USSR.

Erlandson, Jon M., Lisa Thomas-Barnett, René L. Vellanoweth, Steven J. Schwartz, and Daniel R. Muhs

2013 From the Island of the Blue Dolphins: A Unique Nineteenth-Century Cache Feature From San Nicolas Island, California. *Journal of Island and Coastal Archaeology*, 8:66–78.

Essene, Frank

1942 Culture Element Distributions: XXI: Round Valley. *University of California Anthropological Records* 8:1–97.

Essig, E. 0.

1933 The Russian Settlement at Ross. *California Historical Society Quarterly* 2(3):191–216.

Farris, Glenn

1993a Visit of the Russian Warship Apollo to California in 1822–1823. *Southern California Quarterly* 75(1):1–13.

1993b Talacani, the Man Who Purchased Fort Ross. *Fort Ross Interpretive Association Newsletter* September/October 1993, unnumbered pages (7–9).

1998 The Bodega Miwok as Seen by Mikhail Tikhonovich Tikhanov in 1818. *Journal of California and Great Basin Anthropology* 20 (1):2–12.

2001 Russian Counterfeit Wampum: Pomo Quality Control. *Society for California Archaeology Newsletter* 35(2):30–31.

2012 *So Far From Home: Russians in Early 19th Century California.* Berkeley, Calif.: Heyday Books.

2013 Kirill Khlebnikov's California Correspondents, 1823–1833. In *Over the Near Horizon: Proceedings of the 2010 International Conference on Russian America*, pp. 19–25. Sitka, Alaska: Sitka Historical Society.

Farris, Glenn J., Maurice Hodgson, and Andrew David (eds.)

2004 The California Journal of Lt. Edward Belcher aboard H.M.S. *Blossom* in 1826 and 1827. Edited by Glenn Farris, Maurice Hodgson and Andrew David. Annotated by Glenn Farris. Journal of the California Mission Studies Association *Boletín* 21(1):45–67.

Fedorova, Svetlana G.

1973 *The Russian Population in Alaska and California, Late 18th Century-1867.* Materials for the Study of Alaska History No.4. Kingston, Ontario: Limestone Press.

Feest, Christian

1984 Review of *Pleasing the Spirits. American Indian Art Magazine* 9(2):69, 71–72.

Fletcher, Francis

1947 The World Encompassed by Sir Francis Drake. Extract from Francis Drake and the California Indians, 1579. Robert F. Heizer, ed., Appendix II, pp.283–292. *University of California Publications in American Archaeology and Ethnology* 42(3):251–302.

Fuentes, Louise Newcomb

n.d. Recording of an interview in the 1960s. Ms. on file, Tuolumne County Historical Society, Sonora, Calif.

Galbraith, Edith

1924 Malaspina's Voyage Around the World. *California Historical Society Quarterly* 3(3): 215–237.

Galvan, John (ed.)

1971 *The First Spanish Entry into San Francisco Bay, 1775: the Original Narrative Hitherto Unpublished by Fr. Vicente Maria and Further Details by Participants in the First Explorations of the Bay's Waters.* San Francisco: John Howell Books.

Gebhardt, Charles L.

1958 Sutter's Fort: A Study in Historical Archaeology with Emphasis on Stratigraphy. Ms. on file, State of California, Department of Parks and Recreation, Sacramento.

Geiger, Maynard

1969 *Franciscan Missionaries in Hispanic California, 1769–1848.* San Marino, Calif.: The Huntington Library.

Geiger, Maynard, and Clement Meighan

1976 *As the Padres Saw Them: California Indian Life and Customs as Reported by the Franciscan Missionaries, 1813–1815.* Santa Barbara, Calif.: Santa Barbara Mission Archive Library.

Gibson, James R.

1968 Two New Chernykh Letters. *Pacific Historian* 12(3):48–56 and 12(4):54–60.

1969 Russia in California, 1833: Report of Governor Wrangel. *Pacific Northwest Quarterly* 60(4):205–215.

1971 A Russian Orthodox Priest in a Mexican Catholic Parish: Father Ioann Veniaminov's Sojourn at Fort Ross and Visit to Missions San Rafael, San José, Santa Clara, and San Francisco in 1836. *Pacific Historian* 15(2):57–66.

1972 Russian America in 1833: The Survey of Kirill Khlebnikov. *Pacific Northwest Quarterly* 63(1):1–13.

1973 California in 1824 by Dmitry Zavalishin. *Southern California Quarterly* 55(4):369–412.

1978 European Dependence upon American Natives: The Case of Russian America. *Ethnohistory* 25(4):359-385.

2013 *California Through Russian Eyes, 1806–1848*. Norman: Arthur H. Clark.

Gibson, James R., Katherine L. Arndt, Glenn J. Farris, Alexei Istomin, John Middleton, Alexander Petrov, and Lyn Kalani (eds.)

n.d *Imperial Russia Encounters Colonial California: Impressions and Interactions, 1806–1841*. Documents from Russian Archives, A National Endowment for the Humanities & Fort Ross Interpretive Association Collaborative Research Project. Unpublished Manuscript, Fort Ross SHP Archives. [See Gibson 2013 above.]

Gifford, Edward Winslow

1917a Miwok Myths. *University of California Publications in American Archaeology and Ethnology* 12(8):283–338.

1917b Northern and Central Sierra Miwok Field Notes. Manuscript 203, University Archives, Bancroft Library, University of California, Berkeley.

1947 California Shell Artifacts. *University of California Anthropological Records* 9(1):1–114.

1955 Central Miwok Ceremonies. *University of California Anthropological Records* 14(4):261–318.

Gil'zen, K.K.

1916 *Il'ia Gavrilovich Voznesen'skii: K stoletiiu dnia ego rozhdeniia (1816-1871)* [*Il'ia Gavrilovich Voznesenskii: At the Centennial of his Birth*]. St. Petersburg: Academy of Sciences. [*Museum of Anthropology and Ethnography* 3:1–14.]

Glover, Winifred

1978 *The Land of the Brave: The North American Indian Collection in Ulster Museum, Belfast*. Belfast: Blackstaff Press.

Goddard, Pliny E.

1903 Life and Culture of the Hupa. *University of California Publications in American Archaeology and Ethnology* 1(1):1–88.

Goldstein, Lynne

2012 Fort Ross Cemetery: How was it Located, What did we find, and What does it all Mean? Paper presented at the Fort Ross Conference, Santa Rosa, California, April 24, 2012.

Golovnin, Vasilii M.

1864 *Sochineniia i perevody*. St. Petersburg: V tip. Morskago Ministerstva.

1979 *Around the World on the Kamchatka, 1817–1819*. Translated by Ella L. Wiswell. Honolulu: The Hawaiian Historical Society and the University of Hawaii Press.

Grinnell, Joseph and Alden H. Miller

1944 *The Distribution of the Birds of California*. Berkeley, Calif.: Pacific Coast Avifauna 27.

Gunther, Erna

1972 *Indian Life on the Northwest Coast of North America.* Chicago: The University of Chicago Press.

Harrington, John P.

1942 Culture Element Distributions, XIX: Central California Coast. *University of California Anthropological Records* 7(1):1–46.

Heizer, Robert F.

n.d. Notes on the Ethnographic and Archaeological Collections of León de Cessac in the Musée de l'Homme, Paris. Ms. on file, Santa Barbara Museum of Natural History.

1951 Indians of the San Francisco Bay Area. In *Geologic Guidebook of the San Francisco Bay Counties, History, Landscape....* Sacramento, Calif.: *Department of Natural Resources Bulletin* 154:39–56.

1952 California Indian Linguistic Records: The Mission Indian Vocabularies of Alphonse Pinart. *University of California Anthropological Records* 15(1):1–84.

1953 The Archaeology of the Napa Region. *University of California Anthropological Records* 12(6):225–358.

1968 One of the Oldest Known California Indian Baskets. *The Masterkey* 42(2):70–74.

1974 *The Costanoan Indians.* Cupertino, Calif.: De Anza College, California History Center, Local History Studies 18.

1978a History of Research. In *Handbook of the Indians of North America, Vol. 8: California*, Robert F. Heizer, ed., pp. 6–15. Washington, D.C.: Smithsonian Institution.

1978b Treaties. In *Handbook of the Indians of North America, Vol. 8: California*, Robert F. Heizer, ed., pp. 701–704. Washington, D.C.: Smithsonian Institution.

Heizer, Robert F. and Albert B. Elsasser

1953 Some Archaeological Sites and Cultures of the Central Sierra Nevada. *University of California Archaeological Survey Reports* 21:1–42.

Hodge, Frederick W.

1905 *Handbook of American Indians North of Mexico.* 2 Vols. Bureau of American Ethnology Bulletin 30.

Hudson, John W.

n.d.a. Unpublished Field Notes, ca.1899–1902. Ms. on file, Department of Anthropology, Field Museum of Natural History, Chicago.

n.d.b. Word List of Central Californian Languages. Unpublished ms. on file, Department of Anthropology, Field Museum of Natural History, Chicago.

1893 Pomo Basket Makers. *Overland Monthly* 21:561–578.

1899 Letter to Dr. G. A. Dorsey, November 27, 1899, on file, Department of Anthropology, Field Museum of Natural History, Chicago.

1975 Pomo Wampum Makers. In *Seven Early Accounts of the Pomo Indians and Their Culture*, Robert F. Heizer, ed., pp. 9–20. Berkeley: University of California Archaeological Research Facility.

Hudson, Travis

1974 Chumash Archery Equipment. *San Diego Museum of Man Ethnic Technology Notes* 13.

1983a The Kunstkammer's Chumash Baskets. *Santa Barbara Museum of Natural History Bulletins* 66.

1983b Chumash Baskets in Russia. *The Masterkey* 57(3):94–100.

1984 Early Russian-Collected Ethnographic Objects in European Museums. *American Indian Art Magazine* 9(4):30–37.

1987 Hewett's California Arrows. In *Coast, Plains and Deserts*, Sylvia Gaines, ed., pp. 107–116. Tucson: Arizona State University.

Hudson, Travis, and Thomas Blackburn

1982 *The Material Culture of the Chumash Interaction Sphere: Vol.I: Food Procurement and Transportation.* Ballena Press Anthropological Papers No. 25. Los Altos, Calif.: Ballena Press.

1983 *The Material Culture of the Chumash Interaction Sphere: Vol. II: Food Preparation and Shelter.* Ballena Press Anthropological Papers No. 27. Los Altos, Calif.: Ballena Press.

1985 *The Material Culture of the Chumash Interaction Sphere: Vol. III: Clothing, Ornamentation and Grooming.* Ballena Press Anthropological Papers No. 28. Menlo Park, Calif.: Ballena Press.

1986 *The Material Culture of the Chumash Interaction Sphere: Vol. IV: Ceremonial Paraphernalia, Games, and Amusements.* Ballena Press Anthropological Papers No. 30. Menlo Park, Calif.: Ballena Press.

1987 *The Material Culture of the Chumash Interaction Sphere: Vol. V: Manufacturing Processes, Metrology, and Trade.* Ballena Press Anthropological Papers No. 31. Menlo Park, Calif.: Ballena Press.

Iglesias, Mercedes Palau de

1980 *Catálogo de los Dibujos aguadas y acuarelas de la Expedición Malaspina.* Madrid: Museo de America.

Istomin, Alexei A., James R. Gibson, and Valery A. Tishkov

2005 *Russia in California: Russian Documents on Fort Ross and Russian-Californian Relations in 1803–1850, Vol. 1.* Moscow: Nauka

2012 *Russia in California: Russian Documents on Fort Ross and Russian-Californian Relations in 1803–1850, Vol. 2.* Moscow: Nauka.

Ivanshintsov, N. A.

1980 *Russian Round-the-World Voyages, 1803–1849, with a Summary of the Voyages to 1867.* Translated by Glynn Barratt and edited by Richard Pierce. Kingston, Ontario: Limestone Press.

Jackson, Thomas L.

1974 San Jose Village, A Northern Marin County Site: A Preliminary Report on 1972 Excavations. *Miwok Archaeological Preserve of Marin Papers 1.*

Johnson, Jerald J.

1967 The Archaeology of the Camanche Reservoir Locality, California. *Sacramento Anthropological Society Papers* 6.

Johnson, Patti J.

1978 Patwin. In *Handbook of the Indians of North America, Vol. 8: California,* Robert F. Heizer, ed., pp. 350–360. Washington D.C.: Smithsonian Institution.

Kaeppler, Adrienne

1983 A Further Note on the Cook Voyage Collection in Leningrad. *The Journal of the Polynesian Society* 92(1):93–98.

Kelly, Isabel

n.d. Coast Miwok Field Notes. Ms. on file, Bancroft Library, University of California, Berkeley.

1978 Coast Miwok. In *Handbook of the Indians of North America, Vol. 8: California*, Robert F. Heizer, ed., pp. 414–425. Washington, D.C.: Smithsonian Institution.

Khlebnikov, Kiril (Kyrill) T.

1940 Memoirs of California. *Pacific Historical Review* 9(3):307–336.

1976 *Colonial Russian America: Kyrill T. Khlebnikov's Reports,1817–1832.* Translated with introduction and notes by Basil Dmytryshyn and E.A.P. Crownhart-Vaughn. Portland: Oregon Historical Society.

1990 *The Khlebnikov Archive: Unpublished Journal (1800–1837) and Travel Notes (1820, 1822, and 1824).* Edited with introduction by Leonid Shur; translated by John Bisk. Fairbanks: University of Alaska Press.

Kidd, John Dusty (General Editor)

2013 *Over the Near Horizon: Proceedings of the 2010 International Conference on Russian America.* Sitka, Alaska: Sitka Historical Society.

King, J.C.H.

1981 *Artificial Curiosities from the Northwest Coast of America.* London: British Museum.

Kojean, P. M.

1979 Woven Vessels of the California Indians. *Akademiia Nauk SSSR, Sbornik Muzeia Antropologii i Etnografii* 24:124–139. Translated by Wilma Follett in *Miwok Archaeological Preserve of Marin Papers 4.*

Komissarov, B. N.

1964 Dnevnik putesheshtviya F. P. Litke na shlyupa "Kamchatka" v 1817–1819 gg. *Izvestiya Vsesoyuznovo geograficheskovo obshchestva* 97:414–419.

Korsun, Sergei

2012 "Native American Artifacts in the Russian Federation Collection." Paper presented at the Fort Ross 2012 Bicentennial Conference, Santa Rosa, Calif., April 25, 2012.

Kostromitinov (Kostromotinov), Peter (Pyotr)

1839 Bemerkungen ueber die Indianer in Ober-Kalifornien, von Kostromitinow. In *Statistische und ethnographische Nachrichten ueber die Russische Besitzungen an der Nordwestkueste von Amerika*, K. E. von Baer, ed., pp. 80–96. St. Petersburg: Imperial Academy of Sciences.

1974 Notes on the Indians in Upper California, ed. by Robert F. Heizer, pp. 7–20. *Contributions of the University of California Archaeological Research Facility.*

1980 Observations on the Indians of Upper California. In *Russian America: Statistical and Ethnographic Information, by Rear Admiral Ferdinand Petrovich Wrangell with Additional Material by Karl-Ernst Baer, pp. 41–49.* Translated from the German edition of 1839 by Mary Sadouoski. Edited by Richard A. Pierce. Kingston, Ontario.: Limestone Press.

Kotzebue, Otto von

1830 *A new voyage round the world, in the years 1823, 24, 25, and 26*. London: H. Colburn and R. Bentley.

1948 *Puteshestviia vokrug sveta*. Moscow: Gos. izd-vo geogr. lit-ry.

Kroeber, Alfred L.

1925 *Handbook of the Indians of California*. Bureau of American Ethnology Bulletins 78.

1929 The Valley Nisenan. *University of California Publications in American Archaeology and Ethnology* 24(4):253–290.

1932 The Patwin and Their Neighbors. *University of California Publications in American Archaeology and Ethnology* 29(4):253–423.

Kroeber, Theodora

1961 *Ishi in Two Worlds: A Biography of the Last Wild Indian in North America*. Berkeley: University of California Press.

Kroeber, Theodora and Robert F. Heizer

1968 *Almost Ancestors: The First Californians*. San Francisco: Sierra Club.

Kroeber, Theodora, Albert B. Elsasser, and Robert F. Heizer

1977 *Drawn From Life: California Indians in Pen and Brush*. Ramona, Calif.: Ballena Press.

Langsdorff, Georg H. von

1814 *Voyages and Travels in Various Parts of the World, During the Years 1803, 1804, 1805, 1806, and 1807.* Vol. 2. London: Henry Colburn.

Laplace, Cyrille Pierre-Theodore

2006 *Visit of Cyrille Pierre-Theodore Laplace to Fort Ross and Bodega Bay in August 1839.* Translated and annotated by Glenn Farris. Jenner, Calif.: Fort Ross Interpretive Association.

Latta, Frank F.

1977 *Handbook of Yokuts Indians.* Second edition. Santa Cruz, Calif.: Bear State Books.

Lazarev, Alexsei P.

1950 *Zapiski o plavanii voyennovo shlyupa "Blagonamerennovo"....* Moscow: Geografiz.

Lazarev, Andrei P.

1832 *Plavanie vokrug sveta na shliupe "Ladoga" v. 1822....* St. Petersburg: Morskaya Tipografiya.

Liapunova, Roza G.

1967 Ekspeditsiia I. G. Voznesenskogo i ee znachenia dlia etnografii Russskoi Ameriki [I. G. Voznesenskii's Expedition and Its Significance for the Ethnography of Russian America]. *Akademiia Nauk SSSR, Sbornik Muzeia Antropologii i Etnografii* 24:5–33.

Lightfoot, Kent G., Ann M. Schiff, and Thomas A. Wake (eds.)

1997 The Native Alaskan Neighborhood: A Multiethnic Community at Colony Ross. Vol. 2 of *The Archaeology and Ethnohistory of Fort Ross, California. Contributions of the University of California Archaeological Research Facility* 55. Berkeley, Calif.

Lipshits, B. A.

1950 Etnograficheskie materialy po severo-zapadnoi Amerike v arkhive I. G. Voznesenskogo [Materials on the Ethnography of Northwestern America in the Archives of Il'ya G. Voznesenkii]. *Izvestiia Geograficheskogo Obshchestva SSSR* 82(4):415–420.

Loeb, Edwin M.

1926 Pomo Folkways. *University of California Publications in American Archaeology and Ethnology* 9(2):149–404.

1933 The Eastern Kuksu Cult. *University of California Publications in American Archaeology and Ethnology* 33(2):139–232.

Mahr, August C.

1932 *The Visit of the "Rurik" to San Francisco in 1816.* Palo Alto, Calif.: Stanford University Press.

Markoff, Alexander

1955 *The Russians on the Pacific Ocean.* Los Angeles: Glen Dawson.

Mason, Otis T.

1889 The Ray Collection from the Hupa Reservation. *Annual Report of the Smithsonian Institution for 1886*, Pt. 1, pp. 205–239.

Mathes, W. Michael

2008 *The Russian-Mexican Frontier: Mexican Documents Regarding the Russian Establishments in California, 1808–1842.* Transcription, translation, and annotation by W. Michael Mathes with the assistance of Glenn Farris. Jenner, Calif.: Fort Ross Interpretive Association.

Mazour, Anatole G., translation and introduction

1940 Memoirs of California by K. T. Khlebnikov. *Pacific Historical Review* 9(3):307–336.

McKern, W. C.

1922 Functional Families of the Patwin. *University of California Publications in American Archaeology and Ethnology* 13(7):235–258.

McLendon, Sally

1977 Ethnographic and Historical Sketch of the Eastern Pomo and their Neighbors, the Southeastern Pomo. *Contributions of the University of California Archaeological Research Facility* 37.

2001a California Feather Blankets: Objects of Wealth and Status in Two Nineteenth-Century Worlds. In *Studies in American Indian Art: A Memorial Tribute to Norman Feder*, Christian F. Feest, ed., pp. 132–161. Seattle: University of Washington Press.

2001b Les ceintures de plumes californiennes dans les collections françaises. *Gradhiva* 29:77–85.

McLendon, Sally, and Robert Oswalt

1978 Pomo: Introduction. In *Handbook of the Indians of North America, Volume 8: California*, Robert F. Heizer, ed., pp. 274–288. Washington, D.C.: Smithsonian Institution.

McMahan, J. David (ed.)

2002 Archaeological Data Recovery at Baranof Castle State Historic Site, Sitka, Alaska: Final Report of Investigations (ADOT & PF Project NO. 71817/TEA-00003[43]). J. David McMahan, ed., with contributions by Daniel Thompson, Margan Grover, Renee Petruzelli, Timothy (Ty) Dilliplane, and Michael W. Strunk. *Office of History and Archaeology Reports* 84. Anchorage: Division of Parks and Outdoor Recreation.

2012 Science for the Public: Collaborative Investigations and Cultural Events in Alaska and Siberia under the IASRA Umbrella. Paper presented at the Fort Ross 2012 Bicentennial Conference. Santa Rosa, Calif., April 26, 2012.

Meighan, Clement W.

1953 Preliminary Excavation at the Thomas Site, Marin County. Papers on California Archaeology 19. *Reports of the University of California Archaeological Survey* 19.

Merriam, C. Hart

1955 *Studies of California Indians*. Berkeley: University of California Press.

1967 Ethnographic Notes on California Indian Tribes. Robert F. Heizer, ed., Part III. *University of California Archaeological Survey Reports* 68.

Miller, Virginia P.

1978 Yuki, Huchnom, and Coast Yuki. In *Handbook of the Indians of North America, Volume 8: California*, Robert F. Heizer, ed., pp. 249–255. Washington, D.C.: Smithsonian Institution.

Milliken, Randall

1995 *A Time of Little Choice: The Disintegration of Tribal Culture in the San Francisco Bay Area, 1769–1818*. Menlo Park, Calif.: Ballena Press.

2008 *Native Americans at Mission San Jose*. Banning, Calif.: Malki-Ballena Press.

2010 *Contact-Period Native California Community Distribution Model: A Dynamic Digital Atlas and Wiki Encyclopedia. Volume 1: Introduction*. Report submitted to the California Department of Transportation, District 5, San Luis Obispo, California.

Moratto, Michael

1976 *New Melones Archaeological Project, Stanislaus River, Calaveras and Tuolumne Counties, California, Phase VI, Part 2: Ethnography and Ethnohistory*. San Francisco: San Francisco State University.

Moratto, Michael, Lynn M. Riley, and Steven C. Wilson (eds.)

1974 Shelter Hill: Archaeological Investigations at Mrn-14, Mill Valley, California. San Francisco State University, *Treganza Anthropology Museum Papers* 15, Miwok Archaeological Preserve of Marin Papers 2.

Morgan, Dale and George Hammond

1963 *A Guide to the Manuscript Collections of the Bancroft Library: Volume I*. Berkeley: University of California Press.

Mornin, Edward

2002 *Through Alien Eyes: The Visit of the Russian Ship* Rurik *to San Francisco in 1816 and the Men behind the Visit*. Oxford: Peter Lang.

Müller, Claudius C.

1980 400 Jahre Sammeln und Reisen der Wittelsbacher. In *400 Jahre Sammeln und Reisen Aussereuropäische Kulturen*, pp. 11–33. Munich, Germany: Hirmer Verlag.

Nordenskiöld, A. E.

1881 *The Voyage of the* Vega *Round Asia and Europe; with a Historical Review of Journeys Along the North Coast of the Old World*. London: Macmillan.

O'Brien, Bickford (ed.)

1980 *Fort Ross: Indians, Russians, Americans*. Jenner, Calif.: Fort Ross Interpretive Association.

Okladnikova, Elena A.

1981 Kaliforniiskaia kollektsiia I. G. Voznesenskogo i problema drevnikh kul'turnykh sviazei Azii i Ameriki [The California Collection of I. G. Voznesenskii and the Problem of Ancient Cultural Connections between Asia and America]. *Akademiia Nauk SSSR, Muzeia Antropologii i Etnografii* 37:54–66. Translated by M. W. Kostruba, *The Journal of California and Great Basin Anthropology (1983)*, 5(1 & 2):224–236.

1984 Kaliforniiskaia Kollektsiia I. G. Voznesenskogo v MAE [The California Collection of I. G.Voznesenskii at the Museum of Anthropology and Ethnography in Leningrad]. *Sovetskaia Etnografiia*, 4:92–102.

Osborn, Sannie Kenton

1997 *Death in the Daily Life of Colony Ross*. Ph.D. dissertation, University of Wisconsin-Milwaukee.

Palumbo, Patti Jo.

1967 The Archaeology of Amador-23. *Sacramento Anthropological Society Papers* 6.

Parmenter, Ross

1966 *Explorer, Linguist and Ethnologist*. Los Angeles: Southwest Museum.

Pérouse, Jean F. G. de la

1798 *The Voyage of* La Pérouse *Round the World in the Years 1785, 1786, 1787, and 1788*. London: John Stockdale.

Petrov, Viktor P.

1977 *Fort Ross i ego Kul'turnoe nasledstvo (Fort Ross and its Cultural Heritage)*. Los Angeles: Friends of Fort Ross.

Phelps, William Dane

1983 *Alta California 1840–1842. The Journal and Observations of William Dane Phelps, Master of the Ship "Alert."* Introduced and edited by Briton Cooper Busch. Glendale, Calif.: Arthur H. Clark.

Pierce, Richard A.

1972 *Rezanov reconnoiters California, 1806*. San Francisco: Book Club of California.

1986 *Builders of Alaska: The Russian Governors, 1818-1867*. Kingston, Ontario: Limestone Press.

1987 Archival and Bibliographic Materials on Russian America outside the USSR. In *Russia's American Colony*, S. Frederick Starr, ed., pp. 353–365. Durham, North Carolina: Duke University Press.

1990a *Russian America: A Biographical Dictionary*. Alaska History Series, No. 33. Kingston, Ontario: Limestone Press.

1990b *Russia in North America: Proceedings of the 2nd International Conference on Russian America, Sitka, Alaska, August 19-22, 1987*. Kingston, Ontario: Limestone Press.

Pinart, Alphonse

1873 Various Drawings of Artifacts in Museums in St. Petersburg, Moscow, Dorpat, Helsingfors, Copenhagen, and others. 6 folders. Bancroft Library, MS Collections, Box 1, Z-Z 17. University of California, Berkeley.

1955 Pinart's Tcholovone Vocabulary. In C. Hart Merriam, *Studies of California Indians*, pp. 133–138. Berkeley: University of California Press.

Pinola, Billyrene Marrufo

2012 Kashia-Fort Ross Bicentennial Expedition to Russia. *Fort Ross Conservancy Newsletter* 1(2):6

Polansky, Patricia

1987 Published Sources on Russian America. In *Russia's American Colony*, S. Frederick Starr, ed., pp. 319–352. Durham, North Carolina: Duke University Press.

Pope, Saxton

1918 Yahi Archery. *University of California Publications in American Archaeology and Ethnology* 13(3):103–152.

Powers, Stephen

1877 *Tribes of California*. Washington, D.C.: Contributions to North American Ethnology, Volume 3, U. S. Geological Survey of the Rocky Mountain Region, Department of the Interior.

Purdy, Carl

1902 *Pomo Indian Baskets and Their Makers*. Los Angeles; Out West Company Press.

Riddell, Francis

1955 Archaeological Excavations on the Farallon Islands, California. *University of California Archaeological Survey Reports* 32. Berkeley, Calif.

1978 Maidu and Konkow. In *Handbook of the Indians of North America, Volume 8: California*, Robert F. Heizer, ed., pp. 370–386. Washington, D.C.: Smithsonian Institution.

Rokitiansky, Nicholas I.

1977 Fort Ross. *Voprosy Istorii* 7:213–217.

Rotchev, Alexander

1970 New Eldorado in California. Translated by A. F. Doll and R. A. Pierce. *Pacific Historian* 14(1):33–40.

Rozina, L. G.

1978 The James Cook Collection in the Museum of Anthropology and Ethnography. *Akademiia Nauk SSSR, Sbornik Muzeia Antropologii i Etnografii* 23:234–253. Translated in *Cook Voyage Artifacts in Leningrad, Berne, and Florence Museums*, Adrienne Kaeppler, ed. Honolulu: Bishop Museum Special Publication 66:3–17.

Sakovich, Maria

1998 Partners in Preservation: Citizen Participation in the Development of Fort Ross State Historic Park. In *Fort Ross*, Lyn Kalani, Lynn Rudy, and John Sperry, eds., pp. 27–28. Jenner, Calif.: Fort Ross Interpretive Association.

Shabelski, Achille

1826 *Voyage aux colonies russes de l'Amerique fait á bord du Sloop de Guerre L'Apollon, pendant les années 1821, 1822, 1823*. St. Petersburg: Imprimerie de N. Gretsch.

Sherwood, Morgan

1967 Science in Russian America, 1741 to 1865. *Pacific Northwest Quarterly*, 58(1):33–39.

Shipley, William

1978 Native Languages of California. In *Handbook of the Indians of North America, Volume 8: California,* Robert F. Heizer, ed., pp. 80–90. Washington, D.C.: Smithsonian Institution.

Shur, Leonid

1971 *K beregam novogo sveta [To the Shores of the New World].* Moscow: Academy of Sciences.

1974 Khudozhnik-puteshestvennik Mikhail Tikhanov [Artist-Explorer Mikhail Tikhanov]. *Publications of the Academy of Sciences, Moscow,* 5:163–180.

Shur, Leonid A. and James R. Gibson

1973 Russian Travel Notes and Journals as Sources for the History of California, 1800–1850. *California Historical Society Quarterly* 52(1):37–63.

Siebert, Erna V.

1975 Irokezkie kollektsii MAE [Iroquois Collections of the Museum of Anthropology and Ethnography]. *Akademiia Nauk SSSR, Sobrnik Muzeia Antropologii i Etnografii* 31:5–35.

Slaymaker, Charles

1977 The Material Culture of Cotomko'tca, a Coast Miwok Tribelet in Marin County. *Miwok Archaeological Preserve of Marin Papers* 3.

Smith, Barbara Sweetland

2000 *Science Under Sail: Russia's Great Voyages to America, 1728–1867.* Anchorage: Anchorage Museum of History and Art.

Smith, Barbara S., and Redmond J. Barnett, eds.

1990 *Russian America: The Forgotten Frontier.* Tacoma: Washington State Historical Society.

Spencer-Hancock, Diane and William E. Pritchard

1981 Notes to the 1817 Treaty between the Russian American Company and the Kashaya Pomo Indians. *California Historical Society Quarterly* 4:306–313.

Starr, S. Frederick (ed.)

1987 *Russia's American Colony.* Durham, North Carolina: Duke University Press.

Stepanova, V. M.

1944 I. G. Voznesenskii i etnograficheskoe izuchenie severo-zapada Ameriki k stoletiin ego ekspeditsii [I. G. Voznesenskii and the Ethnographic Study of Northwest America on the 100th Anniversary of his Expedition]. *Geograficheskoe Obshchestva Izvestiia* 76:277–279.

Steward, Julian H.

1933 Ethnography of the Owens Valley Paiute. *University of California Publications in American Archaeology and Ethnology* 33(3):233–350.

Tikhmenev, Peter A.

1978 *A History of the Russian American Company.* Translated and edited by Richard A. Pierce and Alton S. Donnelly. Seattle: University of Washington Press.

Treganza, Adan E.

1952 Archaeological Investigations in the Farmington Reservoir Area, Stanislaus County, California. *University of California Archaeological Survey Reports* 24.

1954 Salvage Archaeology in Nimbus and Redbank Reservoir Areas, Central California. *University of California Archaeological Survey Reports* 26.

Tumarkin, Daniil D.

1983 Materials of M. Vasilyev's Expedition: A Valuable Source for the Study of Cultural Change and Intercultural Contacts in the Hawaiian Islands. *Pacific Studies* 6(2):11–32.

Uhle, Max

1886 Ueber einige seltene Federarbeiten von Californien. *Mitteilungen der Anthropologischen Gesellschaft in Wien* 16:15–20.

Vancouver, George

1984 *A Voyage of Discovery to the North Pacific Ocean and Round the World, 1791–1795*. Edited, with an Introduction and Appendices, by W. Kaye Lamb. 4 vols. London: The Hakluyt Society.

Varjola, Pirjo

1981 Suomen Kansallismuseon Yleisetnografinen Kokoelma. In *Eripainos Suomen Museo 1981*, pp. 51–86. Helsinki: Suomen Kansallismuseo.

Vatter, Ernst

1925 Ein bemaltes Büffelfell und andere seltene Amerikanische Ethnographica im Städt. Völkermuseum zu Frankfurt a. Main. *Abhandlungen Frankfurter Gesellschaft für Anthropologie, Ethnologie und Urgeschichte*, Acta 2:75–106.

Viola, Herman and Carolyn Margolis

1985 *Magnificent Voyagers: The U.S. Exploring Expedition, 1838–1842*. Washington, D.C.: Smithsonian Institution.

Wagner, Henry

1937 *The Cartography of the Northwest Coast of America to the Year 1800*. 2 volumes. Berkeley: University of California Press.

Wake, Thomas A.

2013 Early Historic Maritime Hunting Technology in California; Insights from Fort Ross and Two Cached Wooden Boxes from San Nicolas Island, California. Paper presented at the annual conference of the Society for California Archaeology, Berkeley, Calif., March 10, 2013.

Wallace, William

1978a Southern Valley Yokuts. In *Handbook of North American Indians, Volume 8: California*, Robert F. Heizer, ed., pp. 448–461. Washington, D.C.: Smithsonian Institution.

1978b Northern Valley Yokuts. In *Handbook of North American Indians, Vol. 8: California*, Robert F. Heizer, ed., pp. 462–484. Washington, D.C.: Smithsonian Institution.

Watson, Douglas, ed.

1934 *The Spanish Occupation of California: Plan for the Establishment of a Government Junta or Council Held at San Blas, May 16, 1768. Diario of the Expeditions Made to California*. San Francisco: Grabhorn Press.

Willoughby, Charles

1922 Feather Mantles from California. *American Anthropologist* 24:432–437.

Wrangell, Ferdinand P. von

1839 Einige Bemerkungen ueber die Wilden an der Nordwest-Kueste von Amerika. In *Statistische und ethnographische Nachrichten ueber die Russischen Besitzungen an der Nordwestkueste von Amerika*, K. E. Baer, ed. St. Petersburg: Imperial Academy of Sciences.

1974 Ethnographic Observations on the Coast Miwok and Pomo, ed. by Robert F. Heizer, pp. 1–6. *Contributions of the University of California Archaeological Research Facility*. Berkeley, Calif.

1980 *Russian America: Statistical and Ethnographic Information*. Translated by Mary Sadouski and edited by Richard Pierce. Kingston, Ontario: Limestone Press.

Zagumlennyi, V. G.

1964 *Na norskikh putiakh k Kalifornii [On Sealanes to California]*. Moscow: Students' Library.

Index

Note: Page numbers followed by an **f** *or a* **t** *indicate figures and tables respectively.*

A

abalone shells, 155
'ahqha yow 'bakhe ya' (Pomo term for Russians and Aleuts), 52
Aki dance, 157
Aleut Islanders, 24, 52
Alexander II, Tsar, 50
arrow quiver, 88–89, 88f
arrows, 78–87
  assorted, 80f, 81f
    barbed, 81f
  characteristics of, 79f
  Desert Side-notch points, 85, 87
  examples of, 32
  in Finland, 83
  hafting technique, 85
  in Helsinki collection, 78–80
  Helsinki collection, 45
  in Kunstkamera catalog, 78
  manufacturing, 78
  projectile points, 84
  quiver set, 80f
  riband markings on, 82f, 83f, 86, 87
  self-, 81f, 85
  Seuamne arrows, 45–46
  stone-tipped, 87
  types of, 84–87
artifacts, California
  Choris's illustrations of, 40–41, 41f
  collected by George von Langsdorff, 38f
  in European museums, 30–31t, 35f
Azbill, Mary, 143

B

balsa boat, 63f, 64–65
Bancroft, Hubert H., 36
Banks, Joseph, 173
Baranov, Aleksandr, 52, 58
basket hopper, 99f
baskets
  bowls, 102, 102f
  burden, 90, 91f
  ceremonial, 166–67
  Chumash, 100–101, 101f, 108
  "classical forms" of, 177–182
  conical burden, 62
  cylindrical, 173
  fancy, 162–65
  feasting, 168–170, 168f, 169f
  gift, 170–72, 170f–72f, 174f–76f, 178f–181f
  globular feather-decorated, 167
  hopper, 100
  knot-type start, 171
  making, 97
  manufactured, 62
  net bags for carrying, 62
  Ohlone, 164
  one-rod technique, 171
  ornate, 162–65
  Oxford, basket in, 173
  Pomo, 171
  reticular pattern, 177
  serving (*see* food preparation and serving)
  specific tasks used for, 97
  as symbols of wealth and affluence, 163

waterproof, 163–64
Yokuts-type, 102
basket trays, 100–102
Bay Miwok. *See* Miwok
beaded hairnets. *See* hairnets
Beechey, Frederick
baskets, 163, 173
bows, 69
deer decoy headdresses, 67
ear rods, 147
feather belts, 140
beef, use of, 97
Behm, Major, 35
Belcher, Edward, 70–71, 114
bird-bone whistles, 161–62, 161f
blankets, feather, 104–7
Blaschke, Eduard L., 46
Bodega Bay, 24, 58
bodywear
clamshell disk-bead belts, 139
ear pendants, 151, 151f
feather belts, 140–46
feather cape, 135–36
feathered band, 146–47
necklaces, 152–56
women's skirts, 132–34, 133f, 134f
bows, 69–78
construction, 70–71
Cygnaeus bow, 78
Etholen, 76–78
in Helsinki collection, 77f
Monterey Indian hunter, depiction of, 72f
nocks, 72–75
Ohlone, 69
photograph of, 74f, 75f
reflex, 72
self, 72
sinew-backed, 71
unbacked, 71
Brandt, F. F., 47
Brown, Chris "Chief Lemee," 113f
Bryant, Edwin, 164

C

"cabinets of curiosities," 25
California artifacts
Choris's illustrations of, 40–41, 41f
collected by George von Langsdorff, 38f
in European museums, 30–31t, 35f
California Indians. *See* Native Californians
cape, feather, 135–36
Cardero, José, 72f, 88, 104, 105f, 147
cargo balsa. *See* balsa boat
Carmel mission, 100–101
carrying net, 92f, 93, 93f
Central Sierra Miwok. *See* Miwok
ceremonial baskets. *See* baskets
ceremonial dancing
of Chico Maidu, 145
musical instruments used during, 159–160
as prayer, 109
Wokile Dance, 129
ceremonial regalia
handling, use and disposal of, 110–11
materials used, 109–10
photograph of, 117f
significance to scholars, 111
"chambers of rarities," 25
Chamisso, Adelbert von
basketry, 163–64
on bow and arrow construction, 70
as member of Kotzebue's staff, 51–52
on model tule boat, 62
on native peoples, 54, 58
charlil kol, counterfeit currency, 152
Chernykh, Georgii, 46
Chernykh, Igor, 48
Chico Maidu. *See* Maidu
Cholvon (Cholovoni, Tcholovoni, Tchalaboni, Tscholvan), Northern Yokuts tribe, 2f, 54, 55f, 58, 73f
Choo-hel-mem-sel Patwin. *See* Patwin
Choris, Louis
on arrow quiver, 88
on bow and arrow construction, 70
depictions of Native Californians, 40–41, 55f, 64f, 73f, 117f, 183f
on feather belts, 140
on feather capes, 135
on model tule boat, 62
necklaces, 152
on topknot headpieces, 116–18
on tule balsa, 64
Chucumne, Plains Miwok village, 2f, 48
Chulamni Yokuts. *See* Yokuts
Chumash, 42, 67, 100–101, 102f, 107–8, 161
clam disk bead-making, 152–54
clamshell disk-bead belts, 139, 139f
cloaks, 136–39
collection of curiosities, 42
condor-skin cloak, 139
Cook, James, 35
cu' dut,' Nisenan belt decorated with glass beads, 139

curiosities, 25, 42
Cygnaeus, Uno, 26, 45
Cygnaeus collection
  arrows, 84
  bows, 78

D

dance regalia, 117f
dancing. *See* ceremonial dancing
Decembrists, 40
deer decoy headdresses, 67–69, 68f
de la Pérouse, Jean Galaup, 53
Deppe, Ferdinand, 27, 114
Desert Side-notch points, 85, 87
Deutsches Leder- und Schuh Museum, 44
'devil's beads,' counterfeit currency, 152
diet of local people, 95
Dixon, Roland, 41
documentation
  570 series, 34, 37
  absence of, 29
  Cook-Behm, 35
  defined, 29
domestic objects, 97
Drake, Francis, 182
DuHaut-Cilly, Auguste, 52

E

ear ornaments, 147–151, 148f, 149t, 150f, 151f
Erussi, 58
Eschscholtz, Johann Friedrich, 40, 41
Estero peoples, 58
Estonian History Museum, 27
Etholen, Arvid Adolf, 26, 44–45, 83
Etholen collection
  arrows, 84
  bows, 76–78
  feasting basket, 169f
  flicker headbands, 115
  gift basket, 172
  hairpins, 129, 132

F

feather band, 146–47
feather belts, 140–46
  ceremonial use of, 143–45
  checkerboard motifs, 145
  dimensions of, 141t
  examples of, 140f, 141f, 143f
  geometric elements in, 145
  Helsinki collection, 141f
  ownership of, 142–43
  patterns of, 144f
  Pomo feather belt, 141
  technique used, 142
  "winged diamond" motif, 145
feather blankets, 104–7, 106f
feather cape, 135–36, 135f
feather cloaks, 32–34, 33f
feathered hairpin, 131–32. *See also* hairpins
feather ropes, 157–58, 157f
feather topknots, 116–124, 120f, 121f, 122f, 123f, 125f, 137
Feest, Christian, 44, 132, 133
fire-making kit, 103–4, 103f
Fischer, Friedrich, 46
fishing, balsa for, 65
570 series, 34, 37
Fletcher, Francis, 69, 126, 152
flicker-quill headbands, 112–16
  examples of, 112f
  features of, 113–14
  Miwok style, 114
  of Pomo origin, 114–15
  tieless, 113
  Yuki-style, 114
food preparation and serving, 98–102
  basket bowl, 102
  basket trays, 100–102
  hopper basket, 100
  mortar, 99–100, 99f
  pestle, 99–100, 99f
  seed cake, 102
  serving tray, 101f
  sifting tray, 98–99
  winnowing tray, 98
Fort Ross
  depictions of, 24f, 25f
  as Russian outpost, 185
  as way station, 24–25
foundation hoop, 123–24
Franciscan missionaries, 51–52
Fred, Kenny, 65
fur trade, riches gained from, 23

G

games of chance, 183–84
gaming bones, 183–84, 184f
Garbielino, 161
gathering equipment
  burden baskets, 90, 91f
  carrying net, 93, 93f
  seed beater, 90, 90f
Geiger, Maynard, 53

Gibson, James R., 52
gift baskets. *See* baskets
Gillsen (Gil'zen), Karl, 32, 58, 104, 135
Golovnin, Vasilii
  basketry, 164
  on California native peoples, 53, 54
  contributing to Kunstkamera collections, 42
  on headdresses, 118
  photograph of, 43f
  on tule balsa, 64
gourd rattle, 160–61, 160f
"grass" game, 183–84
Gualala, 58
Guaypem (Uaypeymne), Plains Miwok village, 2f, 49
Guymen (Huimen), Coast Miwok tribelet, 2f, 55f

H

hafting technique, 85
Hagemeister, Leontii, 52
hairnets, 126–28, 126f, 127f
hairpins, 128–132, 130f
hair rope, 66–67
"hand bone" game, 183–84
headband, 92f
headwear
  feather topknots, 116–124
  flicker-quill headbands, 112–16
  hairnets, 126–28
  hairpins, 128–132
hearth, 103
Heizer, Robert, 35–36, 51
Helena (vessel), 47
Helsinki collection
  arrows, 45, 78–80, 84
  bows, 77f
  feather belt, 141f
Hernandez, Juan Josef Perez, 23
Hesi ceremony, 143
hopper basket. *See* baskets
household
  basketry in the, 97
  common objects used in, 97
  as focus of everyday existence, 95
household items, 103–8
  feather blankets, 104–7
  fire-making kit, 103–4, 103f
  storage jar, 107–8
  woven matting, 104
Hubby, E. F., 182
Hudson, J. W., 152
Hudson, Travis, 27
humanitarian significance of ethnographic objects, 186
hunting devices
  arrow quiver, 88–89
  arrows, 78–87
  bows, 69–78
  deer decoy headdresses, 67–69
  hair rope, 66–67
  as mementos, 61
  model tule boat, 62–66
  net bags, 89

I

incised bird bone ear decoration, 148–150

K

Kaeppler, Adrienne, 35
kala, feather belt, 32
Kashaya Pomo, 52
Khlebnikov, Kiril
  basketry, 100, 164
  on bow and arrow construction, 71
  on headdresses, 118
  on intelligence of native peoples, 53
  as officer in Russian-American Company, 42
  storage jar, 107
  watercraft, non-Indian use of, 65
knot-type start, 171
Kodiak Islanders, 24, 52
Kojean, P. M., 167, 181–82
Konkow Maidu legends, 135
Kostromitinov, Petr, 46, 54–58, 71, 152
Kotzebue, Otto von
  on bow and arrow construction, 70
  on diet of local people, 95
  on intelligence of native peoples, 54
  Kunstkamera collections, contributor to, 40, 41
  photograph of, 43f
Kroeber, Alfred, 66–67, 139
Krusenstern, Johan von, 37, 160
Kukshui costumes, 32, 33f, 49, 136–37, 185
Kuksu cult dances, 109–10
Kunstkamera collections
  arrow quiver, 88–89
  arrows, 78
  basket jar, 107
  bows, 72
  catalog identification of, 29–31
  Chumash baskets, 101
  clamshell disk-bead belts, 139
  cloaks, 136

ear rods, 150
feather blankets, 106–7
flicker bands, 113
gaming bones, 184
hairpins, 129
hair rope, 66
importance of, 26
integrity of, 186
net bags, 89
seed beater, 90, 90f
shell necklace, 39
topknot headpieces, 122–23
tule balsa, 66
uniqueness of, 26
Kunstkamera Museum, 25
Kuprianov, Ivan, 26, 44
Kuprianov's collection, 44
Kushov, Ivan, 52, 58

L

Langsdorff, Georg von
on basketry, 163
bow and arrow, 69–70
collection acquired by, 37, 39
decoy headdress, 67
drawings of, 63f, 115f
feather blankets, 104
feather topknots, 116
flicker bands, 112, 115–16
gourd rattle, 160
model tule boat, 62
necklaces, 152, 156
shell bead necklaces, 156
tribal designations, recording, 58
language and tribal identity, 58
Laplace, Cyrille, 67, 97
lattice twining, 98
Lelamne, Eastern Miwok village, 2f, 49
Liapunova, Roza G., 32, 37, 59
Livermore, Earl, 164
Locolome, Eastern Miwok village, 2f, 49

M

Macheme, Eastern Miwok village, 2f, 49
Maggentrick, John, 114
Maidu, 49
belts, 66
Chico, 141, 145–46, 157, 163, 172
hairpins, 130–31
map of, 2f
Northwestern, 155
Malaspina expedition, 100–101
McLendon, Sally, 58
Meighan, Clement, 53
Menetrie, E. P., 47
mé-ti'ni, Pomo name for site of Fort Ross, 52
Milliken, Randall, 49
Mission Carmel, 100–101
Mission San Rafael, 32, 48
Miwok
basket, 177
Bay Miwok (Saclan), 55f, 111
Central Sierra Miwok, 89, 120f, 157
Coast Miwok
basketry, 162, 163, 182
deer decoy headdresses, 67
feather ropes, 157
feather topknots, 116
fur headpiece, 119f
man, 56f
necklaces, 152
woman, 57f
map of, 2f
Northern Miwok, 129
Plains Miwok
baskets, 177
ritual objects used by, 111
villages listed by Voznesenskii, 49
Sierra Miwok
arrow quiver, 88
bows, 72, 76
condor skins used in dances, 139
deer decoy headdresses, 67
feather topknots, 118–120
hair rope, 66
mollok cloaks, 139
Southern Miwok, 87
model boats, 62–66, 63f
mollok costumes, 32, 33f, 49, 138f, 139, 185
Monterey Indian hunter, depiction of, 72f
mortar and pestle, 99–100, 99f
Mourning Celebration, 163
Munich shell necklace, 39f
Munin, Efim, 48
Museum of Anthropology and Ethnography, 25, 26
Museum of Mankind, 27
musical instruments, 159–162

N

Native Californians
depictions of, 55f, 56f, 57f, 63f, 64f, 72f, 73f, 96f, 105f, 115f, 117f, 118f, 119f, 183f
diminished populations of, 26
dull mindedness of, 53
intelligence of, 53–54

physical and emotional characteristics of, 54–58
Russian and Spanish attitudes toward, 52–53
technology of, 53–54
necklaces, 152–56
net bags, 89, 89f
New Albion, 25, 49
New Helvetia property, 48–49
Nicholas I (ship), 48
Nisenan
beaded belts, 154–55
beaded hairnets, 127
deer decoy headdresses, 67
feather belts, 143
feather blankets, 107
feather topknots, 137
flicker-quill headbands, 116
mollok costumes, 139
Nomlaki, 131
Northern Miwok. *See* Miwok
Northern peoples, 58
Northwestern Maidu. *See* Maidu

O

Ohlone
basket, 164
people, 58, 67
Okladnikova, Elena, 27
Olivella shell beads on baskets, 108
Olompali (Olumpali, Numpali), Coast Miwok tribelet, 2f, 55f
one-rod technique, 171
ornate baskets, 162–65
Oswalt, Robert, 58
Oxford, basket at, 173

P

Patwin
Choo-hel-mem-sel, 127
condor skins used in dances, 139
deer decoy headdresses, 67
peón, game of, 183–84
La Pérouse, 69
"persons from in the water," Pomo term for Russians, 52
pestle, 99f
Peter the Great, 25
Phelps, William, 105, 107
Pinart, Alphonse, 36
Plains Miwok. *See under* Miwok
Pomo peoples
baskets, 90, 171, 173, 182
bird-bone whistles, 162
bows, 71
clamshell disk-bead belts, 139f
clamshell disk beads, 153
feather belt, 141
hairpins, 128, 130f
map of, 2f
necklaces, 152
tribal identity of, 58
tule balsa, 65
Yokaya, 162
Pomo tule balsas, 65
Port Petropavlovsk, 35
Port Rumiantsev, 2f, 24, 49, 185
projectile points, 84
promyshlenniks, 23

Q

quivers, 88–89
quiver set, 80

R

rafts, 64
reflex bow. *See* bows
regalia. *See* ceremonial regalia
reticular pattern, 177
Rezanov, Nikolai, 24
riband markings, 82f, 83f, 86, 87
ritual costuming, supernatural power of, 159
Rossillon, Wilhelm von, 44
Rotchev, Aleksandr, 48
Rumantzoff Collection, 46
Russia
ethnographic objects taken to, 25
expansion into North Pacific, 23
fur trading companies, 24
good-natured and well-disposed, 53
initial contact between Spaniards and, 24
relations with Indian people, 52–53
Russian-American Company, 23, 39
Russian collections, hunting devices in, 61
Russov, F. F., 32

S

Saclan, Bay Miwok tribelet, 2f, 55f
Santa María, Vicente, 126
Santiago (vessel), 23
Schroeder, E. I., 47
seed beater, 90, 90f
seed cake, 102
Sekumne, Southern Maidu (Nisenan) village, 2f, 49
self arrows, 81f, 85
self bow, 72
serving tray, 101f, 102f

Seuamne, Eastern Miwok village, 2f, 45–46, 49
shaka, reed boat, 65
Shasta feather bands, 147
shell beads, 153
shell necklace, 39f, 153f
Shishmaryov, 64
Sierra Miwok. *See under* Miwok
Sierran peoples, 66
sifting tray, 98–99, 99f
sinew-backed bow, 71
Siuamni. *See* Seuamne, Eastern Miwok village
skirts, women's, 132–34, 133f, 134f
Smirnova, Nina, 146
Sonolomne, Eastern Miwok village, 2f, 49
Southern Miwok. *See under* Miwok
Spain
  colonial expansion of, 24
  compared California Indians to Aztecs, 53
  initial contact between Russians and, 24
  negative attitude toward native peoples, 52
  on Russian ownership of Ross, 52
Staatliches Museum für Völkerkunde, 26
Steppe-Indians, 58
St. Petersburg collection, 84
Suisun (Suysum), Southern Patwin tribelet, 2f, 48, 55f
Suomen Kansallismuseo, 26
Surinam, 161
su-tai-gus, grooving on arrows, 87
Sutter, John, 45, 48–49
Suysum. *See* Suisun (Suysum), Southern Patwin tribelet

T

Tabin, Ohlone tribelet, 58
Tamkan (Tamcan), Yokuts tribe, 2f, 58
Tcholovoni. *See* Cholvon (Cholovoni, Tcholovoni, Tchalaboni, Tscholvan), Northern Yokuts tribe
technology, basketry associated with, 62
tieless bands, 113
Tikhanov, Mikhail
  on beaded hairnet, 126
  depictions of Native Californians, 56f, 57f, 96f, 118f, 119f
  describing California native peoples, 42
  on domestic families, 95
  on ear rods, 147
  on topknot headpieces, 116–18, 119f
Tlingit policy, 52
topknot headpieces, 116–124, 120f, 125f
tribal identity, 58
tricultural system, 52
Tscholban. *See* Cholvon (Cholovoni, Tcholovoni, Tchalaboni, Tscholvan), Northern Yokuts tribe
Tuiban (Tuibun), Ohlone tribelet, 2f, 58
tule boat, 62–66
Turku Academy, 44–45

U

Uaypeymne. *See* Guaypem (Uaypeymne), Plains Miwok village
Uhle, Max, 141
Ululato, Patwin tribelet, 2f, 55f
unbacked bows, 71
Uraga, José López, 104–5
Utschim (Huchiun), Ohlone tribelet, 2f, 55f

V

Valley Nisenan peoples. *See* Nisenan
Valley Yokuts. *See* Yokuts
Valthazar, 56f, 119f
Vancouver, George, 53
Vasilyev, Mikhail Nikolayevich
  on bow and arrow construction, 70
  on complex regalia, 109–10
  on musical instruments, 159–160
  naming native groups, 58
  on watercraft, 64
Vatter, Ernst, 141
Voznesenskii, Il'ia
  as Acting Conservator, 49–50
  basketry collection, 167
  collection acquired by, 25–26, 48–50
  collections, importance of, 50
  death of, 50
  ethnographic objects taken by, 31–32
  feather cloaks, 32–34
  on hairnets, 126
  on *kukshui* costumes, 136–37
  letter to Schroeder, 48
  memberships in distinguished organizations, 50
  on *mollok* cloaks, 139
  notebooks on California Indian people, 32
  origins of, 47
  photograph of, 43f
  in Port Rumiantsev, 47
  returned to St. Petersburg, 49
  specimen collection, instruction in, 47
  tribal designations, recording, 59
  on watercraft, 65
vyvak, paddles, 65

W

Wagler, J., 173
Wallalakh, modern Gualala, 58
Wappo, 2f, 140
waterfowl-hunting balsa, 65
waterproof baskets, 163–64
Watham, Charlie, 142
wild plant materials, 61
Wilkes, Charles, 137
Wilkes expedition, 26, 128
Winnowing tray, 98f, 99f
Wintun, 76
Wokile Dance, 129
women's skirts, 132–34, 133f, 134f
woven matting, 104
Wrangell, Ferdinand von
  ear pendants, 151
  feasting basket, 168–69
  feather belts, 140
  feather blankets, 105
  gift baskets, 171, 181
  as member of Russian-American Company, 42–44
  on native peoples penchant for beauty, 54
  photograph of, 43f
  topknot headpieces, 124

X

"X-wrap" hafting technique, 85

Y

Yalesumne, Southern Maidu (Nisenan) village, 2f, 49
Yokaya Pomo. *See* Pomo peoples
Yokuts
  basketry, 101–2
  Chulamni, 58, 73f (*see also* Cholvon (Cholovoni, Tcholovoni, Tchalaboni, Tscholvan), Northern Yokuts tribe)
  map of, 2f
  Valley, 72
Yuki, 71

Z

Zavalishin, Dmitry
  on bow and arrow construction, 70
  contributing to Kunstkamera collections, 39–40
  feather belt, receiving, 142–43
  on intelligence of native peoples, 53–54
  on watercraft, 65

About the Authors, Editors, and Contributors

Authors

The late **Travis Hudson** was Curator of Anthropology at the Santa Barbara Museum of Natural History (1973–1985). A specialist on the Chumash people of California, he wrote numerous books, articles, and reports on the subject, as well as contributing papers on sailing technology, rock art, archaeoastronomy, and material culture. He coauthored, with Thomas Blackburn, the five volumes of *The Material Culture of the Chumash Interaction Sphere.*

Craig Bates is former Curator of Ethnography at the Yosemite Museum. A specialist in basketry, he is author of over 100 articles and monographs on western Native American material culture and history.

Editors

Thomas Blackburn is Emeritus Professor of Anthropology at California State Polytechnic University, Pomona. He has published extensively on symbolic anthropology and the native peoples of California. He is Associate Editor of the Journal of California and Great Basin Anthropology, and is the recipient of the Fredrickson Lifetime Achievement Award of the Society for California Archaeology.

John R. Johnson is Curator of Anthropology at the Santa Barbara Museum of Natural History and Adjunct Professor of Anthropology at the University of California, Santa Barbara. His research contributions include more than 80 studies devoted to California Indian prehistory and ethnohistory.

Contributors

Stephen D. Watrous is Emeritus Professor of History at Sonoma State University and an expert on the Russian experience in America.

Glenn J. Farris is a retired Senior State Archaeologist for California State Parks and is a Research Associate in Anthropology at the Santa Barbara Museum of Natural History. He is a recipient of both the Fredrickson Lifetime Achievement Award and the Baumhoff Special Achievement Award of the Society for California Archaeology.